MEXICAN AMERICAN FASTPITCH

MEXICAN AMERICAN FASTPITCH

*Identity at Play
in Vernacular Sport*

Ben Chappell

STANFORD UNIVERSITY PRESS
Stanford, California

STANFORD UNIVERSITY PRESS
Stanford, California

©2021 by the Board of Trustees of the Leland Stanford Junior University.
All rights reserved.

Printed in the United States of America on acid-free, archival-quality paper

Library of Congress Cataloging-in-Publication Data
Names: Chappell, Ben, author.
Title: Mexican American fastpitch : identity at play in vernacular sport /
    Ben Chappell.
Description: Stanford, California : Stanford University Press, 2021. |
    Includes bibliographical references and index.
Identifiers: LCCN 2020052605 (print) | LCCN 2020052606 (ebook) |
    ISBN 9781503609969 (cloth) | ISBN 9781503628595 (paperback) |
    ISBN 9781503628601 (ebook)
Subjects: LCSH: Mexican Americans—Sports. | Softball—Social aspects—
    United States. | Mexican Americans—Social life and customs. |
    Mexican Americans—Ethnic identity. | Sports—Anthropological
    aspects—United States.
Classification: LCC E184.M5 C38374 2021 (print) | LCC E184.M5 (ebook) |
    DDC 973/.046872—dc23
LC record available at https://lccn.loc.gov/2020052605
LC ebook record available at https://lccn.loc.gov/2020052606

Cover design: Rob Ehle

Typeset by Kevin Barrett Kane in 10/14 Minion Pro

Dedicated to the memory of
John Limon Jr. and
Reynaldo Gonzalez

CONTENTS

ACKNOWLEDGMENTS

First and foremost, I owe this book to the many people who generously shared their time and space to help me understand and appreciate the Mexican American fastpitch tradition, including Carol Acosta, Geraldo "Jerry" Acosta, Luis Aguayo, Albert "Cocoa" Alcanto, Bob Alonso, Gil Aragon, Lauren Bautista, Cathy Beckett, Jennifer Benavides, Carolyn Benitez, Jesse Berrones Jr., Jesse Berrones III, Fortino Bonilla, Tony Castillo, Javier del Castillo, Elias Castro, Lee Castro Jr., Geronimo "Jerry" Collazo, Frank del Toro, Greg Escobar, Mario Escobar, Richard Escobar, Daniel "BeBe" Garcia, Mario Garcia, Dan Govea, Lucio Govea Jr., Paulie Hernandez, Steve "Sparkle" Jaso, Arthur Juarez, Manuel Ledesma, Richard Lopez, Gilbert Martinez, Hector Martinez, Hector Martinez Jr., Pat Martinez, Raul Meza, Antonio Moya, Louis Murillo, George Ontiberos, Anthony Oropeza, George Perez, Harley Ponce, Ted Ponce, Charlie Porfirio, Israel Rey, Hildebrand Rios III, Michael Rios, Jesse A. Rodriguez, Antonio Sandate, Bob "Güero" Sandoval, Margie Sandoval Titus, Angel Torres, Vicky Torres, Amelia Vega, Paul Vega, Joe and Mary Vela, and Angelo Zuniga.

A few people made me feel especially welcome and showed me the meaning of the "fastpitch family." Our friendship has endured over the years, and I hope I can someday return the abundant hospitality I've enjoyed from Ray and Laura Guerra, Herbie and Diane LaFuente, and David and Yvonne Rios. Manuel Jaso always made sure I was at home in Newton, Kansas, and Todd Zenner has renewed this welcome.

Mexican American fastpitch has generated its own intellectuals and historians, and I have benefited greatly from the generosity and collections of David Acosta, Ray Olais, Gil Solis, and Rudy "Chato" Velasquez. I also couldn't ask for better collegiality from my academic colleagues already deep into the study of Mexican American sport, who welcomed this newcomer with immediate offers of collaboration: thanks especially to Gene Chávez, Jorge Iber, and Richard Santillán. I have relied on the archives of the Newton Public Library, the Austin History Center, the Houston History Archives at the University of Houston, and the Houston Metropolitan Research Center, where I was welcomed by Mika Selley. Chad Frey at the *Newton Kansan* has been constantly supportive of the project, even picking up a T-shirt for me in a year when I couldn't make it to the tournament.

The long gestation of this book was nourished by invitations to speak about it, notably from Kirstin Erickson at the University of Arkansas; James Dorson at the Free University of Berlin; and the Place, Race, and Space Seminar at the Hall Center for the Humanities. I am grateful to Pia Wiegmink and Birgit Bauridl for inviting me to join the German research network on Cultural Performance in Transnational American Studies and present at the Obama Institute of the University of Mainz. Rachel Epp-Buller included me on her Hometown Teams project grant, which supported my talks at Bethel College, Kauffman Museum, and the public panel discussion that provided essential narrative material for the book. The opportunity to take part in a Smithsonian Institution collecting event at the Kansas City Museum was also generative. Over the years of working on this project, I have been inspired, challenged, and motivated by students in my U.S. Ethnography seminars and colleagues in the American Studies Association's Ethnography and Sports Studies caucuses. Preliminary versions of the ideas in this book appeared in the collections *Latinos and Latinas in American Sport: Stories beyond Peloteros*, edited by Jorge Iber for Texas Tech University Press, and *The Everyday Life of Urban Inequality: Ethnographic Case Studies of Global Cities*, edited by Angela D. Storey, Megan Sheehan, and Jessica Bodoh-Creed for Lexington Books.

Key moments for moving the project forward happened in writing groups organized by Rebecca Barrett-Fox, Tanya Golash-Boza, Justin Wolfe, and the University of Kansas College of Liberal Arts and Sciences. Material support came from a resident fellowship at the Hall Center for the Humanities, a grant from the General Research Fund of the University of Kansas, and a Big 12 Fellowship, for which I am grateful to John Hartigan of the Américo Paredes Center for Cultural Studies at the University of Texas for the invitation. Another crucial moment of synthesis was occasioned by the full day of sessions of "la Tejanada," former anthropology graduate students of Richard Flores, José Limón, and Martha Menchaca at the Inter-University Program for Latino Research conference in San Antonio. I owe a debt to those colleagues that runs deeper than the citations of their work in this book and an even greater one to my teachers.

Many individual colleagues have at times buoyed this project even if they did not realize it. For small or large measures of direct support for this work, including letters, suggested sources, or even a random passing comment, I am grateful to Fede Aldama, Danny Anderson, Henry Bial, Melissa Biggs, Mieke Curtis, Jennifer Doyle, Arlene Davila, Betsy Esch, Iris Smith Fischer, Ruben Flores, Jennifer Hamer, David Katzman, Richard King, Alan Klein, Cheryl Lester, José Limón, Michelle Lipinski, John McKiernan-Gonzalez, Valerie Mendoza, David Montejano, Bill Nericcio, Chris Perreira, David Roediger, Gilberto Rosas, Theresa Torres, Lucia Trimbur, Michael Trujillo, Sherrie Tucker, Bill Tuttle, and Sujey Vega. At Stanford University Press, Kate Wahl and Margo Irvin, along with the rest of the team, were fantastically supportive and patient. Kathy Porsch labored in support of my many funding proposals that were ultimately denied—but her faith in the project and constructive feedback made it better. The Jokers Athletic Club presented me with their annual Sportsmanship Award when I first attended their tournament at Del Valle fields—an optimistic vote of confidence in the work I was just setting out to do. I hope the book lives up to their affirmation.

My family, Marike, Calvin, and Felix, have lovingly endured this fixation with a topic that often took me away from home. In an extended family that relies on summers to reconnect, my parents, Terry and Bobbie Chappell, and my sisters and their families—the Chappell-Dicks, Chappell Deckerts, and Chappell-Lakins—have also been patient and forgiving of my work priorities. The Chappell Deckert home in North Newton was an ideal field station for more than one Fourth of July tournament visit, and my in-laws, John and Reinhild Janzen, were always ready to receive me down the road at Heubuden. James Nikkel was a one-person booster organization who made sure I benefited from his network of contacts in Newton and occasionally from the sublime Crust and Crumb bakery. One of the unexpected pleasures of this work has been the chance to visit dear friends Johann Eberhart and Mary Swartz and enjoy their unrivaled hospitality at two different homes over several years of research trips to Austin. Now I have to think up new excuses to return. I ask forgiveness from all whom I've inadvertently left out of these acknowledgments. I assure you it was a momentary lapse.

Several of the people I met and consulted for this long-term project passed away as my work crept along at an academic pace. Two in particular stand out in my memory for their enthusiasm and commitment to the game and communities they loved and for supporting and cultivating my interest. John Limon Jr. and Rey "Chita" Gonzalez died during the year that I was finishing this book, and my greatest regret for the project is that I didn't complete it in time to place a copy in their hands. I dedicate the book to them.

MEXICAN AMERICAN FASTPITCH

⚾ INTRODUCTION ⚾

RAY EVANS WAS A STANDOUT ATHLETE at the University of Kansas (KU), an institution that has produced its share of legends. After enrolling in 1941, Evans went on to become the only KU athlete to be named All-American in both basketball and football and the only one to have his jerseys retired in both sports. His feats garnered recruitment attention from both the New York Knicks and the Chicago Bears before he interrupted his college athletic pursuits to go to war in 1944. As a veteran, he returned to KU and led the Jayhawks to the Orange Bowl, and in 1948 he played a season of football with the Pittsburgh Steelers. Along the way, even the New York Yankees threw in an offer to play professional baseball, which Evans declined (Just 2017; SB Nation Rock Chalk Talk 2014).

Amid this wealth of recruitments came an invitation from a Mr. Bowersock, owner of a gas station in Newton, Kansas, a railroad town situated some 150 miles southwest of the university in Lawrence. Bowersock was one of many people at the time driven to contend for bragging rights in the local softball leagues and tournaments that were ubiquitous in the postwar United States. In August 1947, before Evans's final football season at KU, the Knights of Columbus in Newton hosted a softball tournament, and through some means of persuasion, Bowersock brought in the college star Evans, now remembered as one of the best all-around athletes ever to play for KU, to pitch for his sponsored team, Sox Super Service.

1

Though softball has evolved into several forms, the game that was all the rage nationwide in the postwar era was what is now known as fastpitch. Played on a scaled-down diamond as compared to baseball, the game revolved around pitchers throwing underhand, often as hard as they could, while the batting team scrambled for hits, bunts, and steals to advance around the bases. It was a far cry from the relaxed "slowpitch" version of softball that is a widespread recreation today. Games could easily become duels between pitchers, as each batting team vied for unlikely contact with the ball and a defensive slip that would allow a run to break the impasse. Final scores of 1–0 or 2–1 were not uncommon. In the first game of the tournament, Sox Super Service met a team known in the Newton city league as the "Mexican Catholics." Like Evans, many of the Mexican players were veterans, except when they went to war, they had interrupted not their studies but hard labor as track workers for the railroad. These were the second generation of *traqueros* (track workers) in Newton, whose parents had begun to settle there during the period of the Mexican Revolution, 1910–1920. One of those elders, Canuto Jaso, arrived in Newton in 1919 after a stay in El Paso, Texas, a staging point where many Mexican émigrés would meet the *enganchistas* (labor recruiters), who would then channel them to jobs around the Midwest (Innis-Jiménez 2014, 69). Jaso played baseball while in El Paso, and his children continued playing the family's favored sport after settling in Kansas.

The Mexican traqueros in Newton first lived in boxcars and then in brick houses built by the railroad, forming a community known as El Ranchito. With relatively stable work and residence, some of the men formed a baseball team they called Cuauhtemoc and played in the Newton city league. In the late 1930s, the sons of some of the Cuauhtemoc players and their friends formed a team they called Los Rayos, challenging the older generation and beating them (Olais 2019). Players for Los Rayos were part of the "Mexican American generation"— U.S. citizens who went to war and, on their return, enthusiastically took to the game of fastpitch softball, which had enjoyed a surge of popularity around the United States in the 1940s.

The pitcher for the Mexican Catholics, Joaquín "Chuck" Estrada, had learned to pitch underhand while in the military. Numerous individuals whom I've interviewed in Newton repeated to me the almost legendary attribute that Chuck threw "without a glove," suggesting a kind of naturalistic source of strength, or perhaps simply reflecting the confidence that his pitch would be so intimidating that fielding would not be necessary. Rey Gonzalez, who later played third base for Newton but was younger than the Rayos and served as a batboy in the 1947 tournament, recounted the game to me in an interview over sixty years later, about how the dueling pitchers retired batters one by one:

> Ray Evans from KU came in to pitch for the Bowersock softball team. Had a good team, too. But anyway, they met—in the second round they met our guys. I think they were playing—yeah, Magees, yeah. And it was zip zip zip, too, it was zip zip zip all the way, until the sixth or the seventh inning. . . . I remember the game. They bunted and they got a hit—or no . . . yeah they hit to the shortstop, or the third baseman, a hard grounder and he bobbled it and let it get away from him, and a run scored, and we beat Ray Evans one to nothing! He was so damn mad at those guys.[1]

As the *Evening Kansan Republican* newspaper tells the story, Evans gave up no hits, but a fielding error allowed Lou Gomez to get on base. Gomez proceeded to steal second and advance to third on an out, ultimately scoring on a wild pitch. The newspaper sports page held that Evans versus Estrada was "the best pitching duel seen in many a moon in Newton" ("Pitched No-Hit Game and Lost" 1947).

The story of the mighty Ray Evans pitching a no-hitter but losing in a softball game against an all-Mexican team doesn't turn up in most accounts of his multisport exploits. But the feats of Chuck Estrada and the team that would pick up sponsorship in the next season from an Anglo potato chip merchant named Magee are retold from year to year (see Figure 1). Much later in Newton, these and other stories circulate in Athletic Park each year at the Mexican American softball tournament that the former Rayos players founded the year before the Evans-Estrada duel and won the year after. The tournament has run annually since then, celebrating its milestone seventieth year in 2018. For many of those years, the tournament director has been Manuel Jaso, one of many descendants of Canuto to play in the tournament.

This book is the result of an interactive engagement with softball tournaments and the people devoted to them. In my multi-sited ethnographic research, I followed the sport roughly between Kansas City and Houston. At over eighteen tournaments, in the homes of players, organizers, and umpires and in the neighborhoods where they played, I struck up conversations in the bleachers; listened to announcers, players, and fans in the heat of competition; browsed the archives of historical centers and memorabilia hounds; and recorded interviews with over fifty people. Through this fieldwork, I gained a sense of the importance of fastpitch in the ordinary annual life of certain Mexican American communities.

FIGURE 1 Newton Magee team, also known as the Mexican Catholics, 1948. Photo courtesy of the *Newton Kansan*.

The portrait that emerges here is of people who have endured migration, limited economic opportunity, de facto segregation, and everyday racism, but also have gained a degree of social mobility over time, forming fastpitch teams rooted in friendships and family relations along the way. The particular appeal of fastpitch—what sport theorists call its *illusio*—draws people to the sport and moves them to invest time, energy, and identity into it. The resulting tradition links old-generation Mexican American communities in the Midwest, an area where they have more than one hundred years of history but little representation in scholarship, with the borderlands of Texas, the region that spawned a kind of scholarship that is the basis for this study: ethnographic inquiry into socially embedded cultural poetics.

• • •

A largely Mexican American crowd, clustered in lawn chairs under shade trees and pitched nylon canopies, or seated on aluminum bleachers in full July sun, carries on innumerable conversations while watching men play fastpitch on the red-dirt field. I catch a few snippets from my seat in the bleachers.

"Remember when we faced them in Kansas City? Twenty-one innings and then it was one to nothing. They didn't have time limits in those days."

Two women regale me with their stories of attending fastpitch tournaments in the railroad towns around Kansas, and then they situate their families within more widely known histories: "My grandfather, aunt, and uncle all rode with Pancho Villa. I have documentation."

From the bleachers, a yell: "Come on, baby! Twist it!"

Rick Lopez, having driven over nine hours up from Texas, greets friends and former opponents. His T-shirt commemorates his team, the Baytown Hawks, for their unrivaled record winning "the Latin," a fastpitch tournament that will take place two weeks later in Houston. That tournament is the second oldest to Newton's, and it anchors a circuit of other competitions in Texas cities like Austin and San Antonio, just as Newton shares a summer season calendar with Kansas City and other railroad towns, including Topeka, Hutchinson, and Emporia.

Midmorning on Saturday of the tournament weekend, I run into Rey, known as "Chita," behind the bleachers and he excitedly reports: "Did you see that game? A great game. A tough game. They should have squeezed him in on third with one out." Then he is distracted, because a young man, just off the plane on a military furlough to make it to the tournament, asks if he can use a shower at Rey's house.

"Okay, Mijito. I don't think anyone's there, but you know where the key is, right?"

From the other side, a woman, maybe in her thirties, taps Rey on the shoulder to greet him as the press box PA kicks off a polka. Rey throws a *grito* and dances off with her across the dusty park ground.[2]

Scholars note that people of Mexican descent in the United States have held a ubiquitous and persistent interest in sport that until recently was not well represented in scholarship (Iber and Regalado 2006). This book follows one bright thread in the fabric of Mexican American sport, a continuing tradition of fastpitch softball played in communities throughout the central United States, from the High Plains to Texas. This ethnic sporting practice is maintained through annual tournaments mostly played by men, with Newton's being the longest running (Figure 2). Through fastpitch teams and tournaments, Mexican Americans have practiced a version of cultural citizenship, defined by Renato Rosaldo as "the right to be different . . . with respect to the norms of the dominant national community, without compromising one's right to belong" (Rosaldo 1994, 57). The challenge of cultural citizenship for Latina/os and other people of color, according to Rosaldo, is to achieve full integration and recognition in American society without allowing the historical erasure of their particular identity and experience.[3]

When the players and organizers of Mexican American softball tournaments take part in what was once the very mainstream of public recreation in the

FIGURE 2   Game play at the Newton Mexican American Fastpitch Softball
Tournament. Photo by the author.

United States, they also assert the right to construct spaces of cultural difference,
defined and performed on their own terms. Carrying on with fastpitch into
the second or third generation of players even as interest in the sport among
men in general has substantially declined in favor of the more relaxed slowpitch version of softball or other activities altogether, the historically Mexican
American tournaments now function as reunions that allow people to maintain
ties to their shared past in specific communities and keep up the strong social
relationships that form around the sport. Recognizing fastpitch as a practice
of cultural citizenship situates it within a history marked by migration, marginalization, organization, and struggle, through which Mexican Americans
have navigated complex negotiations of cultural, national, and local identities.

In the process, they found agency by developing rich cultural resources. This book counts sport as one of those resources.

Softball as a differentiated cultural space is evident at the Mexican American fastpitch tournament held every Fourth of July weekend in Newton for over seventy years. This tournament is not only the oldest of its kind still running, but the only one—to my knowledge and that of the organizers with whom I've spoken—that throughout my fieldwork remained a predominantly Mexican American event by rule. In general, players were required to have at least one parent of Mexican descent. A team could bring as many as three players who didn't have this qualifying ancestry as long as they put no more than two on the field at a given time. Non-Mexican players were not permitted to pitch or catch.[4] While maintaining the identity requirement makes the Newton tournament unique, other Mexican American communities in the Central United States have also hosted fastpitch tournaments from the mid-twentieth century, when softball was one of the most popular recreational activities nationwide, de facto segregation was a social norm, and many Mexican Americans who were a generation removed from migration both sought access to public space in everyday life and built their own institutions to avoid or challenge exclusion.

Softball teams—formed around relationships of family and friends, supported by community centers and business sponsors based in barrio neighborhoods, and playing on ball fields nestled into those neighborhoods—are examples of a kind of barrio institution that have survived as the history of their communities continues to unfold. In Kansas City and smaller towns like Newton, softball became a favored activity among the Mexican people whose parents had been recruited to railroad work in those areas around the turn of the twentieth century. In urban centers of San Antonio, Austin, and Houston, softball also took hold in enclave communities facing the daily struggles of segregation and containment that historians have described as "barrioization" (Villa 2000). Throughout this Central U.S. region, which itself has been shaped by an economy and infrastructure that reached across the national border, softball teams and tournaments carry on a vernacular sporting practice that devotees invariably describe as a tradition. Mexican American fastpitch is a tradition because the accumulated years of playing justify playing more. Participants speak of a duty to continue what their predecessors struggled to build. They also speak of the sport as their "culture"—a repertoire of practice marked with accents or shades of difference that embed this sport within the historical particularity of Mexican American experience.

In this multi-sited ethnography of vernacular sport, I argue that the tradition of annual fastpitch softball tournaments has been maintained over generations by Mexican American communities because the sport provides an opportunity to engage in socially approved recreational activity and, simultaneously, remake and perform identity in terms that make sense to participants and speak to their experience. This was critical during a history that saw Mexican Americans embrace many aspects of U.S. national identity while nonetheless having the legitimacy of their citizenship and belonging repeatedly called into question or undermined in practice. Citizenship may not seem to be directly at stake in recreational sports, but with the United States ascendant as a world power in the early midcentury, new energy animated a dominant, national culture that articulated strength and winning with Americanness. At the same time, Mexican American citizens were subject to a longer-standing colonial discourse aimed at keeping them in a subordinate position by figuring them as racially inferior and unworthy of the citizenship that they nonetheless legally held.

This colonial discourse, a feature of Anglo American modernity that traces back to military conflicts over territory in the nineteenth century, justified the segregation of Mexicans from public life, including public athletic activities, in a rhetorical double move. First, pseudoscientific ideas about racial types proposed that mestizos, presumed to have substantially indigenous genetic makeup, were not fit for athletic competition with or against Anglos. Then rationalizations followed that those excluded from opportunities to play modern sport didn't even want to do so, an expression of innate, cultural qualities such as fatalism and a lack of ambition. Actual Mexican Americans exploded these racist stereotypes by not only struggling to get their chance on the playing fields of America, but excelling once they got there. Mexican American fastpitch is part of this history of winning a chance to play.

• • •

During men's fastpitch league night at Shawnee Park in the Kansas City barrio of Armourdale, the Outlaws are getting ready to play. Though some appear to be Anglo, they are talking over plans for the Newton tournament as they gather around the bleachers to get ready for the next game. The players pull wadded-up baseball pants out of duffle bags and put them on over their athletic shorts. Baseball pants, tending to be white or light gray, are iconic in the sport that is their only purpose. These particular pants bear the streaked marks of sliding on red dirt base paths. Remarking on the dirt, one player tells a story about when he used to work out every night. He rewore the same sweaty clothes, and the stink would drive people away at the gym, giving him access to the machines. Those people, he says, were just there to look at themselves in the mirror.

Seeing the players dress for a new game in clothes marked by the efforts of the previous game reminds me of a couple of women I had sat near, behind home plate at another tournament, where I enjoyed their enthusiastic and highly informed cheers. Their running commentary gave the impression that they were also players, as they yelled encouragement and advice to one of the teams: "Get dirty, kid! You got to get dirty!" While being willing to get dirty is a key to success, part of the regular ritual of a game is tidying up. The umpire calls time to brush home plate clean, since it may be completely obscured by dust, and then smooths the loose dirt around it with careful sweeps of his foot. The approaching batter does the same, moving the loose dirt with a shoe and feeling the contours of the batter's box. Over the course of a weekend with back-to-back games, the landscape of a field shifts. Pits start to hollow out where the batters stand, deeper than anyone can fill by brushing into it with their feet. Batters start to prop their feet against the inside walls of the pits, seeking leverage on uneven ground where they have to stand to reach the strike zone hovering over home plate. Fastpitch gets played on ground that is solid but malleable, and the playing field, which is only purely level in an ethical-imaginary way, takes its physical form from the actions that have already played out on it in game after game all weekend of a tournament. The dirt also marks the players, at least their uniforms, so that they carry smudges of the history of a game off the field when it is over, and sometimes they can still find it there on their clothes when they put them on to play again.[5] The task of an ethnography is to draw near enough to let historical dirt make its marks on our scholarship and to carry the marks into our other discursive spaces.

Fastpitch participants repeatedly emphasized to me that the games, leagues, and tournaments that make up their sport are part of something bigger—a tradition. Retired postal worker and veteran catcher Hector "Cuate" Martinez Jr. (as a twin sharing a nickname, he is known as "Cuate the catcher") made this point to me when describing the game that he grew up watching his father play in Houston and that turned Settegast Park in his neighborhood into a festive hub of activity. Over time, he realized that this had a history, embedded in direct, personal relationships. He said,

> So when my dad tells me stories about these guys, it's history because I didn't know about it. You know, it's not like—we didn't have a newspaper to publish

this stuff. Nobody knew this about that, this and that. You know, you had to hear from somebody. Like *lore*, you know? You had to hear, it was like folklore you know, you're like . . . it's history.

To approach Mexican American fastpitch along these lines as a lore, as a vernacular, I take instruction from a prior body of anthropological folklore studies of Mexican America, for which the figure of Américo Paredes is paradigmatic (Limón 2012). José E. Limón, a leading proponent and elaborator of the ethnographic approach that Paredes modeled, suggests that such work remains relatively marginalized by the failure of academia to recognize and appreciate the richness of knowledge that is emergent in lived experience. As Limón notes, the publication of Paredes's landmark work, *With a Pistol in His Hand* in 1958 was overshadowed by the roughly contemporary English translations of a novel by Carlos Fuentes (1960) and essays by Octavio Paz (1961), which together "became a cultural window into things Mexican for American intellectuals, deflecting whatever attention might have been given to a folkloric study by a Mexican American from Texas" (Limón 2012, 86). Limón finds a similar disinterest in the vernacular in contemporary cultural studies, which tends to focus on what he calls "circumscribed textualities" (131), texts that enjoy the spectacular reach of mass mediation, a process that inevitably imposes distance from a vernacular mode of discourse, production, and exchange of cultural material, even as those exchanges may be the very material that is represented and mediated.

Giving the vernacular its due as a source of insight alongside published texts that carry the prestige of being mediated has been hampered by residual associations of the field of folklore with antiquity and potentially romantic notions of authenticity. Softball fits awkwardly into this framework, as a tradition that was clearly begun at a particular point in the modern past. A vernacular form of a modern sport can easily fall into the cracks between old, folkish things and other things that draw more water in the present by virtue of their capacity to attract mass attention or investment. Folklorist Roger Abrahams suggests that scholars might deflect outdated assumptions that folklore is concerned only with the olden and the golden by thinking of the vernacular as the "poetics of everyday life" (2005, 18). This intrigues those of us who understand the vernacular and the everyday to be scales on which history, politics, and culture happen in significant ways. But making this case for the everyday requires confronting possible assumptions of its triviality.

Indeed, the "triviality problem" is one that has hampered study not only of everyday life but of sports in general. Situating play as outside the important matters of work, business, politics, and other similar domains presents a challenge of legitimation for those arguing for sport as a valuable object of contemplation and analysis. As Paul Bowman (2019, 26) observes, musing on the possibility of "martial arts studies," legitimation may come through numbers (as in the billions of people who view the World Cup final), money (as in the massive financial investments in the American National Football League or the college basketball Final Four), politics (as in the explosive reactions to symbolic stances taken by athletes such as Colin Kaepernick and Megan Rapinoe), and other avenues. To assert that vernacular sport, undertaken in urban centers and small towns by mostly nonprofessional athletes for crowds that may not outnumber the players, is interesting and important for scholarly consideration confronts the triviality problem on various levels simultaneously.

The question should be, Trivial for whom? Fastpitch was certainly not trivial to the players who rushed home from work to play in weeknight leagues or who devoted years, even decades, of their life to tournaments. I have pursued an ethnography of Mexican American fastpitch not because I thought it was the most important site from which to understand sport in general, although I argue at various points that it does offer unique insights. Rather, this project arises out of my commitment to understanding Mexican American cultural production and an ethnographic preference for the aspects of Mexican American life that are valued highly by their participants. Fastpitch is important enough to study because it is important to certain Mexican American communities, where I chose to work.

The ethnographic priority that I place on vernacular sport runs somewhat parallel, against the modern grain, with the commitment of fastpitch-playing communities to keep an older way of playing going. Pierre Bourdieu, one of a group of scholars invited to analyze and discuss global sport in the run-up to the Seoul Olympic Games (Besnier, Brownell, and Carter 2018, 9), mused on the gap between professional and amateur sport that emerged in modernity, observing that the development of sport as "a relatively autonomous field reserved for professionals comes with the dispossession of lay people, who are reduced little by little to the role of spectators" (Bourdieu 1988, 160). Comparing sport to dance, the anthropologist/sociologist characterizes such modernization as a distancing from folk forms and rituals, which leads to an increased emphasis on "the extrinsic aspects of practice, such as the result, the victory" rather than on the practice of sport itself (ibid.). Of course the actual players and their physical feats are still very much the point of modern sport. But when we distinguish between "big" and "small" sporting events, this scale is defined by extrinsic factors, such as the money invested in teams or leagues; the reach of broadcast media representation; and articulations of players, teams, and games as emblems of identity claimed by populations of varying size. While there is abundant evidence that mass-spectacle sports can be intensely meaningful for fans, the scale of such sports imposes social distance between players and spectators. The bulk of sport studies deals with some aspect of the "relatively autonomous field" of sport as a large-scale spectacle. Yet orders of magnitude more people play sport than will ever play for a mass audience. Thus, the scale of focus for this project is sport that exists primarily to play and to be enjoyed by an intimate audience that is not necessarily separated from players by a vast social gulf.

Modern sport in general also lends itself to record keeping, often with an aesthetic of precise representations, producing statistics, scores, championships, and halls of fame. This is particularly true of baseball and its derivative games, in which scoring a game can involve collecting and archiving voluminous details about every pitch and play, even details that do not necessarily decide the winner, such as hits and errors. This is one face of what sport produces: indelible marks on history, of clear-cut accomplishments. The box scores for city softball leagues in the 1940s in Newton, Kansas, created a kind of unofficial archive by listing the players and key statistics. Thus, in a newspaper that might usually offer little clue whatsoever that there was a substantial Mexican population in this Kansas town, a softball roster entirely full of Spanish surnames is an intriguing historical wrinkle, adding *we were here* to the narrative reproduced annually in public parks: *we still are.*

Some of the devotees of fastpitch would appreciate efforts to deliver more precise facts and data in order to substantiate this historical presence, such as one interviewee who began our conversation by declaring, "Statistics! That's the key!" But beyond sport as a mechanism for producing scores, results, champions, and records, there is the game itself as something that gets played, watched, remembered, and debated. As an ethnographer, my attention is more drawn to people's ongoing reconstructions of memory and personal collections, some more orderly and comprehensive and some haphazard. In this way, I open my account to be shaped and informed by the voices and practices of participants in rich ways. In the time and place of playing, sport can produce a space that is a "palimpsest dense with meanings"—what Alex E. Chávez calls "moments," formed out of "places, feelings, people thrown together" (2017, 297). This book comes with no promises for a comprehensive, "correct" account of everything that happened in the history of fastpitch, but using whatever historical, ethnographic, and other materials at my disposal, I aim to draw near to the moment of fastpitch, in Chávez's sense.

Following these moments in the path Paredes laid, I approach fastpitch as an idiom of festive, culturally productive events, embedded in the social history of the Mexican American communities that host them. That is, I consider the cultural poetics of fastpitch. In his work on transnational music making in Mexican migrant life, Chávez calls for interactive, ethnographic engagement in order to "ground cultural forms in everyday life" (2017, 296). Like *huapango arribeño*, traditional string music from North-Central Mexico that Chávez follows with a transborder migrant community, the annual fastpitch tournaments rooted in Mexican American communities are a practiced version of what literary scholars have termed a "racial tradition" (53). Similarly, while this is a story on some level about sports in general, and about softball in general, it is always also a story of "our game," of a specific tradition linked to specific histories. This is the scale of vernacular sport.

The vernacular refers to a certain scale of access, answerability, and social interaction. Once taken to mean "face to face," vernacular marks relatively nonelite social spheres, where producers and consumers of cultural texts interact closely and in a marginal relation to capital markets—not always by choice. The event of an annual softball tournament may not be a literal everyday occurrence, but the relationships in which vernacular cultural production is embedded are produced and sustained over time through everyday life. Paredes's ethnographic approach to *corrido* border ballads, verbal art and comparable "folk" forms, demonstrates that such vernacular cultural production is capable of being just as subtle, nuanced, and aesthetically sophisticated as more self-consciously creative work done by specialist artists, who may labor quite apart from their audiences until the work is "released." Emergent forms may in fact present more complexity in their refraction of social experience. Because they have access, people take part in the vernacular whose lives have been shaped by social events and formations that might also have excluded them from "high" aesthetic and intellectual production. Vernacular cultural poetics are "answerable" in the sense that there is close proximity and rich exchange between people involved in the collective production of cultural forms. It is not a transmission across a firm boundary between producer and audience. On the vernacular scale, the circulation of discourse and affect in "democratically constructed and emergent, free-flowing performance" (Limón 2012, 104) often conforms to strict rules of convention, but also can appear unruly in terms of the shifting roles of producer and audience. I propose that the same can be said about vernacular forms of sport, which may include "lower" or more common degrees of athletic achievement, but more significantly, take place outside the large-scale intersection of money and media that frame sport as a mass spectacle.

An analysis of vernacular cultural poetics emphasizes culture as a process of making and social interaction that involves both subtle and spectacular acts of agency, as in the "artful use of language" that is the focus of performance-centered folkloristics (Bauman and Briggs 1990). As "enactments" (Abrahams 1977) carried out with the signifying resources of an established sport, the events that make up Mexican American fastpitch amount to acts of articulation. Much of the cultural work done at the tournaments that were the major sites of my field research is to articulate Mexican American identity to fastpitch softball. To articulate, in the sense proposed by Stuart Hall, is to forge "a linkage which is not necessary, determined, absolute, and essential for all times; it is not necessarily given in all cases as a law or a fact of life. It requires particular conditions of existence to appear at all, and so one has to ask, under what circumstance can a connection be forged or made" (Hall 2016, 121).

The conditions for this articulation are historical and particular. In fastpitch, Mexican Americans have articulated their identities to a sport that was at the very center of public attention across the United States in the 1940s. Over time it has become more marginal, at least as played by men. Yet the commitment of some ballplayers to the sport has been continuous through the specific histories of their local, barrio communities—histories that have featured exclusion, underestimation, dedication, organization, triumph, recognition, and other experiences along the way. This embeddedness in historical particularity is a characteristic of fastpitch as a practice of cultural politics (Figure 3). This is how a study of sport, like the study of other vernacular forms, can "take us to socially situated cultural practices as well as toward an understanding of such culture as intimately tied up with questions of domination, power, struggle, and resistance" (Limón 2012, 122).

Beyond asserting presence and continuity with a specific history, Mexican American fastpitch does not carry any obvious or consensual political position. U.S. patriotism is integral to many fastpitch events, fueled by the patriotic rituals of U.S. sport in general and the historical fact that fastpitch was popular

FIGURE 3 Mike Fernandez of Topeka pitches at the Paul "Waxie" Hernandez fields, Kansas City, Missouri. Photo by the author.

and supported in the U.S. armed forces. But within the fastpitch scene, a wide range of political positions and outlooks is at home within the fastpitch scene. The importance of the multivoiced, emergent cultural swirl that goes on at the scale of the vernacular is heightened in an age when cultural performances like "Make American Great Again" mobilize power in the interest of a very precisely defined, imagined white national subject. The vernacular may not necessarily resist that political theater directly in content, but it does resist the vector of a purifying nationality in the way that vernacular practices tend to be open to multitudes and crisscrossing trajectories. As Chávez argues, the point of identifying and studying a racial tradition is not to solidify a "premodern, authentic specimen."

> Rather, the aim of this discussion is to identify how a performative practice, as part of a racial tradition, operates as part of and in response to the pressures and circumstances of modernity, how it is used to forge collectivity, how it changes and moves as people change and move, how it carries a different kind

of power with it that is conceived against imposed and limiting notions of space and time. (Chávez 2017, 53)

By its form and process, cultural production on a vernacular scale resists purity.

THE ILLUSIO OF FASTPITCH

Games are underway at Washington Park on the south side of Newton, one of three ball fields around town used during the Mexican American tournament. At this one, well into Saturday, a kid is taking a turn as announcer, holding a microphone. He calls the batters by first name over the PA system: "Up to bat is Louis, Roland on deck, Frankie in the hole."

I wander across the street to the Girl Scouts' "little house" that stands in an adjacent city park, where Kansas-style deep-fried flour tacos are for sale. The cool space inside offers respite from the heat, and people linger to reminisce. One woman from Wichita regales me with tales of traveling with teams to Kansas City, Salina, and other places: "I remember when they wouldn't serve Mexicans, so we used to bring picnics." Someone else mentions the football stadium beyond the outfield at Athletic Park across town—teams from Garden City used to sleep on cots under the bleachers and take meals there as well, prepared by women of the hosting community. I recall the conversation at a different tournament, in Kansas City, where the concession stand was behind third base and the old-timers gathered there to tell their stories while following the game. Back in the day, car-pooling teams on road trips tried to economize, opting when they could for all-you-can eat buffets. Food summons up stories as memorable as some of the games:

> "That time in Hutch? *They ran out of food.*"
>
> "My compadre could eat, boy."
>
> "It came from growing up rough. They used to get just tortillas, made the old way" [the speaker demonstrates by patting his hands and turning them one over another] "and one strip of bacon. So later on, he'd get two omelets and eat everything else, too!"

I had heard more stories elsewhere of eating and festivities around the tournaments. In Texas, an often-described image of the old days was the prevalence of barbecuing just past the outfield. In Houston's Memorial Park, Field Number 1 has well-groomed grass in the outfield and a big green wall at the boundary fence like a miniature piece of Boston's Fenway Park, so the mobile smokers are more likely to be set up in the parking lot. There are fewer of them now, old-timers tell me.

"You should have seen it at Settegast, back then," more than one spectator tells me, referring to the city park in the heart of the barrio where the fastpitch tournament began. "The whole outfield was just *lined* with pits!"

I mention that fastpitch seems to be a sport where people tailgate for themselves, an idea that my hosts in Houston seem to like. They are David and Yvonne Rios, from San Antonio but regular attendees at tournaments around Texas, where the Rios's family team, San Antonio Glowworm, competes. They open their circle of lawn chairs for me and a cooler of beer each time I come by. David begins to rave about his love of the sport. Even with most of his playing days behind him, he is devoted to spending weekends at tournaments. "I go back to work and people . . ." He begins to play out both parts of a dialogue scene:

> "What did you do all weekend?"
> "Softball, all day."
> "Whaaaaa?"

Breaking character, he turns to me. "But this is our *life*, papi! I love this! I love it!" He gestures expansively with his beer can and goes on to list all of the other spectacles or activities that he would rather skip to watch fastpitch—Fiesta, Sea World, and others. He smiles and shakes his head, both resigned and delighted by the strangeness of his commitment. Yvonne laughs at this too, commenting that it's not everyone's idea of a romantic couple's weekend.

● ● ●

The festive atmosphere at softball tournaments—the food and drink, music, and storytelling—that accompanies the games situates fastpitch, like other vernacular practices, as a focal point of intensified sociality, standing apart from ordinary life as one of the "fundamentally social acts that stake claims of belonging through a vitality and conviviality otherwise severed or denied" (Chávez 2017, 53). The vitality that was ordinary in an earlier age of presumed segregation is one thing that fastpitch devotees told me about when I asked about the longevity of the tournaments. People started the Mexican tournaments in response to a continuum of overt and implied exclusions. Such grievances are not an ahistorical constant, though. Some things do change and have gotten better. But memories of the bad old days of segregation mix with a nostalgic desire for the sociality of neighborhoods and families that became close-knit partly because of the circumstances of enclosure and containment that structured everyday life. The paradox of achieving the social mobility to move up and out of barrio homes while nostalgically longing for the community experienced there is one of many cultural tensions that overlay a fastpitch tournament.

All of this is premised on multileveled, intensely felt, and publicly expressed forms of caring. Numerous scholars of sport and games focus in on this care—the attachments and attractions of a particular game that amount to a shared affect and investment in the idea that a sport is worth playing. This is the idea of illusio, introduced by Johan Huizinga (Garrigou 2008, 164). Anthropologist Robert Desjarlais glosses illusio as "the investment people make in the activities that give meaning to their lives, their commitment to them" (Desjarlais 2011, 12). This affective tie, which is obvious to those involved and devoted to a particular sphere of practice, can seem arbitrary or oblique to those outside it. Illusio drew Desjarlais's ethnographic attention to chess in a project he calls an "anthropology of passion" (15). In his research on the game and its devotees, Desjarlais pursued questions such as, "Why devote one's energies to a time-intensive pursuit that is little valued or understood in one's own society?" (13).

In a society where sport is everywhere, it is not passion for sport itself that is remarkable. Rather, the specific activities and events that people choose to invest with passion indicate a particular illusio, which can also be understood as a genre in the performance of difference. This has been an important reason to resist treating softball, and the specific softball tradition that is my focus, as a subset of baseball. The legitimacy of softball—and fastpitch in particular—as a sport in its own right was expressed by many of the people I spoke with, and I endeavor to reproduce that priority here. That is not to say that the uniqueness of softball should be my main argument. An intriguing thread throughout this work that I must leave for another researcher to pick up is that the same communities that developed a fastpitch tradition, even the same individuals within those communities, played basketball under comparable circumstances and for similar stakes. Also, it would be foolish to deny the close relationship between softball and baseball outright. For some players, softball was a replacement sport after their prospects in competitive hardball had dried up. But I think it would be a misrepresentation to propose that everything I have observed and heard about fastpitch could just as easily be found in any other sport. The strong commitment that many participants maintained to their sport was to fastpitch in particular—"this game we love," as it is frequently called in social media posts—and taking that seriously in analysis requires considering the specific appeal and character of that sport.[6]

·   ·   ·

A runner is on first base with no outs, and a bunt is tactically in order. I stand behind the chain-link backstop, next to David Rios, who has risen from his folding chair in the shade to come closer and watch the action develop. He nods toward the runner, who is pressing his toe cleats on the leading edge of the base, crouching like a sprinter in the blocks. "You see what they should do?" David asks me.

In softball, base runners may not lead off from a base as they do in baseball, but stealing is allowed as soon as the ball leaves the pitcher's hand. With the path to each base only two-thirds the distance of baseball's ninety feet, a quick runner does not need much time to improve the team's offensive position.

I give my best, rudimentary assessment. "Move him over."

"That's right. Bunt and move him over, Papa."

It looks as if the fielding team concurs, and as the pitcher winds up, both the third and first basemen creep in close to the plate, gloves up. By the time the batter squares off and lowers the bat to a horizontal plane to meet the ball, the space he could be hitting into is excruciatingly tight. The pitch breaks upward, though, and he misses, for a strike. The batter steps out of the box to release tension, taking a practice swing, fixing his helmet, pounding dirt from his cleats. Returning to his stance, it looks as if he might have changed the plan, waving the bat over his shoulder. Just as the pitcher leaps forward and releases, the runner takes off. Swinging hard, the batter drives the ball to near center field. The outfielders sprint for it, but the runner is already rounding second. The shortstop covers third base with his teammates shouting where to throw: "Three! Three! Three!" The throw comes in toward third as the runner slides, raising a billow of dust, and the umpire makes his best calculation of vectors, speed, and timing with limited visibility: safe.

·   ·   ·

My ethnographic approach seeks to draw close to the distinct meanings that converge in fastpitch: the illusio of sports both particular and general; the social determinants of a game and a tradition and their effects that spill over the boundaries of play; and the practices of narration, representation, and memory through which people actively produce Mexican American fastpitch. Any ethnography is necessarily an act of translation between discourses and their characteristic lexicons and genres, if not necessarily between discrete, standard languages. To account for this, I need to situate my use of two key terms throughout this book, since trying to remain close to their use in the field potentially introduces some tension or dissonance with their significance academically. One, *community*, is a risky but sometimes necessary term for referring to collective subjects who make fastpitch happen. The other is the term of identity, *Mexican*, which I use in various ways and in combination with other terms, most notably in unresolved tension with *American*. I have endeavored to follow the lead of my interlocutors in how I understand and deploy these terms, but that is not to say that everyone I conversed with in this project would make the same choices. The language in this book is ultimately my responsibility.

COMMUNITY

I have already made reference numerous times to the "communities" involved in fastpitch, the collective form of the protagonists of this story. Critics who have unpacked its potential to romanticize and smooth over actual heterogeneity and boundary work within groups of people make a strong case that the meaning of community and its use should not be taken for granted (Joseph 2002). In this book, community refers not to the large-scale political entity that Benedict Anderson influentially described in characterizing the modern nation, though the people I interacted with in fieldwork are most likely all engaged in some fashion with the "deep, horizontal comradeship" articulated to the United States by nationalism (Anderson 1983, 7). But that is not the reference here. Instead, when I refer to communities, I am drawing on the sense from linguistic anthropology of a "community of practice" (Mendoza-Denton 2008, 230), a group of participants who take part in a shared repertoire of expressive acts and meanings. In this sense, one could speak of a "fastpitch community," as people sometimes do, though more often the cluster of translocal relationships that develop among people involved in their sport is invoked as the "fastpitch family." Community in this account also serves another important purpose of identifying local, often barrio-based groups of individuals and families, the milieu in which specific fastpitch teams and tournaments developed. These communities are people brought together by the labor needs of specific industries, the shared conditions of segregated residence and limited access to public institutions, a shared ambivalence with regard to the broader imagined community of the United States, and both felt and ascribed cultural attachments to Mexico. All of these shared circumstances of living amount to a common historical experience that is by no means uniform among all the individuals involved. But a substantial number of people can identify that experience as a reference point of difference from the experiences and circumstances of others, notably white Anglos.

The late Nuyorican scholar Juan Flores, in an essay critically considering the prospect of a generalized Latina/o identity, makes some useful points about community. Working subtly with Marxian notions of class, Flores elegantly deconstructs the Spanish term *comunidad* to consider what different referents might exist for terms of identity (1997a). Somewhat ironically, since in this project I tend to avoid the generalization of "Latino" or "Latinx" except when it is used in the source material, I find Flores's analysis compelling as a schema for understanding specifically located communities that are discernible in actually existing, expressive practice. This analysis begins with the delineation of two qualities embedded in the term *comunidad: común* and *unidad. Común* speaks to the shared conditions that bind a community—that which certain people have in common. Among the specific local groups that I routinely describe as "softball-playing communities," I use the idea of común to refer to the circumstances of living, defined by migration in the first decades of the twentieth century (by the relatives of many of the people involved) and by the subsequent circumstances in which they secured housing, interacted with markets of exchange and leisure activities in public, sought education, and so on. Navigating the specific contours of Mexican life in the United States, in a particular place and time, gave people experiences in common, making them a kind of community in itself.

But this is different from a community for itself. Flores goes on to argue that not every historical grouping that forms in such a way is characterized by *unidad*, a shared purpose or interest expressed in coordinated or concerted action. The consciousness or feeling of solidarity between people who share certain conditions in común can lead to unidad, though this is not automatic. To be sure, contrasting and contradictory ideas of a community for itself also makes the existence and outlines of "community" deeply contingent. The question of whether softball, or recreational sports more generally, was an activity and cause to which people should form a unified commitment did not always produce a consensus in the communities I'm talking about. The competing draws of different sports and activities or different associations—playground teams; school teams; a continuum of public, religious, civic, and professional organizations—and different ideas of what was in the interest of "the community" fed a diversity of positions about the relative value of fastpitch to the larger community and the relative significance of playing softball as a practice of community.

All of this heterogeneity needs to resonate in any reference made to "the community," but such considerations also highlight a specific characteristic of sport that helps explain its prominence in communities where, because they are defined to some degree as distinct from society at large, the question of how and whether to draw together in unity carries particular stakes for collective survival and well-being. The relevant characteristic of team sports is they are exercises or rehearsals of unidad. This is partly what has driven other writers to try to articulate the collective benefits of participating in sport—those that extend beyond the obvious aim of winning particular contests. Often the terms available to describe these benefits are examples of human capital, characteristics that develop out of the shared experience of competition and organized unity of a team—such as leadership, pride, and confidence. José Alamillo situates these benefits as collective in his historiographic discussion of the role of baseball in the lives of lemon pickers in California, mentioning that the experience of sport cultivated forms of social organization and personal qualities that would later be applied in more direct social advocacy (2008, 100). Besides the personal development that players take away from participating in sport, they also practice solidarity.

The solidarity of a team is a project of unidad driven initially by the simplified and arbitrary illusio of a game, the shared desire to score points and win. The pleasure of this provides motivation, and the structure of the game determines how much the aim of winning is served by collective agency. Games can be turned by the heroic efforts of exceptional individuals, but when a team manages to unify players' perception, thought, and effort—as in a swiftly and smoothly coordinated double play—the group momentarily acts as a collective subject, and it can stage a palpable drama of unidad above and beyond the obvious and apparent strengths that individuals hold. The unidad of a sports team is not at all immune from the exclusions that can occur in the forming of any collectivity, even in a "community-based" form. But as will be clear in some of the accounts that ballplayers have shared with me, with all its limits, the solidarity built through competition can endure beyond the game.

MEXICANS

In interviews, at moments when it seemed that my interlocutors were thinking about representation, they used a range of terms to identify themselves collectively, including Mexican American, Latino, Chicano, Hispanic, *mexicano*, and American of Mexican descent. The dilemmas of naming have been a persistent feature of Mexican American identity, linking the representations of self and community to material effects of racial categorization in law, citizenship, and everyday life. Ethnographically, the priority of this project is to learn and respect the ways that people identify themselves. In less carefully chosen references, outside of an interview or when the focus is not on naming itself but on the utilitarian task of describing people, it was almost universal in my fieldwork for people to refer to themselves as "Mexicans" and their communities and collective projects as Mexican people, Mexican teams, and Mexican tournaments. These were variously juxtaposed against "Anglos," "white teams," "bolillos," and "mainstream" sports, not at all in equal proportions.

I have adopted this use of "Mexican" to refer to a historically precise but analytically complicated mixture of race, national origin, cultural practice, and kinship. Somewhat in the vein of how W. E. B. DuBois wrote about race, "Mexican" became a badge representing a particular historical experience when used in the way that people did in my chosen field sites. For this reason, I demur on using the term "ethnic Mexicans," which some colleagues have adopted in a well-reasoned effort at precision (Fernandez 2016; Barraclough 2019). Like "social class," "ethnic Mexicans" sounds redundant in the context of my fieldwork, perhaps catering too much to a definition from outside the speaking community I am representing. At fastpitch tournaments, it was only necessary to qualify "Mexican" as "ethnic" if you began with the assumption that the former term denotes national citizenship. I did not find that to be taken for granted in the fastpitch world. In my prior work in some of these communities, I did hear references to "*Mexican* Mexicans," the emphasis implying that when the aim was to refer to nationality, it must be qualified. I defer to many interlocutors who, in my estimation, implied that that it is identity as a lived experience that is fundamental and the identity granted by state documents is secondary.

But this book is also a hybrid document and intentionally made up of a crossing of discourses. In passages where I deploy the analytical registers of my profession, I follow Limón to refer to "Mexican Americans" (1994). The term captures the specificity of the experiences of most of the people I talked to in and around fastpitch. The absence of a hyphen is intentional and important, reflecting that the hybridity of "Mexican American" is not a synthesis but an open dialectic that is lived in tension more readily than it is settled philosophically (see also Bretón 2019). Other analytical frames deployed by my colleagues—for example, sports historians who refer to people of the "Spanish-speaking Americas" (Burgos 2007, 11)—trace important interactions and scales of identity that reach into globalized professional baseball. This transnationalism is also evidence in parts of the Mexican American fastpitch world. During fieldwork, I saw Mexican (Mexican-Mexican), Argentine, Dominican, Cuban, Venezuelan, and Guatemalan players make their appearances at traditionally Mexican American tournaments, usually as sponsored guest pitchers. But while certain pan–Latin American factors, including language, made these visits possible, such hemispheric networks existed in tension with deeply rooted local histories of Mexican American fastpitch. I have focused for this project on the latter.

The ethnoracial character of the tournaments that define these projects is based primarily in relations and networks that developed over time in direct interaction—neighborhood, family, work, and the sport itself. Though *Mexican American* is a usable term to capture the heterogeneous and historically shifting social positions of many people involved in the sport I am looking at, I do not mean to disavow *Chicana/o*. This project, and my analysis, would not be possible without the intellectual history of Chicana/o studies and the social movements that animated it. Moreover, in the field, I recall at least one nostalgic conversation in the bleachers when a fan mentioned "when we were Chicanos" favorably. Movement poet and professor Ramón Del Castillo confirms this overlapping history in his poem "Kansas Fastpitch Softball *a la Chicanada*" (Santillán et al. 2018). But that term, emphasizing political consciousness and autonomy claims, was generally not as salient in my fieldwork during the 2010s. Finally, no one I spoke to in fieldwork used or offered an opinion on the use of Latinx, though the scene could certainly benefit as much as any other from the interrogation of gender binaries embedded in the history of that term.

GAME PLAN

The chapters that follow take up different lines of inquiry in order to draw close to the experience of Mexican American fastpitch. Chapter 1 elaborates on the historical frame I am suggesting for fastpitch as a chapter in a long saga of Mexican people's contested belonging in the United States. The longer histories within which Mexican American fastpitch emerged include the expansion of the United States by military conquest and the attendant racialization of Mexicans for purposes of governing. They also include over a century of Mexicans making their home in the center of what is now the United States, including Kansas, and effectively creating the region I call mid-América, through travel and interaction with the southern borderlands, mainly Texas. I note the emergence of Mexican American fastpitch in temporal proximity to famous moments in Mexican American political mobilization for civil rights and equality, the *Mendez, et al. v. Westminster civil rights* case, and the so-called Longoria affair. I also emphasize that athletic clubs and tournament-hosting organizations are part of a continuum of vernacular organizations through which people have negotiated questions of belonging and identity under these historical circumstances.

Chapter 2 focuses on softball as a national pastime in the early twentieth-century United States and identifies the segregated everyday life of barrio communities as the ground from which Mexican American fastpitch teams and tournaments emerged. Recognizing how fastpitch is deeply embedded in social relationships is key to understanding the enduring interest and commitment to sports in general and fastpitch in particular that are evident in Mexican mid-América. Within that social base, I suggest that softball provided Mexican American communities with a source of both competition and camaraderie.

Chapter 3 digs into specific tournaments, the teams that hosted them, and playing fields to render the processes by which Mexican American communities built a racial tradition of sport. As they did, they negotiated a shifting balance between tournaments as counter-public, barrio institutions, invested in particular people and relationships, and as a staging ground for those interested in presenting their athletic feats and capabilities to a broader audience and field of competition. Throughout the unfinished history of Mexican American fastpitch tournaments, the relative merits and limitations of remaining identified as a "Mexican tournament" as opposed to "opening up" in different ways remain unsettled and debatable, even as the boundaries established under segregation crumble and fade. This remains true for the identity of tournaments across changing circumstances, as well as for the people personally and collectively invested in them.

Chapter 4 examines the figure of the ballplayer, a privileged form of subjectivity that playing fastpitch produced in barrio communities. I note that sport as a kind of discipline of self-making provided Mexican Americans with a resource to counter racist constructions of Mexicanness. Part of what made the prospect of being a ballplayer a path of prestige was that it offered a means of performing generally valorized and legible versions of masculinity. This process produced local legends who distinguished themselves on the field. But many former players maintain that a more important outcome was the camaraderie among ballplayers and their communities, fostering enduring relationships that were ultimately more valuable than victory in a game.

Chapter 5 further develops the implications of the fact that modern sport is profoundly and assertively gendered, and softball itself in particularly complicated ways. Recognizing that fastpitch has been celebrated as a Mexican American tradition mostly as an activity of men, I highlight some of the women who also have participated in this tradition and claim it as theirs. As the position of softball in the gender-divided field of sport has changed over the past century, I argue that the social base of Mexican American fastpitch has made it a resource that endures across generations.

Chapter 6 analyzes softball as a cultural form articulated to Mexican American experience. In conversation with other scholars who have examined sport as a symbolic or narrative idiom, I consider the narratives specific to softball and baseball in terms of what appeal they might hold in a Mexican American context. These include enactments of individual-collective relationships and varying scales of opportunity that are part of the formal structure of the game. Considering how these narrative forms read against the ongoing political dynamics of Mexican identity in the United States sets the form of softball in a particular relation to the larger social formation. On this basis, I argue that a sport that might seem to play an ideological role to support unequal social relations functions differently for Mexican Americans, for whom the demarcated space of the playing field takes on utopian meanings in ways that contrast with social life.

The conclusion returns to the framework of cultural citizenship and the view expressed by people involved in Mexican American fastpitch that their sport of choice is "culture," according to a sense of the term that emphasizes legitimate difference from a mainstream national identity. This discussion underscores the importance of fastpitch to Mexican Americans, arguing further that it is not a naive or even untheorized relationship. Rather, the illusio, or particular and perhaps seemingly peculiar appeal of fastpitch to its devotees, is embedded in the ongoing dynamics of Mexican American history and experience. Indeed, playing the game and maintaining a particular tradition of doing so are ways of materializing and recognizing people's relation to that history.[7]

• • •

At Newton, it is the Friday night before the Fourth of July and the old-timers'
game is getting underway to open the weekend of the Mexican American tournament. Elder men who are veterans of decades of softball have divided into
teams, sporting T-shirts printed for the occasion. All read across the back:
"*Hecho* in America *con* Mexican parts. [Made in America with Mexican parts]"
Paul Vega steps to the pitching rubber, his silver mustache seemingly qualifying him for the retirees' game. His delivery also has a temporal connotation:
he swings his arm back in a slingshot style not often seen these days, changing
the direction of the ball when it is behind him to bring it forward again and
deliver the pitch.

Stiff knees and short breath notwithstanding, the old-timers play a couple
of innings, clearly enjoying their return to the red dirt diamond. Jocular shouts
are a constant accompaniment as players cluster around the chain-link fence
separating each team's bench from the playing field. A foul ball crashes into
the fence, just missing a man who has wandered out to watch the play from
beside first base. "Watch it!" yells a player from the other side. "I don't think
they make parts for that year-model anymore!"

The teams and tournaments that are the living embodiment of Mexican
American fastpitch in mid-América formed under historical circumstances that
continue to inform their complex designation and memory as "Mexican" events.
Though the communities that launched the tradition of Mexican American
fastpitch have seen many of their members move some distance away geographically or socially, the games draw people to return to the ball fields that
are layered with sedimented meaning. They come back for the relationships
formed around playing and to reestablish or shore up their connections to
specific origins and experiences in the past. Fastpitch softball is one way—for
a substantial number of people an exciting, aesthetically pleasing way—to exist
within Mexican American history, and indeed to continue to make it.

⚾ 1 ⚾

MEXICAN QUESTIONS

MEXICAN AMERICAN FASTPITCH SOFTBALL is part of a much longer story, going back at least a hundred more years before the Mexican Catholics in Newton, Kansas, sponsored their own tournament. It was the aftermath of armed conflict over territory in the nineteenth century that created the possibility of the identity "Mexican American"—first, when the Republic of Texas, newly independent from Mexico, was annexed to the United States as a slave state in 1845, and then in 1848 with the Treaty of Guadalupe Hidalgo that ended the Mexican-American War. These measures, which along with the Gadsden Purchase, transferred over half of the territory formerly governed by Mexico to the United States, also shifted the national ground under the feet of Mexican inhabitants of that land, who became the first Mexican Americans. As John-Michael Rivera has noted, this population posed a problem for the ascendant and expansionist white Anglo state (2004, 453). Put another way, when the expanding borders of the United States bumped against and crossed over into Mexico, problematic aspects of its "manifest destiny" doctrine became more plainly apparent.

That term, so familiar from U.S. history textbooks, was coined by the journalist John O'Sullivan in 1845 to describe the inevitable and providential spread of the United States across the continent and promote the annexation of Texas. But what exactly was spreading? Was it republican democracy or white rule? And who was "white," after all? For many Americans at the time, which is to say citizens of the settler republic that was snug against the eastern edge of the continent, the inevitability and rightness of the removal of Indigenous people from the land was taken for granted. Confronting another settler nation to the south, however, also European derived politically but in some ways more hybridized with indigenous predecessors, introduced stumbling blocks into the plot of manifest destiny. A racial dynamic exacerbated the contest between republics as the war effort against Mexico prompted large-scale racialization of Mexicans in U.S. print media, where writers and politicians "promoted racial stereotypes of Mexicans that affected Mexican and Anglo relations for genera-tions" (Rivera 2006, 62). Tireless white supremacist and Senator John Calhoun expressed this problematic in an address to Congress in early 1848:

> We have never dreamt of incorporating into our Union any but the Cauca-sian race—the free white race. To incorporate Mexico, would be the very first instance of the kind, of incorporating an Indian race; for more than half of the Mexicans are Indians, and the other is composed chiefly of mixed tribes. I protest against such a union as that! Ours, sir, is the Government of a white race. . . . We are anxious to force free government on all; and I see that it has been urged . . . that it is the mission of this country to spread civil and religious liberty over all the world, and especially over this continent. It is a great mis-take. (in E. Chávez 2007, 118)

O'Sullivan anticipated this a few years earlier, when, one month after in-troducing the idea of manifest destiny, he published an essay, "The Mexican Question." The question posed by Mexico for manifest destiny was whether the United States should encroach into the territory of the neighboring state—or really for many, how far it should go. If the northern nation could take half the country by force of arms, why not take it all? What was the manifest destiny for expansion southward? But this was also a layered question, opening the issue of how the Anglo state would govern the Mexican people it viewed as racially ambiguous and culturally distinct, who were brought into the "American" fold by war and treaty. Such questions would continue to arise as the population of Mexicans within and subject to the United States grew by migration. If the image of an expanding republic could have been disguised at all as being the advance of a noncoercive idea when O'Sullivan mused over it (despite Calhoun's candidness about "forcing free government on all"), it had hardened into an explicitly racial form by the turn of the century, when the United States found its imperialist feet in the Philippines. The "manifest destiny of the white race" was widely held to be both promising and ordained, including by Theodore Roosevelt and Captain John Bourke, the ethnographer and fighter of Native and Mexican people in Texas (Limón 1994). By the time the upheaval of the Mexican Revolution drove thousands of people to cross north over a border that had relatively recently and just as violently been pushed south, the Mexican question in U.S. society had elaborated from referring to the territorial limits of the Washington republic to questions of how to racialize, contain, and manage populations within its borders who were deemed by the state to be ill fit for self-rule.

José Limón has argued that people of Mexican descent met this historical expansion of the Anglo state with questions of their own, which have been the focus of discourse and cultural production since the mid-nineteenth century. The Mexican question "from below" basically was whether and how to join in the Anglo project of modernity that had been the dominant force shaping American society north of the Rio Bravo (Limón 2012, 10; Flores 2002, 11). The features of this version of modernity not only included national expansion by military conquest but also a notion of citizenship that was explicitly tied to whiteness from its inception in the U.S. Naturalization Act of 1790 (Haney-Lopez 2006, 42). Even as the boundaries of U.S. citizenship were gradually and painfully pried open to allow for a greater diversity of racial identities, full-fledged or "substantive" citizenship (Berlant 2014) remained underwritten by Anglo cultural norms. As Limón phrases the Mexican question that Mexican Americans faced, it was, "How are we to define ourselves and make our way in such an American society?" (2012, 10).

From 1848 on, this was a question of advocating for cultural rights that were initially promised in treaty, such as the right to practice the Catholic religion or speak Spanish, but forgotten or negated in practice. In the post-immigration era, the question of Mexican identity under U.S. governance continued to run up against the normativity of white, Anglo citizenship. A so-called ethnic model of migration proposed that social mobility, prosperity, and acceptance by the Anglo majority would all follow specific acculturations such as English language dominance and intermarriage. From the perspective of the Mexican American experience, none of these correlations turned out to be guaranteed.

AN AGE OF MOBILIZATION

If the question of what it would mean to be Mexican in an Anglo-dominated nation-state was initiated by military territorial conquest and its aftermaths in the nineteenth century, it was shaped in the twentieth century by the conditions and effects of transborder migration, including assimilation as an expectation of citizenship. Political-economic developments, such as the agricultural revolution in Texas (García 2002, 105) and industrialization in the Upper Midwest drove a need for labor, while problems of governance and inclusion were refracted through racial logics presuming that a homogeneous nation was superior, producing deep contradictions that determined many of the experiences of Mexicans in the United States (Innis-Jiménez 2013, 26; Molina 2014, 21). Mexicans were scapegoated for the palpable economic woes of the Great Depression and infamously subject to deportation and new immigration restrictions. A legal classification of Mexicans as "white" as a workaround for racially defined citizenship became a slippery foothold in the Anglo-ruled nation as restrictionists and white supremacists sought to rationalize and codify their presumptions about Mexican inferiority. In 1930 the U.S. Census introduced "Mexican" as a racial category, despite the fact that legal whiteness had already been the basis for some Mexicans to claim citizenship successfully in court (Molina 2014, 5). Even in the midst of early-twentieth-century processes of racialization aimed at preventing Mexicans from realizing a full social and political franchise in the United States, people offered their own answers from below to the Mexican question by mobilizing to claim rights.

Historians have made much of the role of World War II in this process, which no doubt had a massive impact as a moment at which Mexicans proved indispensable to the nation at war, serving and taking casualties in disproportionate numbers, as well as being the most decorated ethnic group in the U.S. military (Valencia 2005, 399). There was also the motivating, contradictory experience of going overseas to fight an overtly racist form of fascism and then returning to second-class citizenship at home. This was part, but not all, of the picture of an upswing in Mexican American activism.[1] After all, the war was still on when Gonzalo and Felicitas Mendez of Westminster, California, sought to enroll their children in elementary school in 1944–45. They were turned away, ostensibly due to English deficiency, despite the fact that their cousins had enrolled in the same school. Since the cousins were lighter complected, with a different last name, and since all of the children in question were legally classified as "white," the Mendezes and four other parents filed a class-action lawsuit on behalf of children of "Mexican and Latin descent," claiming discrimination on the basis of national origin (Valencia 2005, 399–400).

The 1947 ruling in *Mendez et al. v. Westminster*, that segregation into separate schools was unconstitutional, would presage the antisegregation landmark ruling in the 1954 case of *Brown v. Board of Education*, which unlike *Mendez*, would be heard in the U.S. Supreme Court. Richard Valencia notes that *Mendez*, the first case to argue that separate was not equal in K–12 education, was partly enabled by shifts in social science research from hereditarian to environmental explanations for social and economic disadvantage (2005, 398). Charging that segregation was based on arbitrary discrimination by national origin interrupted a commonsense logic that attributed the deprivation of Mexican children to their own racial shortcoming. But if an environmental explanation was ascendant, racial logic also pushed back, as "expert" researchers had very recently testified in the Sleepy Lagoon case that Mexican boys' innate "Aztec" bloodthirst made them a threat to society (Chávez-García 2012, 2).[2] These unsteady intellectual and legal currents, and crisis moments of spectacular anti-Mexican violence like the so-called Zoot Suit Riots betrayed an instability in the racial order, which was pressed further as Mexican Americans organized on their own behalf in the early midcentury (Barajas 2006).

A famous and influential focal point for this organizing was the Felix Longoria affair. Longoria, an oil field worker and fence builder from Three Rivers, Texas, was drafted into the war in 1944 and died in action less than a year later in the Philippines. Private Longoria was buried in a common grave when the Army pulled out two weeks after his death, and his remains were not repatriated to the United States until 1948 (Garcia 2002, 106). Felix's widow, Beatrice Longoria, who had moved to Corpus Christi in the meantime, made arrangements with the Rice funeral home in Three Rivers for Felix's burial, but its manager, Tom W. Kennedy, balked at her request to use the chapel for a viewing. Assuring her that he had "lots of Latin friends," Kennedy reportedly said that "the whites won't like it" if a wake for a Mexican was held in the chapel. He offered instead to furnish and decorate a room of their former house, which Beatrice still owned, for the viewing. Hearing Beatrice's dissatisfaction with the arrangements, her sister, Sara Moreno, approached the American GI Forum, a newly formed civil rights organization under the leadership of Héctor P. García in Corpus (García 2002, 108–110).

García sprang to action, mobilizing a protest rally overnight and wiring the governor, state attorney general, two congressmen, the secretary of defense, and a few other state officials, as well as President Truman. Perhaps most critically, García wrote a longer note to Senator Lyndon B. Johnson, underscoring Longoria's sacrifice in the war and the routine nature of anti-Mexican discrimination in Texas (García 2002, 113). The campaign to bring to light how a casualty of war had been slighted in his hometown resulted in Longoria's being buried with honors in Arlington National Cemetery, with dignitaries in attendance.

These landmarks in early midcentury Mexican American civil rights, the *Mendez* case argued in 1946, and the Longoria affair in 1949, roughly mark out a period in which Mexican Americans were also organizing ball clubs and starting to host softball tournaments. In 1947, the second year that the successful Mexican American softball team in Newton, Kansas, hosted its own tournament, a group of veterans who liked to play sports together in Argentine, Kansas, decided to form a club. Argentine, part of Kansas City, Kansas, was home to a Mexican barrio from at least 1907 and the location of a major rail yard of the Santa Fe system. As recounted in an oral history narrated by community member Loney Sauceda in 2011, the group that had first called themselves the Argentine Eagles Vets Club approached the local American Legion post and were turned away by the commander, who stated that Mexicans could not be members. With the help of another post from the Rosedale neighborhood, the Eagles organized a commission for their own American Legion Post 213, meeting in the Methodist mission building across the street from the rail yard. The post supported teams that competed in softball and other sports, and the Eagles Nest ball field adjacent to the post kept busy with fastpitch.

The Mendez and Longoria stories are well known to students of Mexican American history, but the efforts to organize and participate in sports might seem to be an activity removed from the politics of campaigns and legal cases. From the outside, a critic may even wonder whether investing in recreational activity would divert people and energy away from promoting social change. Within Mexican American communities, however, no such divergence was evident. For example, the influential Fraga family of the East End of Houston, who are recognized for their impact on law, politics, business, and community service, were actively involved in sports including softball (Chambers 2015).[3] Felix Fraga, the first Latino to play baseball for the University of Houston, was also the first president of the Rusk Athletic Club when it took over the state Latin American softball tournament that had been run by the Second Ward Athletic Club. Fraga went on to serve on the Houston City Council as part of a long career in community and public service. Politics and fastpitch overlapped in a similar way in Austin, where Richard Moya, the first Mexican American elected to public office for Travis County, Texas, worked at the Pan American Recreation Center in the Eastside barrio (Barnes 2014) and ran the Aces fastpitch team.

For years, players would head from league games at Pan Am to the nearby Rabbit's Lounge, where they might drink alongside political figures such as state senator Gonzalo Barrientos, who was an honorary member of the Austin Jokers athletic club. Tony Castillo, former manager of the Jokers, related to me that softball players were "a big part of the political movement in Austin." Coach Castillo himself was courted by political organizers to run for office, but the public scrutiny that would entail did not appeal to him. "That's not me," he told me in an interview, "even though I knew what the hell's going on. The respect of the community we did have." Organizations like the GI Forum and the League of United Latin American Citizens (LULAC) joined church and mutual-aid societies in sponsoring softball teams. Across the board, sports featured prominently in everyday life at a time when Mexican Americans were seeking to solidify their social and political standing in the United States.

MID-AMÉRICA

In 1969 the Chicano Youth Liberation Conference in Denver brought activists together from around the country—many of them students but also representing a range of self-organized groups. Reflecting on the experience of encountering Chicana/os outside the Southwest, the celebrated poet Alurista famously recalled, "I didn't even know there were Mexicans in Kansas!" (Fernández 2016, 62). A little more than twenty years later, when I traveled down the logistical spine of mid-América that is interstate highway I-35, from the center of the country toward the borderlands, I did not expect that much had changed in that regard. I had studied in Kansas, following family and community connections as well as a scholarship, and was proceeding to Texas for graduate school. As an undergraduate at Bethel College in North Newton, Kansas, I had been aware of the local Mexican community primarily because of Chuck's Familia, a restaurant beloved by students like me, as well as townspeople, for their burritos "smothered with pork chili," as was typical of the region. This was not Tex-Mex, but a Kansas version of Mexican cuisine, developed over generations out of ingredients available to the Mexican-descended families in the century or so since the Santa Fe railroad company recruited them to the area. I have only seen one restaurant ever try on the label "Mexi-Kans" for this food, but a softball catcher from central Kansas who moved to Colorado shared with me that his friends there called a particular dish made with fat-fried, wheat flour tortillas "Wichitacos."

Every time I enjoyed the smothered burrito with cheese at Chuck's, however, and what I took to be the charming code-switching of the name "Chuck's

Familia," I was ignorant of the fact that Joaquin "Chuck" Estrada, the namesake of the restaurant, was called that by virtue of his skills and success as a softball pitcher. For most of my time eating at Chuck's, which roughly overlapped with my undergraduate years, I was also unaware that each Fourth of July weekend, Mexican American softball teams crowded into Newton to compete in the annual fastpitch tournament. One summer that I spent in Chicago for an internship was an eventful one back in Newton, as the Houston Nine, a formidable tournament-winning team assembled by an ambitious sponsor bent on bragging rights, flew to the tournament by way of the Wichita Mid-Continent Airport. That arrival made the local papers, and the Houston Nine went home to Texas with a trophy.

But I was unaware, so a couple of years later when I went to Texas to study, drawn by the graduate program founded by Américo Paredes, I didn't really expect anyone to know better than Alurista that there were Mexicans in Kansas. I was taken by surprise meeting a fellow student when we both joined the university mariachi ensemble, Mariachi Paredes de Tejastitlán, after the director found out that I had some experience on the violin. My bandmate was from the Rio Grande Valley of South Texas, and when she politely asked where I had come from, I replied that I was raised in Ohio but had studied in Kansas.

"Oh, Kansas? Where?" she asked.

"A little town called Newton. A lot of people around here haven't heard of it."

Immediately she replied, "Oh, I know Newton. My high school mariachi played at a softball tournament up there."

By that time, I had vague recollections of hearing about "the softball tournament," but it had never struck me as something that a high school music group (and South Texas school mariachis can easily include dozens of members) would drive over thirteen hours for. When I had heard reference to "the oldest continuing Mexican American men's fastpitch softball tournament in the country," like many from outside the community that hosted this annual event, I was probably prone to hear "oldest" and think "only." Clearly, though, there were people in Texas who knew that there were Mexicans in Kansas.

Thanks to the work of Paredes on the *corrido*, the typically heroic ballad form born in the conflicted borderlands that are now South Texas and northern Mexico, we know that the oldest extant, complete version of the form is the "Corrido de Kiansis," dating to the 1860s. There are two versions of the song, known as "Kiansis I" and "Kiansis II," and both recount how Mexican vaqueros drove stock to Kansas City. The song form that would later be known for accounts of revolutionary adventures, and more recently of contraband border crossing in the context of cartels and drug wars, focuses in these early examples on the risks and challenges of the drive, of fording rivers and facing killer bulls. Both texts describe "Americans" as being in awe of the riding prowess and courage of the Mexicans—in "Kiansis II," thirty American cowboys are unable to corral five hundred steers, but five Mexicans make quick work of the job, leaving the Anglos "staring in amazement" (Paredes 1995, 53–55). The nineteenth-century texts provide an intriguing historical background to the Houston Nine's odyssey to Newton to showcase their athleticism in "Kiansis," and also to the Austin Jokers who a little earlier had traveled to win the annual Kansas City Amigos tournament in the 1980s. The corrido shows there is nothing new about Mexicans traveling deep into mid-América to display their physical skills in competition. As for besting the Anglos, scoring similar intercultural points as the five Mexican cattle drivers of Kiansis II required less travel for teams from segregated and sometimes isolated barrios during the mid-twentieth century. In Austin, teams from the Eastside, based at the ballpark adjoining the A. B. Cantú Pan American Recreation Center, traveled west across the boundaries of de facto segregation to compete at Butler Fields with "white" teams, often stunning their opponents by winning the game.

The contested dynamics of belonging and exclusion that I've glossed as "Mexican questions" were as evident in the center of the United States as in the borderlands. A letter published in the Newton *Evening Kansan Republican* on August 19, 1946, from Ignacio Martinez expresses the frustration of unmet promises of full citizenship, addressing a merchant whose establishment inspired the letter's headline, "No Mexicans Allowed": "Not very long ago, the Mexican boys from all over the United States were fighting and dying side by side your own friends and perhaps your own relatives, Mr. Doy. Do you know why they were fighting and dying, Mr. Doy? They were fighting and dying for Democracy!" (Martinez 1946).

Despite softball box scores in the pages of the same newspaper reporting rosters entirely populated with Spanish surnames in the city softball league, people I have interviewed from this community pass on different family stories: being unwelcome in Little League play or passed over for invitational weekend softball tournaments. "You see," said Manuel Jaso, "we were the first cut, without a tryout." But recreational softball may have offered some points of access in a context that was generally even more closed off. A quirky feature of the illusio of sport is that even while widespread attention and investment attest to its high social value, there is also a sense that this value lies precisely in sport's nonimportance, that is, in being "just a game" (Garrigou 2008, 165). It is plausible that this sense of the triviality of sport made it seem relatively harmless to the boundaries of segregation and allowed an all-Mexican team to play in the Newton city softball league. At a time when downtown merchants were free to turn nonwhite people away, the league also included a team composed entirely of African American players, the Wolverines. The logic of the day apparently allowed for teams representing different racial communities to face each other but not for any of the teams to be integrated. Separate racial teams represented separate racial communities in a culturally legible form. The soft confrontation of play between them reinscribed their presumably inherent difference in ways preferable to more direct social confrontations over material stakes. Former Newton player Mario Garcia described a similar dynamic persisting during his youth in the 1950s and 1960s:

> Because a lot of times we couldn't take our fight to the street. And I'm talking
> about being able to live as a normal person. We weren't allowed to go places
> in town. There was some confectionaries, cafes, restaurants, we just weren't
> allowed to go in. Even walking to school, people used to tell us to walk on the
> other side of the street.

Moreover, in this small town, where high school basketball was a point of pride (the nostalgic filters of the film *Hoosiers* come to mind), nonwhite students were not allowed on the varsity team in the 1940s (Schmucker 2019).[4] Newton High had a separate Black basketball team, and Mexican youths played hoops for their church in Catholic Youth Organization tournaments and other events. In one memorable year, Newton High School won the state basketball championship while a team of track workers' children won the state Mexican tournament, sponsored by the Catholic church. Newton artist and community-based historian Ray Olais included the Mexican basketball teams from the 1940s as part of a historical display that he mounted at the seventy-first annual tournament. As we viewed the display, former softball pitcher and college basketball player Paul Vega pointed out the 1948–1949 team to me, which included Mario's uncle, Bernie Castro, who would become one of the first nonwhite basketball players for Newton High in 1951. "That was one hell of a team," he told me. "That year Newton High School won state, but on the weekends at the Y, they couldn't even stay on the court with the Mexican team."

VERNACULAR INSTITUTIONS AND CULTURAL CITIZENSHIP: ANSWERING MEXICAN QUESTIONS ON THE FIELD

Softball was not only part of the history of Mexican Americans seeking to gain entry into social arenas controlled by Anglos. It was also the focus of barrio-based vernacular organizations. As the birthright U.S. citizenship of Mexican Americans was rendered precarious or limited through various practices of discrimination, including de facto segregation that extended from work and residency to education and recreation, Mexican Americans built their own popular institutions to provide a means of belonging and social activity. As in the question of political engagement raised earlier, it is not useful to try to place athletic clubs on one side or the other of a sharp binary divide between resistance and accommodation. Rather, sports teams are part of a wide continuum of Mexican American vernacular social organization that also encompasses church festivals, *mutualistas* (mutual aid organizations), social clubs, musical groups, restaurants, and other entities. In his San Diego–based documentary on lowrider car style, *Everything Comes from the Streets*, Alberto Lopez Pulido (2014) includes historical accounts of drag-racing teams and the social "jacket clubs" of Southern California, informal youth groups who marked their affiliation by naming themselves and wearing matching clothes. Pulido's film makes clear that direct lines of interaction and mutual influence tie aesthetic and leisure clubs, radical movement groups, and recognized civic organizations together.[5] It is striking that one of the social clubs Pulido mentions, Los Chicanos, adopted that term of self-reference in 1955, well before the political movement that made *Chicano* a household word (García 2015). A question that the founders and participants in all of these diverse organizations negotiated was what particular balance they would strike between two competing interests: autonomy as a group and recognition from outside. This was cultural citizenship practiced in social organization.

Sports were part of this institutional life in which Mexican Americans worked to find a balance between the aim of winning acceptance from white-Anglo-dominated society and retaining autonomy over self-definition and community priorities. The concrete clarity of athletic contests provided opportunities for players who experienced exclusion or marginalization to seek respect in socially acknowledged recreational activities. Athletic success seemed relatively indisputable: a ball dropped through a hoop or hit over a fence could not be called back for arbitrary reasons (at least not easily, though visible and concrete results were sometimes minimized, diminished, or reversed). Playing a sport that historically has been associated with wholesome, law-abiding citizenship, and even deployed as a kind of participatory propaganda for Americanness, fastpitch teams embedded in communities geographically and socially bounded by segregation offered a means for participants and spectators alike to develop and display identities that made sense to them and spoke to their experience.

Other ethnographic and historiographic scholarship makes it clear that playing fields have repeatedly provided the scene for addressing Mexican questions, even as the stakes and specific terms shifted with context. Like fastpitch players and fans in the railway world of mid-América, Mexicans in Chicago during the Great Depression avidly played baseball and basketball, "not only to persist and persevere, but as a vehicle to create organizations to improve their everyday lives" (Innis-Jiménez 2014, 70). Like Mexican soccer associations much later, also in Chicago, fastpitch tournaments and leagues provided "a social space to initiate political participation, contest the dominant culture, defy urban segregation, construct and display transnational ethnic loyalties and celebrate a notion of Mexicanness based on the Mexican experience in the United States" (Pescador 2004, 355). Like the *charros* of California—"Mexican cowboys" who to this day display unambiguously Mexican styles of horsemanship and cattle handling in aestheticized and competitive spectacles—fastpitch "allows ethnic Mexicans to resist the core processes through which they have been racially subjugated in the United States" and implicitly "galvanizes hope for a more autonomous, dignified, and equitable future" (Barraclough 2019, 5). As in other communities and other sports, fastpitch has served as "a mechanism for enjoyment, resistance, and developing ethnic identity, pride, and solidarity" (Iber 2016, 7).[6]

In our conversations, devotees of fastpitch freely discussed how the benefits and effects of playing extended far beyond the foul lines, but they also enthusiastically extolled the intrinsic value of the game itself. More than a few interviewees, when I asked why softball had such appeal and staying power in certain Mexican American communities, answered immediately, "The competition!" Other times when I asked, "Why fastpitch?" thinking in my own mind that playing the sport was a choice made over a wide range of other activities—say, in the arts or more explicit political activism—interviewees would muse something like this: "Well, slowpitch wasn't around yet, and we didn't have a Little League," as if playing ball were taken for granted, and it was only a question of what particular version one played. In line with Adrian Burgos's work on "baseball's infusion into Latino cultures," then, fastpitch softball in mid-América is not simply a matter of "America's game" being imposed on an immigrant population like the English language, despite the imperial ambitions of A. G. Spalding that baseball should "follow the flag" (Burgos 2007, 71). Navigating the contradictory currents of Anglo-dominated social structures that simultaneously sought to contain Mexicans in segregated spaces (including barrio ball fields) and to "Americanize" them through pedagogical deployments of activity such as sport (Innis-Jiménez 2014, 72), Mexican Americans made fastpitch softball their own. As Burgos found with professional ballplayers, fastpitch in barrios was, and remains, a complicated process of exchange and negotiation (2007, xiii), part of a larger, unfolding history of cultural citizenship.

Contested belonging has animated Mexican American cultural production in many idioms of expression, as artists, writers, practitioners of folklore, and so many others have grappled with the predicament that scholar Alma Gaspar de Alba calls being "alter/native" (1998). This is the specific experience of subjects being figured as "other" in a colonial sense, when it occurs within a nation that to some extent made those precise subjects, and indeed depends on them for its existence, its economy, its defense, and its own, normative sense of identity. Mexican American fastpitch, a history that continues to unfold, is rich with examples of people who, consciously or not, decided to answer the Mexican question—"How are we to define ourselves and make our way in such an American society?"—by being good at sports. In the mid-twentieth century, fastpitch softball provided a means to do so that was fully embedded in the social fabric of communities that had been partially cordoned off from full participation in public life. At the same time, fastpitch offered limited channels to enter into competition in the broader public sphere. While resisting the boundaries imposed on them by this containment, Mexican Americans also refused to give up certain cultural practices marked as "different," resignifying them as "ours." At the same time, they organized and persistently claimed space within American culture, including on the playing fields of schools and parks.

⚾ 2 ⚾

HECHO IN AMERICA CON
MEXICAN PARTS

I WAS SITTING IN THE BLEACHERS at Athletic Park when a small ruckus a little way down the bench drew the attention of the fans away from the field. A young man had shown up on furlough from military service to surprise his friends and family, who had no idea he was coming. Shouts of laughter rang out as relatives clapped him on the back and embraced him tearfully. He had been stationed in East Africa and chose to use up his only leave (in place of Christmas) to fly the twenty-four-hour itinerary home for the tournament. Taking a furlough to attend a sporting event that can more or less accurately be called "amateur" is a noteworthy choice, but to many in attendance at Newton, it was a logical one. Manuel Jaso, the tournament director, told me when I first met him that everyone in the extended families of people involved in the tournament here knows that "you don't get married on the Fourth of July." That date, or rather the weekend close to the Independence Day holiday, is reserved for softball. Interviewing Mel Vega, the daughter of the pitcher in the old-timers' game, about why, after moving from her childhood home to Kansas City, she travels back when possible to visit the field and the tournament where her father earned a reputation as one of the local legends, she replied, "My Dad always said, 'Newton is the center of the world.'"

I have yet to hear anyone challenge the claim made by the Newton Mexican American Athletic Club that their event is the oldest Mexican American fastpitch tournament in the country. Members of the Rusk Athletic Club in Houston generally accept the view that their tournament, held annually two weeks after Newton's, has the second-oldest continuous run by one year, though the Second Ward Athletic Club of Houston hosted a precursor tournament, the first annual Latin-American State Tournament, in 1940. Newspaper archives also show evidence of an all-Mexican tournament in Newton as early as 1940. Records were spotty and some years were rained out, but by generally accepted consensus, Newton celebrated its seventieth annual tournament in 2018, and Houston did so in 2019. These are only the oldest of the tournaments that are the current manifestation of Mexican American fastpitch.[1] In addition, other tournaments with more than a half-century behind them include those hosted by the Stateline Locos of Kansas City and the San Antonio Glowworm. Still others that began a little later include tournaments hosted in cities like Austin and El Paso, on both sides of State Line Road in Kansas City, and in Kansas railroad towns like Topeka and Emporia. These tournaments, hosted by teams such as the San Antonio Compadres, the Austin Jokers, and the Kansas City Angels, Eagles, and Indios, reflect local communities that have been playing, cheering on, and organizing softball since the 1930s and 1940s, when the so-called Mexican American generation was coming of age after their parents took part in the mass migrations from Mexico to the United States around the time of the Mexican Revolution.

Richard Santillán has documented the depth of ball-playing history in the Mexican American Midwest (2008; see also Iber 2016, chap. 2).[2] The tournaments I have attended in six cities over summers since 2011 fall within a geographic column joining the Midwest to Texas, the region I call "mid-América" and that the *Houston Chronicle* in the late nineteenth century called "The Railway World" (Blevins 2014). Extending from the borderlands north into markets for beef, oil, and labor, this region charts many of the destinations of the wave of migration from Mexico that occurred during that country's social revolution of 1910 to 1920. In fact, Newton and Houston, the sites of the two longest-running tournaments, basically sit on the spine of the railroad system that links the Central United States and Mexico.

Softball in the early to mid-twentieth century was one of the most popular recreational and entertainment activities nationwide. Cities large and small hosted weeknight leagues and occasional weekend tournaments, which sometimes reflected the social boundaries and hierarchies of the time by being segregated. In Newton, railroad workers and their families participated in the city softball leagues that were popular before and after World War II, but also relate memories of discrimination like Manuel Jaso's of being "first cut, without a tryout" from high school sports teams. After World War II, Newton ballplayers, like many other veterans who were emboldened by their experience with the military to form organizations to advocate for civil rights, founded the annual Mexican American tournament on their return from the war. For years, the Newton tournament was affiliated with Our Lady of Guadalupe church, and the team represented the Holy Name Society lay organization. The Rusk tournament in Houston grew out of the Rusk Settlement House in the Second Ward and eventually served as a state Mexican American championship, colloquially known as "the Latin." The metropolitan area of Houston, much larger than Newton, drew ballplayers from a variety of occupations, including from the families of mule team drivers who had been recruited from Mexico to nearby Baytown to work the oil fields. Some members of these families played ball while pursuing careers in law, business, and accounting. This generation of professionals with barrio roots has been active sponsoring teams for the Latin and organizing the tournament.

The two oldest historic tournaments are focal points of circuits of similar events in Kansas and Texas. As vestiges of a time when de facto, if not de jure, segregation was the normal state of affairs for recreation as well as other aspects of daily life, these tournaments and the teams that hosted them were known to be predominantly, if not exclusively, "Mexican," and only shortly before I initiated my fieldwork in 2011 did most of them become open to players of any background. Despite some diversification of the participants, the tournaments that I count as part of Mexican American fastpitch retain that ethnic identification by virtue of their history and the individuals and families who predominantly take part. These events are not only competitions. Because each is typically held at the same time of the summer every year, they become family reunions and opportunities to construct a collective memory that asserts and celebrates the specific historical experience that members of these communities share. The stakes involved in launching and maintaining their own sporting institutions have certainly changed for Mexican Americans since the 1940s, but as one arena among many in which to claim belonging to the larger society while resisting the erasure and negation of Mexican American experience, fastpitch softball offers a view into a continuous, unfolding history.

• • •

In Athletic Park in Newton, Kansas, an exuberant Tejano polka is blaring over the PA system as crowds arrive at the softball field (Figure 4). Handshakes, hugs, and kisses accompany the music and laughter as people stake out their

FIGURE 4 Newton Mexican American Fastpitch Softball Tournament, Athletic Park, Newton, Kansas. Photo by the author.

areas in the shade. Groups of twenty or thirty wearing matching T-shirts arrange coolers, chairs, and softball gear under portable canopies. The music pipes down, and the tournament director, dressed to play in the old-timers' game, introduces the local priest, who gives an invocation at home plate and sprinkles holy water on the field. Beyond the first-base foul line in the distance stands the vacant Harvey Building, where passenger trains bound from Kansas City to Santa Fe used to stop to take on clean china and fresh food for passengers.

A color guard of ROTC students advances on the pitching rubber, bearing flags of the Republic of Mexico, the United States, and Newton's Mexican American Athletic Club. The flag bearers split up so that Mexico ends up at first and the athletic club at third, with the American flag at center in the pitching circle, while a young woman takes the microphone to sing an a cappella rendition of the "Star-Spangled Banner." The flags seem to map out some kind of continuum, an identity mix echoed in the code-switching slogans that appear on the back of the T-shirts that men in their sixties and older are wearing for the old-timers' game that will open the weekend's competition: "Hecho in America con Mexican parts."

The tradition of Mexican American fastpitch softball began as Mexican people navigated the race-segregated landscape of public recreation in the early to mid-twentieth century. This history has always been a mixture of struggling for inclusion in playing spaces like city and industrial leagues or tournaments like the massive, multiweek competition once sponsored annually by the *Houston Chronicle*, while also assembling the resources and space for teams based in community and family relationships to have their own competitions. The latter trajectory produced the tournaments that continue today and are the site of Mexican American fastpitch as an ongoing vernacular practice rather than a distant, finished history.

In this chapter, I focus on how Mexican American fastpitch teams and tournaments are embedded in the social circumstances of their communities. To tie this to the historical frame of Chapter 1, I first discuss what softball represented as a participatory national pastime in the midcentury United States and then consider the circumstances of segregation that fastpitch players have described as motivation for maintaining a distinctive tradition of softball. Finally, I render the sport's embeddedness within the relations of everyday life, the site where the dynamics of cultural citizenship remained a poetic tension in fastpitch as a vernacular social and cultural form.

A NATIONAL PASTIME

Athletics provided one of many areas in which Mexican Americans confronted the question posed by life under conditions of de facto segregation: how to inhabit a citizenship that was not always fully recognized. Softball was one of the sports for which this was true. To understand the particular appeal and staying power of softball requires some perspective on how widely popular this sport was in midcentury, notably as participatory recreation, as well as being a spectator sport that brought exciting live entertainment into communities before the era of ubiquitous televised sports. Softball also became nearly universal as a social intervention saddled with pedagogical aims and other good intentions (depending on the eye of the beholder) as it was promoted throughout the urban neighborhoods and community parks around the country.

The origin of softball is widely held to have been an impromptu indoor baseball game taken up in Chicago in 1887 by Ivy League alumni waiting to hear by telegram the results of the Harvard-Yale football game. To pass the time while awaiting the outcome of their bets in a boat club gym on Lake Michigan, the sports fans bound up a stray boxing glove and played ball with it, batting with a broomstick. A reporter in the group, George Hancock, published a set of rules, formalizing the game as indoor baseball and promoting it as a seasonal placeholder between football and baseball, as basketball had not yet taken its place as the indoor winter sport (Dickson 1994, 47–48). By the turn of the century, the scaled-down version of baseball that had been popular indoors was catching on in playgrounds and parks around the country. Paul Dickson, in a tome on softball published by the Worth sporting-goods equipment company, argues that the sport variously known as kittenball, playground ball, twilight ball, army ball, and other names was a flexible game open to experimentation and change, thanks to its distinction from tradition-bound baseball (1994, 58). Being by definition "not really baseball," softball developed in a marginal state that gave it a kind of freedom and flexibility. Along with the effect of producing many sets of rules and styles of play, this left softball open to participation by people who had been excluded from more formalized recreational activities—notably women, who played softball virtually from its beginning. Requiring less real estate than baseball also made softball appeal to people and communities for whom recreational opportunities and resources were scarce during the Great Depression.

According to writer Erica Westly's history, softball was promoted by factory owners in the early 1900s in the interest of a healthy and happy workforce. Industrial softball was also the beginning of a quasi-professional system in which the effort to recruit particular players to a sponsor's team might include hiring them on at the factory or commercial business that supported the ball club (2016, 2). In 1933 the sport got a boost and a reason to organize into a universal, common game when it was featured at the Century of Progress International Exposition, otherwise known as the Chicago World's Fair. Promoted by a sportswriter and a sporting-goods merchant, the World's Fair softball tournament drew sixteen teams of men and eight teams of women, competing in both fastpitch and slowpitch versions of the game. The teams played by a common set of rules and drew over 350,000 spectators over the course of three days. The competition got little attention from the press, but the fan turnout established softball as a spectator sport (27, 3).

The compact scale of the game that began as indoor baseball accounted for part of its rapidly growing appeal. The short base paths and possibility of stealing made base running fast and competitive, earning fastpitch the nickname "lightning ball." Morris Bealle, author of *The Softball Story* (1954), noted that the emphasis on speed and agility also opened the door for the "small, wiry player" to be a valuable asset. Bealle considered speed a mark of modernity as well, writing elsewhere in the same book, "In this age, when streamlining is the order of the day, from automobiles to radios, from airplanes to munitions of war, the streamlined brand of baseball has definitely surpassed the orthodox version of America's national game" (quoted in Westly 2016, 32, 61). The appeal for both players and spectators was such that the Amateur Softball Association (ASA), which had formed after the 1933 fair in Chicago, reported that 250,000 teams contended to play in the association's national tournament each year in the mid-1930s, again with both men and women playing. Nationwide, 125 million people watched softball games each year (Westly 2016, 73). Enthusiasm for the sport quickly reached the railroad hub town of Newton, Kansas, with a population of about 11,000 at the time. A 1934 article in the *Evening Kansan Republican* reported that the city league would have eight teams, as it had the year before, and with electric lights being installed at a local college field, games would be played four nights a week ("Soft Ball Season Starts" 1934).

By 1938 the ASA reported that 5 million people played in organized leagues around the country. The popularity of industrial leagues, and the potential role of the popular sport in maintaining labor peace, was referenced by Lowell Thomas and Ted Shane in a softball-promoting book in 1940: "Were old Karl (Whiskers) Marx alive today, we venture to guess he'd have to do something about softball. . . . There are rumors around that Detroit, spawning bed of the hottest softballers and unionists and a swell place to start a revolution, has been pretty well tamed by softball" (quoted in Dickson 1994, 69). Whether or not it was motivated to quell workers' resentment in that way, the Works Progress Administration built over three thousand athletic fields as part of its multibillion-dollar impact on the landscape of everyday U.S. life between 1935 and 1943, emphasizing softball fields and often including lights to make nighttime play possible (Dickson 1994, 72; Leighninger 1996, 226). In 1940, when L. H. Wier, the director of the National Recreation Association, addressed the ASA's annual meeting, he extolled the democratic nature of the sport and its positive social influence, by implication on marginalized populations: "Softball fields . . . are cheaper to build and maintain and will build stronger character than penal institutions" (Dickson 1994, 82).

When Mexican Americans stepped onto these fields prepared by public investment, ideologies of social welfare and public health, and articulations of physical competition with gendered notions of nation and citizenship, they came ready to play. Despite innumerable measures of de facto segregation that organized the spaces of work, residence, education, and public life so as to isolate and contain Mexican American communities and regulate interactions across racialized social boundaries, softball offered a chance to take part in an activity that was being enthusiastically practiced and celebrated throughout American society. At the same time that they built civil rights campaigns and organizations, Mexican Americans started sports teams. While pushing schools to integrate rather than exclude their children, they were playing in softball leagues. And when paternalistic encouragement to play America's playground game began to run a little thin, they held tournaments for Mexican teams only, creating a version of the sport and a venue for playing that would never make them feel unwelcome due to their ethnic background or shared history.

The Newton tournament advertised its seventieth annual iteration in 2018, though the team that was the forerunner of the Newton Mexican American Athletic Club, responsible for the tournament today, hosted a tournament in 1946, and newspaper reports mention a Mexican softball meet as early as 1940. Taking into account a couple of rained-out years, though, the tournament celebrated its thirtieth anniversary in 1978 and fiftieth in 1998 (Figure 5). What began as an invitational event drawing Mexican teams from several surrounding, small railroad towns and the nearby metropolis of Wichita eventually became a pivotal tournament on a circuit of similar Mexican events, serving as a de facto championship for teams from the state capital of Topeka and Kansas City and drawing visiting teams from Colorado, Nebraska, Oklahoma, and Texas at its peak.

Houston's tournament, once promoted as the State Mexican American championship, dates from 1949. The Rusk Athletic Club began as a project of the Rusk Settlement House, a social services organization in Houston's Second Ward barrio that had been established in the first decade of the 1900s as part of the international settlement house movement. Houston ballplayers involved with the club organized a Mexican tournament as early as 1940, but as in Newton, consecutive annual events were interrupted by the war. Later known as the State Latin American championship, and colloquially as "the Latin," Houston's tournament marked seventy years in 2019.

From the time of the *Mendez* decision in 1947, during at least twenty-five years of desegregation efforts by Mexican Americans, the organizers of tournaments for Mexican teams cultivated them as a kind of racial tradition of sport—an annual cycle of tournaments that accrued enough cultural value to their host communities that organizers accept it as a duty to keep them going

FIGURE 5 Souvenir program cover, Newton Mexican American Fastpitch Softball
Tournament, 1998. Used with permission of the Mexican American Athletic Club.

from year to year as a sign of respect and even an obligation to those who came
before. To understand the obstacles to that longevity, it is important to consider
the conditions of segregation from which the Mexican tournaments emerged.

THE CONDITIONS OF SEGREGATION

The organizers of the Newton tournament talk about its identity rule, which
limits the participation of players without Mexican ancestry, as maintaining
"our tradition," and continue to draw justification from the history of their own
segregation and exclusion. As Manuel Jaso, who directs the Newton tournament
as his father, Nicholas Jaso, once did, said to me in an interview:

> From what I've gathered, my dad told me . . . they were not allowed to play
> alongside the Anglos, so they started, basically a league of their own. And not
> just them but the blacks had a league, and they could play against each other,
> but not necessarily with the Anglos, which uh, you know. . . . Just a sign of the
> times, you know?

"The times" referenced here were just before the mid-twentieth century, and segregation was taken for granted as the order of everyday life in much of the United States. As part of the background for his biography of Mike Torrez, the major league pitcher and denizen of the Oakland barrio of Topeka, Kansas, Jorge Iber describes how segregation in Kansas as experienced by Mexican people was uneven and often contradictory. Local practices effectively barred Mexicans from some parks and places of business. Exclusion of Mexican Americans from public life was not always official or absolute, and economics played a key role. Certain employers, such as the Santa Fe Railroad, took stands in defense of their workforce by refusing to comply with federal repatriation orders (Iber 2016, 14). Railroad companies had actively recruited Mexicans to work on their track throughout the 1920s and even before, in some cases providing housing in modest *casitas* that would form enclave communities in small towns along the line. Beyond this relationship to the railroad, Mexican American fastpitch was established in a period when cracks were beginning to show in the edifice of segregation. But even as the *Mendez* decision heralded desegregation advances that were still to come, the appeals process of that case and events like the Longoria affair showed that the struggle by Mexican Americans to demand full status as Americans would proceed unevenly, with steps forward and backward. They were far from the only such situations.

This is why anthropologist Jennifer Najera, providing context for her historical ethnography of race in a small South Texas town, argues that the history of segregation experienced by Mexican Americans is not a story of steady progress from premodern ignorance to equality (2015). On the contrary, Najera shows how patterns of segregation were crosshatched with contradiction and exception, and the greater part of the twentieth century can be characterized not in terms of a binary between segregation and freedom but what she calls "accommodated segregation." In this social formation, certain individuals of Mexican descent (in her specific area of focus and mine) may have experienced a measure of social mobility and opportunity, often because they were deemed exceptional in their racial, financial, educational, linguistic, or other characteristics. And yet the notion of Mexicans as "racial others" could come back into play at any time to throw up and enforce social barriers.

Najera joins other scholars who argue that the segregation of everyday life and public space emerged in the early twentieth century as a response to what Anglos viewed as the "Mexican problem"—what I have been tracking here as the Mexican question. In Texas, an ascendant Anglo order displaced traditional ranch society with the coming of the railroad and new forms of commercial agriculture. The Mexican question, for Anglo rule, was that people from Mexico served an urgent need for labor and yet challenged the hegemonic project of associating "America" with specifically Anglo ethnicity, including English language use, uncomplicated national allegiance to the United States, and, for some, physically observable racial distinction from both African and Indigenous descent. In other words, the order being established in Texas under Anglo rule in the early twentieth century needed the presence of Mexican bodies at work but equally desired the absence of Mexican bodies from the imagined community. The presence of Mexicans who were more than bodies—who appeared in fact as autonomous subjects organizing in their own interests—exploded the contradiction and refused erasure.

These dynamics also played out in Newton, now a town of just over nineteen thousand people, about 14 percent of whom are Latina/o, that sits a half-hour north of Wichita, Kansas. Newton is a railroad town that at one point played a pivotal role in the middle section of the Santa Fe system and is still home to a BNSF rail yard. The families that first made up Newton's Mexican-descended community were drawn there in the 1920s by what historian Jeffrey Garcilazo describes as the "seemingly insatiable demand for labor" that accompanied the construction of the western railroad (2012). It was the community of railroad workers in Newton who formed the team known as "the Mexican Catholics," later taking on the name of the church's Holy Name Society.

In the letter from Ignacio Martinez discussed in the previous chapter, we see a version of the narrative of postwar political awakening that has become common in Mexican American historiography: after joining the total war effort against fascism, Americans of Mexican descent would not settle for second-class citizenship. The prewar social formation of accommodated segregation was crumbling, though it would hold on for decades longer in some quarters. It would take sustained and vigorous resistance to begin to dismantle the segregated racial boundaries. Yet this kind of engagement was not universal: Mexican American sports traditions were not an expression of militant politics, but neither can they be dismissed as assimilationist or, for that matter, a substitute for politics. Rather, they reflect the messiness of accommodated segregation and struggles to move beyond it. The founding of local sports institutions represents a community that was at once resisting exclusion, making claims to play in leagues dominated by Anglos, and also turning the condition of segregation into an opportunity to build and exert authority by forming teams and tournaments of their own.

As for the vantage point of Mexican Americans themselves, for many the question of their own "Americanness" was settled, but what remained open was the degree to which their inclusion into U.S. society would be recognized, through what means, and at what cost. The Newton softball team known as the Mexican Catholics often dominated the standings in the city league. When weekend tournaments came along, however, with the chance to win trophies and even money, those events were often invitational. The politics of getting invited to such events, or excluded from them, belong to the contents of history that are not recorded in the *Evening Kansan Republican* sports pages. The collective memory formed around Mexican American fastpitch serves as a reminder that being formally allowed in a city league did not always equate with being made to feel welcome. The memory of informal but palpable boundaries and barriers to full inclusion is reconstructed annually at the Newton tournament as people renarrate the past to each other. Such narrative, albeit messy, is key to understanding the history of exclusion and integration of Mexican American communities in the United States, which requires close attention to the finer points of de facto segregation. One theme in this history that interviewees reported to me is a pattern across decades and generations of Mexican American athletes being blocked in their desire and efforts to compete by a systematic underestimation of their potential. This alone would be reason enough to motivate a community to run tournaments of their own.

The Newton tournament acquired importance to the community as a contrast from the general marginalization they felt in everyday life. Mario Garcia, a veteran of the Newton tournament whom I interviewed, said, "There were so many things we couldn't do at the time, that this became a big release." The experience of being barred arbitrarily from certain cafés, theaters, and other businesses, enduring degrading comments while walking to school, and otherwise navigating the racial minefield of the era of normalized, accommodated segregation motivated the Newton ballplayers to develop a winning softball team, as well as institutions such as the Fourth of July tournament and its organizing committee. In Newton, as in other communities that cultivated a fastpitch tradition, enduring the conditions of segregation formed tight bonds among neighbors, developing a social base that supported collective efforts to play ball.

SOCIALLY EMBEDDED SOFTBALL

The social conditions of early Mexican American fastpitch required resourcefulness and strong bonds of friendship to endure. Over generations, these qualities became more deeply articulated to the game for participants and spectators.

The specificity of this historical experience is as important to the fastpitch tradition as some universal or generic appeal of sports. In other words, the fact that Mexican American fastpitch exists is not necessarily an argument that American bat and base games hold universal appeal. Although Mexican American people built their own tradition of fastpitch when it was widely popular, perhaps even the most popular recreational sport in the country, in the ensuing years, fastpitch played by men has dwindled to the status of a niche sport. Yet the sport shows staying power in Mexican American communities. More important, when Mexican Americans continue to invest fastpitch with their interest and significance as part of their personal and collective identities, there is no suggestion that such investments make them any less Mexican. Thus, certain reformers' dreams of base games as engines of assimilation seem tenuous. On the contrary, ballplayers and tournament-hosting communities have made these ways of being Mexican in the United States at least partial answers to the Mexican question.

Mexican American fastpitch endures on a mix of different versions of illusio—that particular and at times peculiar appeal that accounts for people's otherwise unaccountable investment in certain games. There is the appeal of softball as a quick-paced and accessible form of baseball, but also the continuation of a specific historical experience and the social bonds cultivated by the challenges posed under certain social circumstances. When fastpitch players invoke the tradition of Mexican American teams and tournaments, it is not a general baseball tradition but a specific barrio one. In other words, Mexican American fastpitch is ineluctably Mexican *and* American, and what makes it so is not just that Mexican people play it but that it has a long history rooted in Mexican American communities. This rootedness has at least two sides, evident in different ways throughout its history. On one hand, the origin of specifically Mexican American fastpitch under conditions of segregation is part of a longer story of ongoing forms of discrimination that people in Mexican American communities face. On the other hand, being embedded in the everyday life of barrio communities facing those social conditions, fastpitch took on an attractive cultural vibrancy as a site of collective pleasure and conviviality.

• • •

In the Kansas City, Kansas, neighborhood of Armourdale, a high foul ball clears the batting area and descends toward the yard across the street where a team that was eliminated several hours earlier has set out their beer coolers and lawn chairs. Several spectators yell a warning from the field before the ball hits the sidewalk with a respectable crack. A guy beside me in the stands says, "They wouldn't have felt it anyway. They've been drinking beer since they lost."

Armourdale was incorporated in 1882 and named after Armour & Company, the Chicago meatpacking firm that opened shop in the area and employed workers from Mexico. Today around 65 percent of its residents identify as Hispanic or Latino, and about 35 percent of the population is "foreign born." Tony Oropeza, the player-manager of the Stateline Locos, told me that the community is surrounded by the river and railroads, so everyone has to take a bridge to get in or out. When he was a kid, this meant freedom, since he and his friends could ride bikes all around the town, following a simple parental rule not to cross bridges. The "island" of Armourdale is situated within an oxbow curve in the Kansas River, with Interstate 70 and railroads behind. In the middle of the island is Shawnee Park, with a softball field. The outfield is bounded on the left field side by Kansas Avenue, a major thoroughfare and the beginning of an industrial area that includes railroad maintenance facilities. Beyond right field is a commercial street lined with businesses. Behind home plate and across a narrow street is a row of houses leading to the Catholic church that was desanctified by the parish and is now home to a social services organization.

Adjoining the field are traces of a second ball diamond, now grown over with grass and weeds. When I first visited during the Locos' tournament, playground equipment on the defunct ball field was busy with kids. A handful of them congregated near the road, tugging on imaginary cords each time a semitruck came through, begging to hear the horn. There was a fairly regular stream of trucks coming off the highway and then turning left, away from the park, toward the industrial expanse. One was loaded front to back with railroad car wheels. When a driver obliged and gave the kids a blast, they erupted into shrieks of delight.

I had driven to Armourdale on the occasion of the Locos' fiftieth anniversary fastpitch tournament in 2011. But before I found all this, I had to stop at a used tire shop to ask directions. The proprietor was decked out in Norteño gear, including a cowboy hat, belt buckle, and the curl-toed ostrich boots that were high fashion at the time. He spoke Spanish with a customer who came in just before me, translating to English for his Latino employee behind the counter. When I asked for Shawnee Park, he said, "Oh, that's far—a long way from here. Shawnee Mission?" No, I said, I was not looking for Shawnee Mission Parkway, the major route running from the affluent southwestern suburbs to the Plaza shopping district. Not that, but Shawnee Park. I thought it was around here. "Oh. For the baseball? It's right over there."

Right over there, in the center of town. If I had taken a wrong turn and was looking for my way to the Missouri side of the city or the interstate, I might have driven past without noticing the ball field and the players spread out over the grass and brick dust. So easy to miss. Yet rumor has it that someone's ashes lie buried behind the pitching rubber, a decidedly unofficial tribute to the last wishes of a ballplayer to be planted in ground he held dear. Certainly plenty of dramas have played out there. When I did approach the field to attend the Locos' anniversary tournament, I was still unaware of the site's geography that I would learn about in a later interview—an unwritten map drawn over years and generations of habit, something like what I remember from church in my small midwestern hometown, where everyone knows which family sits in which pew. I'm not sure I caught the schema exactly, but it was something like: the Talaveras sit on the concrete platform next to the concession stand behind third, the Garcías sit in the bleachers, the Moraleses sit on their *abuelo*'s porch just across the street beyond the first baseline. Standing behind the Talaveras during opening ceremonies, some aging veterans (of both war and softball) reminisced about how things used to be done. One of the old-timers who was watching the game nodded toward the diamond and said, "I played my first game of fastpitch here in 1946." Photographs of teams from that era and before adorn the concession stand in posterboard displays brought out to commemorate the occasion and the longevity of this tournament, the sport, and the community that kept them going (Figure 6).

If the enduring appeal of the historically Mexican tournaments, and fast-pitch in general, in these communities has to do with the way the sport was embedded in everyday social life, this was partly by design. As noted, softball was promoted by proponents of recreation, such as the YMCA, whether as a means of assimilation or general social uplift. Around the time that the Mexican team in Newton's city league was organizing a tournament to invite other Mexi-can teams from surrounding cities, a private women's service club in Austin, Texas, the Pan-American Round Table, sought city support to convert a defunct schoolhouse at Third Street and Comal in the Eastside barrio into a recreation and community center. La Comal, as it was named, became a center of gravity for Eastside kids, including Richard Moya, who recalls "practically living" at the center as a youth (Buckholz 2004). La Comal was also the base of operations for *The Blah, Blah, and Blah*, an alternative newspaper highlighting Mexican

FIGURE 6   Display at the Stateline Locos' tournament, Shawnee Park, Armourdale, Kansas. Photo by the author.

American students that Moya and his friends from Austin High published ("Richard Moya Obituary" 2017). Later Moya became one of Austin's most prominent Mexican American residents, rising through state and local politics to serve on the Travis County Commissioner's Court and as deputy chief of staff for Governor Ann Richards, among other offices. Moya joined the fastpitch softball team, the Aces, formed by La Comal's activity director, Roy Guerrero. In 1948 the Pan Am Aces went undefeated in the seventeen-and-under Junior League, traveling to Houston for the state tournament, where they were finally beaten by a Galveston team. A rough, unattributed newspaper clipping on the 1948 Aces in the Austin History Center's vertical files attributes the Aces' success to relationships formed off the diamond:

> A great deal of credit for the successful season which the Aces enjoyed is due to the fact that these boys have been playing together for several years. They have formed themselves into an athletic club in order to stay organized the year round. Every season they participate in whatever sport the season calls for: baseball, basketball, softball, or football. The recreation leaders at the Pan-American

Center try to assist them in every way possible, but the Aces have long since learned to manage themselves without having to depend on adult aid.

Moya's teammate on the Aces, Louie Murillo, would go on to help found the Austin Jokers, a team that competes and hosts its own tournament today (Figure 7).

According to an undated booklet published for a commemoration of the team's fiftieth year of competition, the Austin Jokers had their roots in pickup softball that kids in the Zaragoza and Comal playgrounds of East Austin played. As these players reached adulthood, in 1961 Louie Murillo and Tony Castillo formed a team to compete in the fastpitch league based in Pan Am Park. According to Dan Govea, who played on that first team, the prototype for the Jokers team was assembled the year before as Louie, who had just quit the Pan Am Aces, put together a team called the Austin All-Stars to take to the Rusk

FIGURE 7   Louie Murillo "the original Joker," at his home, Austin, Texas. Photo by the author.

invitational tournament in Houston. Louie knew Mexican ballplayers from around the city and converted a fair number of baseball players to fastpitch. Dan was playing with the Montopolis Rebels at the time, based in another barrio further east, and Louie recruited him for the All-Stars by coming earlier in the morning to pick him up for Houston. Despite being thrown together at somewhat the last minute, the All-Stars took fifth in the tournament. and the next year, the Jokers were born.

The accounts of how they came into their name vary. One attributes it to their rivalry with the Pan Am Aces: the Jokers presented themselves as a wild card team that could trump the highest card in a deck. Both Tony Castillo and Charlie Porfirio, an Italian American neighbor who also played on the original Jokers, told me that the name originated with Dr. Hepcat (Lavada Durst), the first Black radio DJ in Texas. An announcer for Negro League baseball before he took to the airwaves in 1948, Durst also worked for the city at the Rosewood Recreation Center, which served the Black community of East Austin. The city ran a league for teams representing various neighborhood parks, and when Comal faced Rosewood, Castillo handed over a lineup full of nicknames for the Comal side—Scratch, Fancy, Cobra, Güero, Baron. Dr. Hepcat scanned the list and remarked (Charlie said), "What are these? A bunch of jokers?"

As the initial group that had grown up playing softball together in the parks came of age, Murillo and Castillo picked up more players with high school or semiprofessional baseball experience, some of whom played in a Mexican hardball league in East Austin's Zaragoza Park. Other exceptional athletes also joined the Joker Athletic Club, which had a basketball team in winter as well as softball in summer. Rene Ramirez was one, the "galloping gaucho" who was a rare Mexican American standout for the University of Texas (UT) football team in the late 1950s. Albert Almanza also played recreational sports with the Jokers while playing basketball for UT and the Mexican Olympic team, which he co-captained in 1960. Later, Texas football legend Earl Campbell was an honorary member of the Jokers Athletic Club and joined them on the basketball court at Pan Am.

Tony Castillo had grown up two blocks from Pan Am Park. He managed the Jokers while putting in over two decades as the basketball coach at Johnston High School and serving as president of the Pan Am advisory board. Coach Castillo told me in an interview that the basis for such lasting Eastside softball teams as the Jokers was friendship. Kids who played Little League baseball together, as well as park league softball, formed lasting bonds.

They were mostly friends. . . . Some of these guys, we play about every Wednesday, we still . . . growing up from elementary school, and we still gather today. We still socialize. They baptize my children, I baptize their children. Birthdays, we all go. Especially when we were very young, any time there was any kind of occasion—Boom! We were there. All of us. En masse.

Similarly close relationships grew out of segregation in Baytown, Texas, just outside Houston. Baytown had a close-knit Mexican colonia, established to house people recruited to the area by oil companies. In 1955, Baytown resident and future ASA Hall of Fame manager Daniel "Bebe" Garcia also started a softball team that became the Baytown Hawks, one of the longest-running and most successful fastpitch teams in the state. Bebe's nephew David Acosta, known as "Wheel" in fastpitch, told me,

Baytown—one of the reasons that it's so close compared to other places (I guess in the country) is that when they built the Humble Oil refinery, they brought—a bunch of Mexicans came down to build it and work at it. They put these Mexicans in barracks so they lived in these shotgun houses, and they all started marrying each other. Their kids—my grandfather was working—he worked forty-four years there. . . . But they came from different parts of Mexico. And they married the children of the workers, and before you know it—we were all cousins, and we were all friends. I'm one of eighty-six first cousins. I have twenty-two aunts and uncles, before they started to pass away. I have fifty-six first cousins on my father's side here in Houston. I have thirty first cousins in Baytown.

David and Geraldo "Jerry" Acosta, were among five brothers who had been standout high school athletes. Growing up in the barrio known as Old Baytown, the Acostas and other neighbors fashioned rag balls for impromptu ball games or played basketball on dirt under the only streetlight not yet shot out by "hoods," as Jerry told me. The boys' uncle Bebe could do a unique whistle, Jerry told me, that would summon players to practice, and Bebe's sister had a distinctive yell to call her sons home for dinner.

The social basis of fastpitch in Mexican American communities continued across generations. Jesse Rodriguez, a former tournament director for the Rusk Athletic Club in Houston, recounted to me how his father, Lupe Rodriguez, played for teams such as Los Compadres and Lone Star in the Second Ward center for fastpitch, Settegast Park:

Going around with my dad, at the parks, they used to have what they call the league games. At Settegast Park we used to go, and play, and I used to bat-boy. . . . He made me learn to keep score. . . . It was just a way of keeping me busy, keeping me occupied, keeping me out of trouble, keeping me from running around, you know? Somewhere he could watch me, so . . . you know, I got to the point where I really loved keeping score, you know, it kind of got to being an art form for me.

Back then it was entertainment. You couldn't go to a ball game or an Astros game, because either money or the bus wasn't going in that direction, but so for entertainment, you know, all these guys wanted to, or came to, um, Monday, Tuesday, Thursday nights and watch the fastpitch softball game, watch the men play. And I guess in hopes and their dreams that they would, they were gonna be playing there someday. And a lot of them are.

Jesse studied physical education at college and went to work for the city Parks and Recreation Department in the 1970s. Assigned to direct recreation activities at De Zavala Park, which he described to me as "one of the toughest areas of Houston," he formed a softball team of boys aged twelve and under to play teams from other neighborhoods. When he took them to play in Moody Park, Jesse, from the East End, faced his counterpart coach from the Northside, Alfred Gordy Rodriguez, who drove his team to the game in the back of a pickup truck. Jesse recounts:

And they're all boys coming in, all barefooted and you know, torn jeans and T-shirts and they had one glove so he had to ask us, can we borrow your gloves for the thing? And they had one bat and one ball. [laughs] So at that time, we'd had, our supervisor had came through so we had a lot of bats, we had a lot of balls, and I had all the gloves, so I kept the gloves. . . . I said yeah, so I always tell them hey, make sure you partner up with somebody, switch gloves when somebody comes in the inning.

After sharing equipment so their teams could compete with each other, the two coaches became friends and discovered their common interest in Tejano music. Later they developed a loyal following on radio as the Chorizo Crew, playing requests and reading dedications as "Jumpin' Jess" and "the Boogeyman." Jess kept coaching youth teams, and when a national fifteen-and-under tournament came to Houston, parks director Richard "Rock" Rocamontes, who was also the ASA metropolitan commissioner, asked his recreation division if there were any fifteen-and-under teams, since it would look bad for the city not to field a home squad. Jess in fact was coaching a team at that age group, but they were playing in an eighteen-and-under division for lack of opponents. This park-based team of Mexican kids represented Houston in the tournament. The pageantry of the national tournament, as well as the opportunity to play at Memorial Park's field number 1, an immaculate diamond with actual below-ground dugouts and a huge outfield wall, thrilled Jess and his players, motivating them to prepare for more tournaments. As coach, Jess drew on the barrio fastpitch tradition as a resource, bringing his fifteen-and-under and eighteen-and-under teams to play in the Rusk tournament against adults when they were preparing for national competition in their age group.

The Rusk Athletic Club, like its counterparts in several other cities, maintains a hall of fame for players who have excelled at their tournament, and at each annual induction ceremony, the honorees are invited to say a few words about their memorable experiences. At their induction into the hall of fame in 2019, brothers Andy and Gilbert Martinez recalled the experience of winning a city championship and then playing on the only "Hispanic" team in the national youth tournament in Houston. Two of the players Jess recruited as boys, the Martinez brothers continued to play into their fifties.

TOUGH COMPETITION

It was late on a hot Saturday afternoon in Texas, and many of those in attendance at the tournament had been there all day. The fans of each team, gathered into bleachers set along the first- and third-base foul lines, cheered on the tightly contested game. A little farther back from the field, under shade trees, the teams and family members had established their areas, little campsites almost, defined by coolers, lawn chairs, and portable canopies. The game was close, and it was the time of the weekend when teams were starting to collect their second losses, which would mean getting sent home in the double-elimination format. A woman stood close to the backstop fence around home plate, taking photos through one of the gaps in the chain-link. Her T-shirt matched the uniforms of one of the teams, and she took issue with a call that went against them, addressing the umpire with the colloquial reference to the color of his shirt, "Blue": "They're kicking our ass already, Blue. They don't need your help! How much they paying you? . . . I'll buy you dinner if that's what they're doing."

A woman on the opposite-side bleachers from the one with the camera called out from her seat, "Don't listen, Blue. You're doing fine. *I'll* buy you dinner." The two fans finally turned toward each other as all pretense was lost about whom they were addressing. The first cursed the umpire again.

The second replied, "Hey, lady, leave him alone. That's my brother."

"I don't care. He's an umpire."

"I don't care. He's my brother. Be quiet, lady." And then back to the field, "Don't listen to her. You're doing good."

The first woman took a step forward, "We can take it to the streets, baby girl."

The infield umpire approached the backstop to say, "Ladies, please, just step back and quiet down. I will call this game. Just step back and let them play."

The fans acquiesced and play continued. When the first woman finished with her photos, she walked casually past the other toward her team's area, muttering comments about the umpire and opposing fan as the tournament director subtly positioned himself between them. A boy supporting the same team took her vacated seat on the bleachers. The next pitch was called a ball, and he looked up from a plastic tray of nachos to yell, "Come on, Blue. That one was so pretty it had a dress on it!"

· · ·

Just because fastpitch is embedded in social relationships doesn't mean it is necessarily idyllic, though players frequently profess their love for each other, their community, and the game. Jumpin' Jess Rodriguez recounted to me his father Lupe's memories that in the 1930s, Mexican children who showed up to play at Settegast Park expected to have to fight white kids for access to the space. The experience of being driven from the park that would eventually be the heart of Mexican American fastpitch in Houston provided part of the impetus for community members to begin organizing their own tournament in 1940. Conflict over playground space or access to recreation was always framed by the larger social context, but community members who promoted softball and other recreation had direct, local interest in occupying the attention of youths whom they feared would be drawn to less wholesome pursuits on the streets. In the late 1930s and early 1940s, Houston authorities raised concern about "juvenile issues" in the growing Mexican colonias. While the Houston police proposed in 1943 that a designated "Latin American squad" of officers was an appropriate response, community groups, including the League of United Latin American Citizens, argued that park space and recreational activities would do more (Kreneck 2012, 52). Support for the Rusk Settlement House, Ripley House, and other community-serving projects followed this line of reasoning: providing positive activities was a better approach to dealing with youth crime.

When Roy Guerrero worked at La Comal in Austin in the late 1940s and 1950s, a set of youngsters who went by the name Los Tigres came around and "gave Roy hell," according to Richard Moya (Buchholz 2004, A6). "Mr. G's" approach was to put them to work, instructing the kids that if they wanted to be a club, they had to elect officers and take part in the activities and work of the center. Guerrero hired one of the biggest young men hanging around at the center, Oswaldo Cantú, who had been incarcerated for attacking a police officer along with thirteen other kids. Oswaldo bore the nickname "A.B., " for "Atomic Bomb," after he single-handedly defended himself from three attackers in an attempted mugging. Cantú himself later reflected that the opportunity Guerrero offered him was strategic, figuring that with an accomplished street fighter on staff, other kids wouldn't "tear the place up" (Bryant 1969).

Cantú was drafted into the Army during the Korean War, returned to work at Frito-Lay, and in 1956 founded the Pan American Boxing Club at the newly built Pan Am recreation center. In a long career working with the Austin Parks and Recreation Department, Cantú became a local celebrity for his work to reach kids through sports and recreation. Upon his death in 1996, the Pan Am center was renamed in his honor, and remains known as the Oswaldo A. B. Cantú/Pan American Recreation Center, at the time the only recreation center in the city named for an Austinite with a Spanish surname, and the center of Eastside fastpitch.

Periodically the intense competition that fastpitch engenders produces an altercation, though a quick ejection by the umpires tends to put a stop to it. Joe Fraga, a former Rusk Athletic Club committee member and one of the influential "Fraga Six" family from Houston's East End (his brother Felix was the first president of the Rusk Athletic Club), told me that for years, Rusk brought in umpires from outside the community for their tournament. The concern was that the players would not respect them and even possibly seek payback in the neighborhood if calls didn't go their way. But the directors' aspiration was to draw from the community for officials as well as players. Jumpin' Jess said that the Rusk tournament organizers' dream was to put three "Hispanic" umpires on the field for the championship game, which finally took place under Rock Rocamontes's direction. By the time of my fieldwork, umpires at Mexican tournaments were fully part of the community. Ray Guerra is one of the stalwart figures in blue, umpiring at the Latin as well as many other tournaments after growing up around Settegast Park, playing ball in the Navy and as an All-Star Hall of Famer in the Mexican tournaments before joining the Rusk Athletic Club organizing committee.

CAMARADERIE AND THE SOLIDARITY OF RIVALS

When I ask former players about their motivation for getting involved in fastpitch, a common answer is that the game offers intense competition. As a scaled-down version of baseball that could be played in more constrained settings like urban parks, softball nevertheless offered fast-paced action and required skill and strategy, especially before the slowpitch version of softball became prominent, with its regulated delivery of the ball. The intensity of fastpitch presented an opportunity for Mexican Americans whose athletic potential was constantly underestimated in Anglo-dominated sports to put their athleticism on display. Yet a recurring theme in my interviews was also how competitiveness ultimately fed solidarity among players. John Limon, tournament director for the Castro Concrete Jokers, told me,

> That was the beautiful thing about what we have in softball, is that when we're on that field, we'll play—you know, bite, scratch, tooth, nail, you name it, you know? But when we're done—let's drink a beer together. Let's have a good time, let's talk and let's eat.

This view was confirmed to me by Herbie LaFuente, whom I met as an umpire based in the Austin area and who had also distinguished himself as a player by earning hall of fame status in both Texas, as a Joker, and Kansas City, where he played for the Amigos. Herbie told me repeatedly, "Between the lines, we will go hard, but after the game, I'll crack a beer with you like a brother."

Ali Solis, the daughter of former Newton tournament director and Newton Metros manager Gil Solis, who was an elite club softball player in her own right, reflected on her experience growing up as a "dugout rat" in the Mexican American fastpitch scene. In an oral history interview collected and archived by Gene Chávez, she said,

> Growing up and being a part of that team, I thought they were all my brothers. When I found out that they were not my actual brothers, and they had different moms and dads, oh my gosh, that threw me for a loop. . . . I was like, "Huh? But you treat me like I'm your sister.".

For Ali, who is raising her son in a south suburb of Kansas City, maintaining a connection to the fastpitch tradition of her Newton childhood is crucial.

Depicting it as a model of sociality in danger of being lost as an effect of generational social mobility, she observes:

> When watching my son play in his tee-ball leagues here in Overland Park, watching how the adults interact, the children interact, it's just so different from the leagues that I grew up in. I think the first thing that comes to mind is the area. These kids did not grow up in the area that my family did, that my ancestors did. And growing up in an area where wealth is common, you treat people different, and I don't necessarily want my son to treat people that way. We're all equal. And it's so important for me to get Andre to the Newton Mexican American tournament . . . to see that camaraderie, to see how everybody else in the world relates to each other, because you have to have that kind of base foundation first.[3]

Ali's reverence for the "area" of Newton, her parents' home, is not innocent of the struggles that earlier generations faced. But now in the process of social mobility, Ali sees a special form of authenticity in the working-class social bonds and camaraderie that her community of origin expressed through softball.

Hector "Cuate" Martinez Jr. also emphasized camaraderie when telling me what appealed to him about the game he watched his father play in Houston and that became a focus of his own social life:

> We made friends with them—lots and lots of friends, you know it was people from Austin, mostly Austin and San Antonio, Brownsville, Corpus. . . . First we were—we weren't enemies but we were opponents. . . . Once the game was over, we were friends, we drank beer with them and it was, you know we had a, a hard slide—[breaks off to greet passersby]. But you know, you took a hard slide, and the guy'll get mad at you. After the game, you drank a beer with him, shook it off and it was over with. There wasn't, you know, like baseball, it wasn't feuds like that. . . . It was a friendly rivalry. It was a few . . . skirmishes, you know. . . . But for the most part, everybody got along, everybody drank beer together afterward, because that's how we were. It's a family thing, you know—our wives knew each other, our kids, you know. Everybody got along.

The solidarity of rivals is also a theme that comes through in Gene Chávez's Kansas City–based video documentary, *Mexican American Fast Pitch Softball* (2015). Interviewed for that project, Ralph Sauceda said, "A lot of my best friends are guys I played against, you know not so much my teammates, but I mean they're my friends. But I mean you earn the respect of other players." Kansas

FIGURE 8   Rusk Athletic Club committee members and families at Houston's
Memorial Park Field Number 1, 2014. Photo by the author.

City standout pitcher Paulie Hernandez credited tight social bonds with increasing the level of competition, and vice versa: "Back then when we played, we'd
argue on the ballfield but after the game, we'd drink together. Socialize" (ibid.).

When the barriers of segregation relaxed somewhat or, in a different narrative, when the barrio teams got good enough, the focus of these softball scenes
switched to different spaces: across the river to Penn Valley Park in Kansas City,
Missouri; across I-35 to Butler Fields in Austin; or to the central Memorial Park
in Houston, which boasts one of the "top two or three softball facilities in the
nation" (Figure 8). As barrio softball teams moved outside the neighborhood to
compete with Anglos in city leagues and mainstream tournaments, sometimes
competition built respect and cautious relational bonds across racialized social distance and the barriers of segregated everyday life. But it was a different
intensity within local communities and between barrio teams from different
cities, when people who shared certain experiences and lived within common
circuits of everyday life competed hard with each other. Paradoxically, intense
competition in this kind of setting is effectively a kind of collaboration, as all

players share an interest in making it a good game. The intensity of competition heightened the games in neighborhood ballparks or community-organized tournaments as events, making them something more special for players and fans alike. Sharing that experience, especially as it accrued over years and generations of play, both drew on and deepened the social base of fastpitch.

⚾ 3 ⚾

HOME TEAMS

Making Place for Mexican Tournaments

IN ARMOURDALE, a final fastpitch game is underway on a chilly and overcast Sunday afternoon in April. The Locos' fiftieth annual tournament has drawn all the local teams, made up predominantly of Mexican American men, that play each other regularly on this field in a summer city league. This is an open tournament, though, accepting any team that can put together the entry fee, and visitors from out of town are carrying the day: a team sponsored by a Des Moines bar, whose owner wants a trophy badly enough that he has paid a pitcher to drive up from Oklahoma and meet them, plays through to the final game.

The catcher, wearing baseball pants, cleats, and a hooded Harley-Davidson sweatshirt under his protective gear, starts to chatter in a high, clear voice that would be an asset on an auctioneer's team:

"Hey, shooter! Hey, shoot! Come on, now! Where y'at! Shoot it in here, now!

"Hey, big'un! Go to work, now! Come on, you!"

A Day-Glo yellow ball arcs over the plate and smacks the catcher's glove. The umpire summons a bellow from his gut, designed to be heard by many more spectators than the dozen or so in the bleachers behind him. "Hike! Hree!" The batter whirls to face him, but the umpire catches himself and checks the clicker in his left hand. Next I hear what is more recognizable as a speaking voice: "Aw, my bad. That was two."

The "shooter," a tall, lanky Native American man whom many of the players on other teams address by his first name, dispatches enough of the hometown hitters to win for Iowa. The Locos, lacking a standout pitcher, had struggled through their own bracket. Other local teams they would face in the Tuesday evening city league also gradually fell before the visitors; actually there were two Iowa teams. Even the mighty Kansas City Indios, who were tough to beat in the city league, and in any given game might fill seven out of the nine positions with a member of the Garcia family, eventually lost, to make it an all-Iowa final. The old-timers watching next to me remarked that this might not have happened in the days when the tournament was invitational, before the Mexican tournaments on the Kansas summer circuit had "opened up" to "white" teams. Earlier, Tony, the tournament director, had told me stories about before the tournament opened up. One player represented the third generation in his family to play, but (Tony gestured toward my face as he recounted the story) he looked white. Tony reenacted the scene for my benefit: "'What's he doing here?' But we said, 'He ain't no white guy! He's Jesse's grandson!'" But those days were gone, and a mostly Anglo team would take the trophy back to Des Moines, while their Native pitcher drove home to Oklahoma, having dispensed his weekend duties.

After the game, Tony carried a wireless mic to the pitching rubber to award trophies and all-tournament honors, most of which went to the winning team, as usual. Reading from a scrap of paper over the press box speakers, he stumbled over some Germanic syllables while naming all-tournament players from the Iowa team. With a self-deprecating shake of his head, he said, "Man, I need some Mexican names!" After congratulating the victors, Tony announced that the barbecue that had been sold as a concession all weekend was now free for the taking, and that there was cold beer as well for those who had hung around to the very end. Another tournament, and a half-century of fastpitch, came to a close.

Later I sat down with Tony, and he briefed me on the annual tournament circuit as I scribbled in my notebook:

- The Locos play their tournament the last weekend in April. It usually rains, but that's the start of the season. "Plant your peppers when we have our tournament."
- Haskell Indian Nations University in Lawrence, Kansas, has their fastpitch tournament on Mother's Day weekend, and some of the Kansas City teams go.
- The Kansas City Angels are on Memorial Day weekend.

- The Kansas City Indios are on Father's Day.
- Newton is the Fourth of July, and Hutchinson is the week before that.
- Topeka has its tournament the week of the huge fiesta [which has run over eighty-five years], a couple weeks after Newton.

This calendar outlines a season and a circuit of tournaments among the railroad towns of Kansas where Mexicans have settled since the early twentieth century. Organizers try to space out the tournaments throughout the summer to allow for rescheduling in the event of rainouts. There is an ethos of reciprocity whereby if one team plays in another's tournament, the host returns the favor. These days, the tournaments take on the atmosphere of a reunion. Today's veteran players and the parents of those just entering their athletic prime remember growing up around tournaments. Kids would spend the weekend playing cupball with crumpled paper cups under the bleachers, pitching the rough paper ball and smacking it with an open hand to bat. Every foul ball from the real game would send a small pack of kids scurrying after it. Bringing the ball back to the press box earned them a quarter or a piece of gum. The same tales get told every year, about teams coming from afar and sleeping on cots under the bleachers because hotels wouldn't take them. Or when the hotels started booking rooms to Mexicans, an enterprising sponsor might pack twenty men into two rooms to save money. Some players remembered subsisting on a per diem of baloney sandwiches ("the Joker special") or, preferably, home-cooked meals as guests of the families of the home team.

Founded as recreational events in segregated working-class communities, the annual fastpitch tournaments that persist today in mid-América have developed through stages of consolidation, expansion, and reunion. Despite having these stages in common, the story of the "Mexican tournaments," as I have heard them called by some participants, is not one of uniform, linear development, even though it is tempting to chart an epic rise and fall in their history. Rather, across the shifting circumstances under which Mexican American communities have hosted fastpitch tournaments, a dynamic tension in the relation of sport to identity persists, remaining important but in different ways and never getting entirely settled. In particular, within these home-grown institutions that gave people a chance to play ball and to get good at playing, a tension emerged between prioritizing the sport as a community-based activity, as opposed to seeing how far home-grown athletes could go in larger metropolitan, regional, national, and international scales of competition. The tournaments have served multiple purposes, sometimes in concert with each other, sometimes in conflict.

The outcome, then, of developing the social base of fastpitch as a local tradition was not always clear in terms of how it came to bear on the collective and individual position of Mexicans in the larger society. It was a version of the Mexican question of cultural citizenship played out on the field, not so much settling the question as keeping it alive: Should the barrio keep its own talent close, nurturing the game in parks where fans could enjoy it from their front porch? Or send the neighborhood's best off into the world to show what barrio ballplayers could do? As the Mexican tournaments endured when other opportunities for men to play fastpitch faded, they took on a special appeal, attracting the interest of outsiders looking for the best places to play a game that had become more niche or even throwback, rather than being in the mainstream of recreation. This raised another form of the Mexican question, one resonating with the tensions around gentrification, when outsiders suddenly take note of the appeal or potential of barrio neighborhoods as real estate. Multigeneration barrio residents may take pride in their newly appreciated neighborhood but not want to lose it. Should cultural institutions formed under segregation retain their differential identity or welcome outsiders to compete on the fields they had "built," sometimes literally and others figuratively?

In this chapter, I explore the historically Mexican tournaments, which are more often than not hosted by specific teams. To elaborate how these teams and tournaments have anchored a racial tradition in vernacular institutions, I lay out stages they all seem to have gone through across shifting historical circumstances. Moving beyond the two oldest tournaments that have been my focus so far, I relate some of what Cuate the catcher termed "lore" connected to other, also long-running, tournaments hosted by enduring clubs. I also discuss some of the ball fields and institutions that have grounded this tradition in particular places. Finally, I consider the stakes and debates involved in opening up the tournaments, thereby loosening some of their ties to a particular racialized history.

BUILDING A TRADITION

The questions and dynamics of looking inward or outward are implicated in the notion of a racial tradition, which I have adopted from Alex Chávez's (2017) ethnography of vernacular music, a usage that he in turn draws from the study of literature. In the case of fastpitch, there are overlapping layers of tradition belonging to the sport in general, as well as to the specific versions, embedded in the social experience of racialized segregation, survival, and perdurance. Participants in Mexican American fastpitch express their love of the sport in general, some treating it as an acceptable substitute for baseball, more accessible and less demanding on time and the body than hardball, and others extolling a preference for the smaller-scale, faster sport of softball as a first choice. With reference to the particular history of fastpitch in Mexican American communities, though, it is common to speak of a commitment to the particular, locally rooted "tradition."

The Mexican tournaments formed a racial tradition in acts of collective memory that have kept connections alive to people's shared, specific experiences within a history that was shaped in part by the violent and coercive sorting of society into races and classes. This does not mean that there is a consensus within Mexican American fastpitch about identity, as my conversation with one tournament director makes clear. When I interviewed Manuel Jaso in 2014, he had been the tournament director of the Newton Fourth of July event for thirteen years. I asked him why fastpitch had such prominence in Newton's Mexican American community, and our conversation quickly swerved into questions of identity:

MANUEL: I think baseball was first, obviously, uh, in the bigger community. Scheme of things, I should say. . . . But when you started playing fastpitch, yeah, it really became a big thing with the Mexican Americans in this, in this city. Or I like to say, Americans of Mexican descent, but [laughs] I catch a lot of flak for that. [laughs] I always like to put the "American" first.

BEN: Yeah? Yeah, and you get flak from who?

MANUEL: People, 'cause they say we're Mexican Americans, and I say no we're not, we're Americans. Yeah, so.

BEN: Is that [crosstalk]

MANUEL: I mean, for *me*, that's a big [crosstalk] . . .

BEN: Well, is that an idea that you grew up with or came to on your own, or—

MANUEL: Uh, little bit of both. My dad didn't necessarily preach that, but my grandfather did. ' Cause he's always, when I was younger, "What are you?"
   I said "I'm a Mexican."
   "Nope. You're American." So, it just kinda stuck with me.

BEN: And, your grandfather was, uh . . . was he the generation that came from Mexico, or was it—

MANUEL: Uh, yes, he was. He was actually born in Aguascalientes. "Hot water,"
which is why I'm always in hot water. [laughs]

Manuel's grandfather, Canuto Jaso, may have embraced his new country
as the focus of his identity, but Anglos generally did not allow the "Mexican"
modifier to become optional, a fact that is no doubt relevant to why the tournament that Manuel directed for years is officially called "Mexican American."
In our conversation, Manuel went on to describe the context of the original
tournament as one in which segregation kept African Americans and Mexican Americans from competition with Anglos, though teams of color would
sometimes play each other. The tournament was started for the Mexican teams
in the Newton area, he said, "more than anything" to provide an opportunity
to compete. De facto segregation in all aspects of daily life taught Mexican
Americans not to expect full access to public spaces and activities. As Manuel
put it, this was "just a sign of the times."

I asked him about the Newton tournament's continued closed status, which
I assumed took some effort to keep going. The organizers of other tournaments had expressed to me that they opened up reluctantly, out of concern that
with only Mexican teams invited, low participation would ultimately make
the shrinking tournaments unviable. But even as he adopted his grandfather's
chosen identity as "American of Mexican descent," Manuel recognized a special
value in the ethnic definition of the tournament—value that arose from continuity with the past and that in turn justified ongoing continuity:

BEN: Well, I mean you've kept it going as an invitational tournament, too, and
that—I'm sure that's taken some doing because there are a lot of tournaments
that have opened up.

MANUEL: Yeah. As far as I know we're the last one, and uh . . .

BEN: Yeah.

MANUEL: It's sad. I used to enjoy going to all those closed tournaments, just because the camaraderie. You know, I—everybody keeps telling me, says, "When
you gonna open it up?" And I—I eventually think we probably will. Because
we're just getting less and less teams. I think kids are now gravitating to soccer;
they have other things going. . . . But, you know, as long as I can get it going,
keep it going the way it is right now, I want to do that. I mean I have nothing
against my Anglo friends or black counterparts, I really don't. I just love the
tradition of it. You know, it got started this way. Let's try to keep it as long as we
can. That's kinda the way I look at it.

Manuel's take on Mexican identity is not necessarily typical within the New-ton Mexican community or the wider fastpitch family. He indicates as much by noting that he "gets a lot of flak" for identifying principally as an American. But the question does not seem to be one of disavowing Mexicanness so much as a matter of differing interpretations of it. Perhaps Manuel and his friends and relatives find more consensus around a concept of Mexican heritage rather than race or nationality. In any case, as an identifying feature of the tournament, Mexicanness for Manuel is a valued characteristic, something connected to the everyday life of the community, respect for family ties with the founders, and the memory of their historical experiences of racialized exclusion. The move by elders and ancestors to found the tournament as resistance to exclusion is one that Manuel and others wish to keep alive.

Keeping the tournament "Mexican American" maintains ties to family and community forebears and to the frustrating and oppressive experiences that they overcame in order to play ball. This is why, even if Manuel's identity term of choice diminishes or denies the potential racial content of "Mexican," the tournament itself represents a racial tradition—a line of continuity with a particular history determined in part by the racialized power structures of the United States. Like similar lines in literature or other art forms, identified by the common experiences of racialization among their creators, the racial tradition of fastpitch is a marked thread in the fabric of softball history more generally, and its constituency wishes to keep it visible.

Consolidation

Establishing teams and tournaments under these conditions, Mexican Ameri-can communities consolidated their own tradition of fastpitch by building mystique and renown around team names, colors, and records. They also de-veloped the tournaments into annual events constituting a circuit among Mexi-can ball-playing communities, and heightening the events with features and characteristics of a festival. Some tournaments were attached to church events, such as a fiesta or *jamaica* (fundraiser), or national holidays such as the Fourth of July or *El Dieciséis de Septiembre*, Mexico's independence day. As circuits of teams and tournaments consolidated in this stage of fastpitch history, so did the network of relationships within and between local communities, many of which took on the intensity of kin relations, even developing into formal rela-tions of family through marriage or *compadrazgo*.[1] As the excitement and lure of strong competition drew spectators and participants to the Mexican American fastpitch tradition, questions arose about how much a locally based sporting tradition could expand. How many teams and fans could a tournament draw, and for home teams, how far could they go?

The stage of consolidation saw the Mexican tournaments and barrio leagues become important social institutions. Even as segregation in recreation began to break open in the 1950s and 1960s under the pressure of social activism, tournaments continued as specifically Mexican events. Teams and hosting communities developed strong reciprocal relationships, supporting each other by participating in each other's tournaments, even while competing vigorously. The seasonal calendar of tournaments became relatively reliable, and the circuit was a framework for social life, as tournaments were occasions not only to play ball but to travel, feast, and dance with an extensive "fastpitch family." As tournaments became focal points for local and regional fastpitch communities in this process of consolidation, the Mexican American fastpitch scene in both Kansas and Texas took on some of the character of a "public" (Fraser 1990; Flores and Benmayor 1998). Events organized primarily to provide opportunities for athletic competition for players and entertainment for spectators became meeting places; venues for announcements of general interest to the community; sites of fundraising for various causes, such as educational scholarships or church building funds; and channels of advertising through sponsorship, program ads, and in other ways. Eating, drinking, and dancing made the tournaments into occasions of conviviality supporting bonds of friendship, camaraderie, and sometimes romance.

But even as these events successfully consolidated a space for Mexican communities to enjoy a festive sporting event without worrying about being made unwelcome or sold short, like any other public formation they also looked outward, beyond the boundaries of the locally defined común (Fraser 1990, 67). In the process of getting known in the neighborhood, ballplayers were also at least tacitly projecting toward a broader public, even within the idiom of fastpitch. This was partly an effect of loosening segregation. As the tournaments fostered the development of better teams and higher levels of competition, the question of how Mexican American fastpitch teams would fare against Anglos or in open competition became more salient. The national popularity and organization of fastpitch gave standout players and teams a ladder to climb, even if it didn't reach to the major leagues. One of these was Paul "Hoss" Lopez, who went to the ASA World Tournament with his hometown Phoenix Lettuce Kings in the late 1930s, pitching a no-hitter at the age of sixteen, the youngest pitcher to play in a world tournament. Later, Lopez and several other Mexican American teammates played with the El Paso Dautrich Realty team that won back-to-back International Softball Congress World Tournaments in 1961 and 1962. The success of exceptional players like Lopez raised the issue within communities hosting Mexican tournaments of whether to continue to cultivate the league of their own or engage with the broader softball world.

Expansion

Expansion is an imperfect metaphor for the ensuing stage, because it is not simply a question of growth from smaller events to larger ones. Indeed, this stage of fastpitch history saw vectors open up for tournaments to expand both out and in. By "expand out," I mean that players and teams who developed their skill within the Mexican fastpitch scene began to look beyond their own neighborhoods and tournaments to compete on a broader stage. This could have meant leaving the barrio to compete in open city leagues or traveling to play in sanctioned events such as the ASA's regional, state, and national tournaments, or even up to the International Softball Congress's world championships. That path represented an expansion of the horizons and pool of opponents that those teams faced, as well as experiences of integration as exceptional players got picked up by mostly Anglo teams. At the same time, the tournaments were "expanding in" by allowing more players who were not from the immediate, local community to play. The desire to win tournaments that held a prominent place in local communities somewhat paradoxically prompted some team managers and sponsors to look outside the community for talent. This became most noticeable in the late 1960s when teams sought an advantage by bringing in pitchers, sometimes from abroad, which required sponsors not only to cover travel and accommodations for the specialist players but eventually payment for their services as well.

Another overlapping dynamic of expanding in emerged when interest and participation in fastpitch began to decline among men in society at large; according to many devotees, this was because of the rise in popularity of slow-pitch softball. This process began in the 1960s, according to Erica Westly (2016), when men began to leave company-sponsored fastpitch as professional opportunities in baseball, football, and basketball grew more respectable to pursue. As fastpitch faced more competition for strong, competitive athletes, the appeal of slowpitch softball also grew, for the opposite reason: as a "sport that paired well with beer and picnics" (128). By the 1970s, slowpitch was the most popular form of softball played by men (152). By the time the NCAA instituted a women's national championship in 1982, fastpitch in general had undergone a regendering turn such that Westly characterizes contemporary fastpitch as "a women's sport without a male counterpart" (177). In Westly's account, the decline of men's fastpitch driven partly by increasing opportunities for men in other sports occurred while softball remained a rare opportunity for women to thrive as competitive athletes—"an open window in a room full of closed doors" (130). But not everyone encountered this landscape of opportunity in the same way. If professional sports became less socially marginal and softball became more a focus of leisure, these developments occurred first for white men. The 1970s and 1980s are remembered as a golden age for men's fastpitch in Mexican American communities, where tournaments sometimes drew up to forty teams.

Thus, the fastpitch tournaments embedded in marginalized communities gained relatively more status as the men's game declined overall. At the same time, however, the general sexism that devalues women's athletics in the United States meant that as fastpitch became a predominantly women's sport, it coincided with a decline in public support and funding. Notably, the "decline" narrated from the men's point of view and the "growth" of fastpitch for women roughly map onto a history in which public athletic resources in the form of parks and city leagues were replaced by private pay-to-play clubs, as discussed in Chapter 5. Fewer fastpitch teams and leagues supported by public recreation resources overall led to fewer people, particularly young boys, learning the essential skill of underhanded pitching. This is part of a larger historical trajectory that prompted numerous participants to tell me in the 2010s that they played "a dying sport."

Most of the Mexican tournaments eventually accepted the entry of whole teams without players of Mexican American ancestry or any connection to the local community or the tradition that identity-marked tournaments had begun to represent. They became open tournaments, and removing identity require-ments to try to court more participation and maintain the level of competition is what participants refer to as "opening up." Despite retaining its nickname, the Latin opened up shortly before I began my fieldwork in 2011. As noted, Newton is the last fastpitch tournament I am aware of that retains the identity requirement, and it does so with some exceptions.

●   ●   ●

At the Rusk tournament, the Latin, I'm again watching games with David Rios of the Glowworm family of San Antonio. David fills me in on the Baytown Hawks, the team to beat. They have brought in Lucas Mata to pitch, an Argentine ranked third in the world. They also have a Dominican batter and some Mexican nation-als on the roster. David guesses the team has sunk $10,000 into the tournament.

Mata throws "a lot of junk, but also heat," and racks up around nine strikeouts before hitting a batter, who takes first base. Even as the opposing team, the Misfits, move him to second on a bunt, the Hawks manage to shut down the inning, and soon they are leading 8–0. The Misfits have also brought in pitching: Tony Mancha from New Mexico. David tells me Mancha, who played some professional hardball, pitched seven games at the Glowworm's Fourth of July tournament and also batted over .400, a feat reminiscent of earlier times. In the 1980s, for example, the Kansas City Amigos traveled to Austin for the Jokers' tournament and their ace, Paulie Hernandez, batted over .500 while pitching. The Hawks are hitting Mancha this time, though, led by their Dominican guest.

• • •

Bringing in specialist players and opening up the Mexican tournaments are both widely accepted as facts of life now but also remain controversial. The chance to see world-class pitching in a local tournament amplifies the excitement in some ways for fans and heightens the prestige of the tournament, creating new challenges for batters and making success at bat all the sweeter. But at the same time, the idea that being able to put together the funding to support a ringer would determine which team would win the local title and claim the year's bragging rights struck some participants I spoke with as being against the spirit of the tournaments. The issue was somewhat of a gray area with players like Tito Florencia of Mexico, who helped the Baytown Hawks win the Latin in Houston several times, beginning in the late 1960s. Tito was not from Baytown, but also was not Anglo, and over time he developed strong friendships with his Mexican American teammates and especially manager Bebe Garcia. In hindsight, a change in the name of that tournament, from the State Mexican American Championship to the State Latin American Championship, may appear to have tacitly allowed Latin American internationals to participate.[2]

Players with no discernable "Latin" or "Mexican" heritage also sometimes turned up, with their sponsors trying various means of rationalization: Stony Burke, an Anglo pitcher who made his mark on the national fastpitch scene, still gets mentioned by those recalling his controversial inclusion on a team playing at the Latin before it was open. One former player quoted an imaginary critic when recalling the episode for me: "Just because he's from New Mexico doesn't make him Mexican." Some team sponsors and tournament directors now take pride in bringing in pitchers rated in the top ten in the world, sometimes drawing from Australia, New Zealand, Central Europe, or throughout Latin America.

Despite the decision of most tournaments to open up, many participants worked to keep attention on the specific history of the sport in the hosting community. This ushered in what I call the reunion stage, a time when people were drawn to the tournament not only because of the intrinsic appeal of the games themselves or the star power of the players, but to maintain a connection to the hosting community's past, including the history of the tournament itself.

Reunion

Today tournaments function as reunions for former players and fans, and their deeply embedded social roots make these events a powerful means of maintaining and rekindling connections with the circumstances—local and historical—that they grew out of. With declining participation in the sport overall among men and unsettled debates about whether opening up tournaments was the cause or effect of drawing smaller numbers of teams, the Mexican tournaments began to be increasingly not only about the competition itself but about gathering to remember the glory days and players who came before (Figure 9).

FIGURE 9 Historical exhibition of previous tournament posters, Rusk Athletic Club Latin tournament, Memorial Park, Houston, 2014. Photo by the author.

My fieldwork at fastpitch tournaments took place within this reunion stage—the gateway for my understanding of all other parts of Mexican American fastpitch history. My task as an ethnographer is to enter into the conversations and the spaces of these reunions as multivoiced cultural swirls and learn what I can from them. What I can learn is not always a perfect picture of "back then," and in a sports context, it is worthwhile to remember the retired athlete's joke: "The older I get, the better I was." But the chance to be there as people gather to commemorate the past and rekindle the relationships and other social and cultural forms that continue to unfold from the past—including the social and cultural form of a good softball game—has taught me plenty about what is important and interesting about the specific history marked by the seasonal rhythm of games.

At the two oldest tournaments that I visited repeatedly during fieldwork, a festival atmosphere was marked by formal opening and closing ceremonies, with a weekend of socializing in between. In both Newton and Houston, the festivities typically begin on Friday night. The Newton tournament was run for years by the Holy Name Society before formally separating from the Our Lady of Guadalupe church, but the priest of that congregation usually still offers an invocation. The presentation of U.S. colors by young cadets or veterans, sometimes accompanied by the Mexican and club flags, marks both the specific relationship of many tournament participants to the military and a general relationship to the pageantry of national identity that is a mainstream part of U.S. sporting ritual. A singer from the hosting community performs "The Star-Spangled Banner," often a cappella, into a wireless mic.

Opening ceremonies also include philanthropy. Both Newton and Houston tournaments regularly present scholarships to young people in the community selected on the strength of essays. The Rusk Athletic Club announced at its seventieth tournament that it had distributed some $90,000 in scholarships over the years, donated by members and fans of the tournament. The Newton Mexican American Athletic Club typically presents four or five awards of $500 and also reports the academic achievements of previous awardees. At a recent tournament, for example, a previous scholarship recipient announced his acceptance into a doctoral program in physical science. While the scholarships are an established feature of the oldest tournaments, occasionally organizers also make space available for other fundraising efforts to support the urgent needs of people in the community. A fifty-fifty raffle is one way to do this: an organizer sells tickets to people in attendance throughout the weekend and draws a ticket to determine the winner. Whoever holds the winning ticket then receives 50 percent of the proceeds as a prize, while the other half goes to the fundraising cause, although it is not uncommon for a winner to donate part of the winnings as well. One of these raffles supported a family connected to a visiting team with an infant who required expensive medical care. Another time, a young pitcher in Austin was struck in the face by a line drive, and tournaments in other cities throughout mid-América raised money for his treatment.

An important part of an established reunion tournament is the Hall of Fame induction. Several of the older tournaments maintain halls of fame, in the form of lists of outstanding and accomplished players. The organizing committee of the tournament accepts nominations and votes on induction to the hall, a highly valued honor among players with a long relationship to a particular tournament. Some outstanding players, such as Herbie LaFuente, who made a mark playing for both the Austin Jokers and the Kansas City Amigos in the course of his fastpitch career, belong to more than one hall. Occasionally people are inducted who did not play in the tournament, as in Newton's hall, which includes a sponsor and batboy in order to recognize the entire original hosting team, or in Houston's hall, which in the last induction by the Rusk Athletic Club included a member of the organizing committee in recognition of her long service to the tournament. Induction is greatly prized by players who have devoted a substantial portion of their lives to fastpitch. Each year's hall of fame class is announced in advance so that extended family and friends of the honorees may attend. Those inducted have the opportunity to speak, which typically includes some reminiscing and plentiful acknowledgment of peers and competitors. At the Rusk tournament, each awardee was also introduced by a speech from another player, recounting more achievements and experiences over their long-term participation in the tournament.

The celebration of past exploits continues when a reunion tournament hosts an old-timers' game, a chance for aging players to play a few innings of relatively relaxed ball with friends and former opponents. Two teams are assembled regardless of previous affiliation to take a kind of all-star form, and the mood of the game is jocular. The divide between the old-timers' and regular competition is not as sharp as it would be in some sports, given that master's divisions for forty- or fifty-and-older age groups are popular in Mexican American fastpitch, and it is plausible for players to compete into their sixties or older. The low-key old-timers' game offers a chance for those who have been sidelined by injury or are no longer competing for other reasons to revisit the playing field briefly.

In Kansas City, an annual stand-alone old-timers' game known as Los Sabios (the wiseguys) is a popular gathering, with a reception following at American Legion Post 213, the "Eagles Nest," which has supported fastpitch throughout its history (Figure 10).

After the opening ceremonies, the tournament transitions into a weekend of games played on several fields running simultaneously. The preferred format tends to be double elimination, though when turnout is small, a round-robin format is a way to produce more games. In the latter, teams are divided into pools in which they all play each other before entering a knock-out phase in which each game eliminates one team. The more common double elimination format arranges teams in brackets and eliminates them after two losses. The flow of a well-designed double elimination tournament rewards teams for winning by granting them rest. A team that wins its initial game moves to the winner's bracket, where it will be matched against other undefeated teams. Many of those games are reserved for Sunday, leading up to the undefeated game, a semifinal between the two teams that have not yet lost. Meanwhile, teams on the "loser's bracket" who drop their first game have to grind out a long day on Saturday to try to get to the final. For this reason, to be able to say, "We were still playing on Sunday," is a mark of accomplishment, either by an early victory or persistence.

FIGURE 10 Los Sabios old-timers' gathering, Eagles Nest, Argentine, Kansas, 2017. Photo by the author.

The final game, between the winners of the winner's bracket and the winners of the loser's bracket, is ironically not always the best attended, coming later on Sunday, when eliminated teams and their supporters may have already left for home, especially those with a long drive and work on Monday. In a double-elimination format, the rule that elimination requires two losses applies to the final match-up as well, so that unless teams agree in advance to a one-game final because of time or other constraints, the team coming out of the loser's bracket may have to beat its rivals twice to claim victory. In other words, if the undefeated team wins the final, that would represent its opponent's second loss, and the tournament would be decided. But if the team with one loss wins, it must play again to beat the winner's bracket team a second time. This is called "double-dipping" and is a highly prized accomplishment for a team that has clawed its way out of the loser's bracket on Saturday. Such a path to the trophy is the subject of many legendary narratives, especially when a single pitcher carries his team all or most of the way by winning seven games or more in a row.

Throughout the weekend, a festive atmosphere makes a reunion tournament much more of an event than the simple staging of softball games. Concession stands offer barbecue, ballpark hot dogs, or Mexican fare. It is not uncommon for a larger tournament to host a dance on Friday night, which in the early years would have provided rare opportunities to socialize among the far-flung railroad towns of Kansas or the barrios of bigger cities. Tony Castillo recounted the scene when the Austin Jokers' tournament got big enough in the 1980s that it needed to expand beyond Pan Am Park to more fields:

> It used to be a very social thing. We used to—Butler complex, if you go by there, [there's] big, semicircle seating, bleachers. Those things used to be packed, and East Austin was there en masse. You could park your cars on the outfield fence, and as early as 10 o'clock in the morning, there come the barbecue pits. See the barbecue pits, and music playing back there, and the beer and the kids would be crying and playing, and oh my goodness! It was very, very colorful. 'Course the tournament always had a dance affiliated with the tournament. People would hang around. Great—it was a great atmosphere.

Lee Castro Jr., whose father sponsored the Jokers, also told me about a nightclub next to Butler fields, where players would take off their cleats and dance in socks right after the games as children took over the field to play cupball into the night. The San Antonio Glowworm tournament, sponsored like its host team by a lounge with the same name, would get city permission to block off the street for their dance.

Continuity and Change

These stages of consolidation, expansion, and reunion track certain ways that the cultural presence of tournaments, and fastpitch more generally in Mexican American communities, has changed over time, responding to and affecting shifts in the social landscape, including the degree and kind of segregation in society at large, the reach of social mobility enjoyed by members of ball-playing communities, the shifting ground of public support in the form of funding and land designated for softball, and the changing appeal of the sport to the general public. The stages also reflect certain continuities, including the game of fastpitch itself as the home base that people return to year after year. Across all of these conjunctures, athletic versions of the Mexican question have been answered and then forced back open again. Enthusiasm for softball has exploded and declined. Arguments about the relative value of seeing a world-ranked pitcher visit a local field in your colors versus going as far as you can with a team that all grew up in the same neighborhood—these carry on and probably will never stop, for there is no time limit or tie-breaking rule for such contests. Different people's accounts of this history suggest trajectories of advancement or decline, sometimes changing direction. Since there is not a clear and steady telos to Mexican American fastpitch, the stages should not be treated as a tidy chronology, only as reference points to locate different events roughly in their historical context.

The oldest tournaments under study here, in Newton and Houston, started with the coming of age of the Mexican American generation. Fastpitch softball presented opportunities by virtue of its paradoxical, ordinary status. On one hand, it was "just softball," not freighted with the same representational stakes as organized baseball or school teams. This relative marginality functioned as opportunity for those on the restricted end of segregation. But at the same time, "just softball" was everywhere—one of the most widely played sports and a highly valued part of the vernacular landscape of communities around the country. This unique status of softball carried over into the postwar era, when most tournaments that continue today began their run. In the 1950s and 1960s, a growing consumer base supported barrio-oriented businesses and philanthropy, connecting the fastpitch scene to sponsors. Another of the oldest continuous tournaments in Texas, hosted by the San Antonio Glowworm team, gives a sense of these developments.

Hildebrand "Chilolo" and Mary Rios were, according to their children, city champion jitterbug dancers and the gregarious owners of the Glowworm lounge in San Antonio. Chilolo was Hildebrand Jr., the son of Hildebrando Rios from Monterrey, as Hildebrand III told me in an interview at the family's fastpitch tournament. In San Antonio, as in other cities, there were Mexican hardball teams early on, such as the Aztecs, who won a semiprofessional West Side championship in 1926 (Santillán et al. 2015, 24). Chilolo played baseball growing up but developed an interest in fastpitch after World War II. Fastpitch was popular on the South Texas U.S. Air Force bases—Brooks, Randolph, Lackland, and Kelly Field—and players from around the country stationed there played in San Antonio's city leagues. In 1957 Chilolo and Mary opened the lounge, and in the same year they founded the Glowworm team.

In our interview, Hildebrand, III and his brother Michael told me that the name of the Glowworm lounge came from the song that was on the jukebox in their parents' lounge—probably the number-one recording by the Mills Brothers in 1952—that was a favorite of some regulars. Their brother David told me another story: that Chilolo had been stationed in New Zealand during his service as a paratrooper and had visited a cave full of glowworms. When he returned to San Antonio, Chilolo retold the story so often that "Glowworm" became his nickname. Regardless of its origin, the Glowworm name became known in softball circles. In 1959, the team won the Rusk Latin tournament, which was effectively the Mexican state championship, as part of a ten-year-straight run of San Antonio teams taking first place in Houston. In 1964 the Glowworm started hosting their own tournament, which still runs annually on Fourth of July weekend.

The Glowworm players were adults, but Mary and Chilolo's seven sons started to play in their teens and recruited friends from Brackenridge High School to join them. The team traveled to other cities to play, and Hildebrand III told me that his father took great satisfaction in "representing San Antonio" on these trips. Chilolo became close friends with Bebe Garcia, manager of the Baytown Hawks, who also hosted a tournament. There was an ethos of reciprocity when teams supported one another by playing in tournaments: "We'll play in yours and you play in mine." Bebe also recruited teams for the Glowworm tournament when the Hawks played elsewhere. The Glowworm team traveled to Kansas numerous times from the 1970s to the 1990s, and teams like the Kansas City Amigos reciprocated. It was at the Glowworm tournament in 1979 that Kansas City's Paulie Hernandez pitched twenty-five innings in a stalemated game. In the interview, I mentioned that I knew Paulie and would ask him about that. Hildebrand and Michael both grew excited: "Ask him! Ask him! He'll tell you. It was in the seventies. He was in his prime." Currently the grandchildren of Mary and Chilolo are in charge of the team, which returned to Kansas City in 2017 to take third place at the Angels' tournament and played in Newton for the first time in 2018.

HOME FIELDS

The home field for many Mexican American fastpitch-playing communities is situated in the barrio. This is likely part of the appeal that led to softball's meteoric rise in popularity: the scale of the game makes it well suited to urban playgrounds and limited playing space (not to mention the diverse fitness levels of enthusiasts who are past their high-school-age prime). A softball field is smaller than a baseball diamond, and the larger ball, struck with a lighter bat, doesn't go as far. Whether these are decisive characteristics, when people tell me their memories of fastpitch, they tend to take me back to the old home field. Shawnee Park in Armourdale is matched by Pan Am Park in Austin and Settegast Park in the Second Ward of Houston. "You should have seen it back in those days," people are likely to tell me in the bleachers as we watch the younger ones play ("younger" could mean those in their forties). "At Settegast, that outfield would be lined with pits! People would get the barbecue going, music playing, sitting under the shade trees, drinking a six." When barrio teams were able to join city recreation programs, there might be league play two nights a week and then a tournament all weekend. Kids tore around the perimeter and chased foul balls to collect their bounty. People came out of their houses and crossed the street or just took in the scene from their front porches.

Early players who competed not only against opponents but against considerable social barriers and challenges to even reach the field in the first place did so while deeply embedded in local relationships and everyday life. Though a sport like softball represents leisure and a measure of freedom from the necessity of work, Mexican American participation in it often depended on resourcefulness in a condition of poverty. People exercised this resourcefulness to field a team, sometimes by drawing on family relationships or by taking advantage of public resources, particularly those channeled through recreation centers like Pan Am in East Austin, and social service organizations like the Rusk Settlement House in Houston.

The largesse of other organizations, like Guadalupe Centers in Kansas City, supported the building of fastpitch teams and tournaments. Founded in 1919,

Guadalupe Centers is recognized by the National Register for Historic Places as being the "longest continuously operating agency serving Latinos in the United States" (Guadalupe Centers 2019). The center originated as a settlement house by the Agnes Ward Amberg Club for Catholic women to provide a clinic and school for Mexican immigrants to Kansas City's Westside. The center sponsored youth recreation programs in the 1930s, including a baseball team that Paul "Waxie" Hernandez played for. Waxie went on to play and coach fastpitch for sixty years in Kansas City, including for the Aztecas in the 1960s, a team that Rey Gonzalez of Newton Holy Name told me "dominated the state until we came around." Waxie's sons boosted the name of Kansas City with the fastpitch teams the Amigos and the Angels. The Amigos are well remembered in Texas, but also for winning three straight titles in Newton without a single loss from 1984 to 1986 (Solis 2018). Paulie, Jr. was a standout pitcher, and Manuel "Rabbit" Hernandez still manages the Angels as well as serving as athletic director for Guadalupe Centers, which runs year-round programs in multiple sports for children. Kansas City, Missouri, honored Waxie Hernandez upon his death in 1992 by naming the ball fields at Penn Valley Park after him.

Mexican Americans built some of these institutions at the same time as pursuing sports opportunities, as in the development of the Eagles Nest American Legion Post in Argentine, Kansas. The history of building and consolidating fastpitch traditions infused ball fields with significance as sites whose material formation remains layered with memory and affect. Ball fields take on a heightened importance as spaces where the illusio of a sport and the memory of a community interlace to form iconic places, almost like secular shrines. The question of opening tournaments to players and teams from outside established communities and networks is not necessarily a decisive turn away from this social base, but such moments engender debates that bring to light valued aspects of a socially embedded vernacular sport.

Dan Govea walked with me to the pocket park that now stands where La Comal once was on the Eastside of Austin, recalling outdoor basketball games on the playground with warming fires in 55-gallon oil drums during the winter. The building that had been Comal elementary school was renamed the Pan American Recreation Center at the suggestion of University of Texas professor George I. Sanchez. In 1956 the center would move a few blocks east into a dedicated building constructed by the city. Like the Rusk Settlement House and affiliated Ripley House in Houston, Pan Am offered English and citizenship classes in addition to a wide range of recreational activities. The adjoining park was the site for a weeknight fastpitch league.

Surveying the park, Dan painted a picture for me of the days when fastpitch was a major source of neighborhood entertainment (Figure 11):

> The field didn't have a fence like they have now. The bleachers were full. There were people sitting in lawn chairs all the way around. They would really pack in the people out here. . . . The old-timers . . . maybe some of them had played ball but they were out here, supporting the teams. . . . They had sno-cones, concession stand, you know. People would come out early, after they get off work, they would eat out here at the field, cause they had a game coming. They wanted to be sure and get the parking.
>
> Night games, especially when known teams was going to play, people knew the schedule.
>
> It was real nice.

The ball fields where barrio leagues and tournaments have taken place over generations are sites that become rich, layered focal points for collective memory as they are infused with meaning through play that is intensified by the passion

FIGURE 11 Pan Am Park, East Austin, Texas. Photo by the author.

of the fastpitch illusio. As a city-owned building, the Pan Am Center remains one of the most prominent sites in the rapidly gentrifying Eastside that still reflects the barrio history of the neighborhood. The vibrant community center founded initially to reach troubled kids survives even as more and more families are priced out of the rapidly changing neighborhood. In Austin's Eastside, decades of ball field exploits leave their traces, such as on the exterior wall of Louie Murillo's home on prime Eastside land, which he has refused to sell even after the gentrification of the area produced rumored offers of over $1 million. Inside Pan Am, a mural by Martin Garcia depicts the Comal schoolhouse, fastpitch play at Pan Am Park, and representatives of specific neighborhood teams all as part of the fabric of Eastside life.

Popular aesthetics make and mark space (Chappell 2012). As practices embedded in the social life and history of a neighborhood repeat over time, they generate rich forms, or "moments," of vernacular space (Chávez 2017, 297). This is the sedimented history of a place, memories and traces of spaces and moments produced out of material copresence, people interacting, living, making scenes in particular ways that make land in a city much more than blank territory. It was the forces of segregation and barrioization, social machinations in the service of organizing and reproducing inequality, that turned Austin beyond East Avenue into the Eastside. It was public investment in wartime, when there were limited ideological pathways available for public funds to flow toward minority groups, that gave many of the neighborhood's social dynamics a material framework in the Pan Am Center.

But Pan Am now stands almost like a trace itself, surrounded by private land thrown to the market in one of the most rapidly gentrifying ZIP codes in the United States (see Chappell 2020), and the market has little time for the thick fabric of traces and memory only partly charted at the center and park, in the mural art and the softball league games that have started up again on Sundays. It's still largely Mexican men who play, and the Jokers field a team, but others drive in from surrounding areas, some from eighty miles away in San Antonio. In the new East Austin, the games may seem almost like a historical reenactment of when the neighborhood would come out and gather at the field. As fragile and ephemeral as the traces of barrio social space are under conditions of gentrification, they still exist as long as a handful of people get together on a vernacular scale of transaction, trafficking in the "traditions of the oppressed" that Walter Benjamin recommended we consult for historical consciousness (1940, thesis X).

The Newton tournament initially began in 1948 as part of a fundraising effort to build an Our Lady of Guadalupe Church to replace the mission chapel that stood on Santa Fe Railroad land. The church was finally constructed ten years later. The next year, work began on a ballpark behind the church, again with the Santa Fe donating the land. In a historical booklet, *Our Lady of Guadalupe All-Stars, 1947–1970*, compiled by Raymond Olais, Reynaldo Gonzalez describes the ballpark as a project undertaken by the parish men "to overcome the unfairness of the city park officials not always granting access to little leaguers of OLG to practice or for church to use city diamonds, come tournament time." Rey then describes how the ballplayers he profiles in the rest of the booklet built the field:

> While the All-Stars were recognized for their play on the ball field, they were also deeply committed to the park and embraced the work needed to accomplish its construction and upkeep through the years. The field was initially just weeds and a little hill before they turned it into a baseball diamond through their hard work and perseverance. They used their appropriate skills and connections with the city and local businesses in acquiring the supplies, materials and equipment to make their own Field of Dreams.

It took until 1963 to build the field with volunteer labor and donated supplies, and that year, the tournament moved there from the city's Athletic Park. The field at Our Lady is legendary to those who have regularly attended the tournament (Figure 12). With covered seating, lights, and actual dugouts for the teams, it provided a big league atmosphere that several former players remarked on— that playing at the Newton tournament, for those active on the Mexican American fastpitch circuit, was like the "world series."

The Newton team that was at home at Our Lady Park was Holy Name, organized by the parish's lay society, and at the time the park was completed, the team was defending champions of the Mexican American tournament and tied for first place in the area industrial league. Paul Vega, who pitched for Holy Name as a second-generation player after his father, Elmer Vega, who had helped found the tournament, told me about traveling in later years to play in the Austin Jokers' tournament. The Texans were taken aback by Holy Name, according to Paul, one of them remarking, "This ain't no church-league team."

The long project of building and maintaining Our Lady Park gave Newton's Mexican American community a facility they could control, so that the continuation of the tournament would not rely on the largesse of the city. Somewhat in the reverse of Pan Am Park in Austin, where the public status of the recreation

FIGURE 12 Detail: Quilt made from previous years' tournament T-shirts from the Newton Mexican American Fastpitch Tournament, image of Our Lady of Guadalupe ball park. Photo by the author.

facility has allowed it to survive gentrification, Our Lady Park provided access through the private control of the parish. But this would prove impermanent. In the 1990s, a change in leadership at the church brought a priest who, according to some tournament veterans, thought the "tail was wagging the dog" with the softball team and decreed that the land would be better used as a soccer field. The field was dismantled, the tournament returned to city parks, and Our Lady Park became a painful memory of loss to those who had attended the tournament annually. Today the dugouts stand as a ruin (Figure 13).

As barrio residents took to softball, among other activities on offer in public parks, church and industrial leagues, and similar social spaces of recreation, many developed and excelled as ballplayers by pulling together certain specific resources available to them. These included social ties from living and working together: younger ballplayers built teams out of friends and neighbors who all occupied a similar social space, faced similar problems, and seemed at times to be able to marshal the común factors of living in a

FIGURE 13   Ruin of a home field: the dugout at the former Our Lady of Guadalupe ball park, Newton, Kansas. Photo by the author.

tightly knit barrio community into the unidad of becoming a team focused on winning. By showing the resourcefulness to assemble the pieces for an effective sports club, they did more than win ball games; they also began to build institutions. As these developed into important sites in each community under discussion, the community organizations, recreation centers, and playing fields became rich sites of memory, cross-hatched with stories, *dichos* (sayings), images and memories of the ball game that was played there in the not-too-distant past.

THE DEBATE: OPENING UP

In Houston's Memorial Park, tarps have been stretched over the bleachers to provide shade at the pristine Field Number 1. The shaded sections are packed, but beyond them there are a lot of empty seats. On the PA system from the press box, a local radio personality is building anticipation for the games to come and urging the crowd to partake of the wares of the beer distributor that is a major sponsor. The space behind the grandstand has been turned into an impromptu museum, with rows of posters and photographs from decades of prior tournaments on display, alongside trophies, plaques naming the inductees to the tournament's hall of fame, and old tournament bracket charts. The bracket for this year is different from those of prior decades: more teams have shown up for the over-forty division than the open. An elderly gentleman sitting beside me as we watch the game takes up a refrain I have heard all weekend long at the annual Rusk Athletic Club softball tournament: "You should have seen it back in the days in Settegast Park. All the stands were full, and everybody put their pits out there past the fence—smoking brisket, drinking beer, music. That was something to see."

Between games, Ray Guerra, head umpire and Rusk tournament committee member, takes me around the park just outside the Memorial 1 stands to visit some barbecue pits. A few of the giant, welded contraptions on trailer wheels are parked near picnic tables for owners to smoke meat and feed an endless stream of family and friends who will stop by to visit over the course of the weekend. I meet a pitmaster, and soon I am properly weighed down with a sagging paper plate of brisket, ribs, and sausage. I have to get eating, and the conversation goes on without me. One middle-aged man who stops by to chat with Ray nods toward the entrance to the ballpark: "What's with the false advertising?"

The wry rhetorical question comments on a banner decorating the chain-link fence: "Rusk Athletic Club 64th annual tournament—'The Latin.'" Everyone on the Mexican American fastpitch circuit in Texas, and quite a few others beyond those borders, know this event as the Latin. Over the seventy consecutive years that it has gone on, the Rusk Athletic Club's tournament has gone through some name changes, being founded as the "Latin American State Tournament" in 1940 and changing to the "Mexican American State Championship" in 1977 and back again. But it was colloquially known as the Latin, which one old-timer explained to me as reflecting the preferred nomenclature of the Mexican American generation that founded it in the 1940s: "Back then, we were 'Latin American,' not 'Mexican.'" More to the point, the Rusk tournament had recently made the decision to open up just before I first attended for research, changing from an invitational format mostly restricted to players of Mexican descent, to being a men's fastpitch tournament of undesignated ethnicity. Reportedly, some prominent teams had decided not to attend the first year it was open. Ray diplomatically refrains from taking a position on the "false advertising" charge. We return to the game at Memorial 1: not all the players on the field are Mexican American, but it is still the Latin.

• • •

The Mexican tournaments that began in segregated circumstances and continued through the tumultuous middle of the twentieth century overlapped with political projects for some participants and probably offered an alternative for others. What is intriguing in the contemporary moment is how an ethnic designation, whether by design or association, has persisted. When the Newton tournament proclaims itself the "oldest Mexican American fastpitch tournament in the country," it is also sometimes unofficially called "the last." That is because the tournament remains invitational, and according to the rules, no team may include more than two non-Hispanic players. No one without Mexican ancestry is allowed to pitch. Officially these restrictions are meant to be enforced by a requirement that players bring birth certificates to show a Spanish surname from at least one parent, but in practice, such documentation is rarely necessary because of the tightly knit nature of the fastpitch community: everyone generally knows everyone else. The Newton organizers talk about the restrictions as maintaining "our tradition" and continue to draw justification from the history of segregation and exclusion. In practice, the restrictions place priority on local and family connections to the original network of ballplayers. The tournament remains a central event in the fastpitch season for predominantly Mexican American teams in the region.

Every other tournament I have visited—in Kansas City, Topeka, Austin, San Antonio, and Houston—has changed to an open format, welcoming all teams that can come up with an entry fee. Many participants express ambivalence about this change. On one hand, there is widespread pessimism that fastpitch is a dying sport. With a smaller constituency of players for the men's game, many tournaments are viable only if they accept all comers. Opening up fosters competition and keeps tournaments going.

On the other hand, this more cosmopolitan, less rooted version of fastpitch, like many other outcomes of the negotiation of identity, represents something gained and something lost. Participants whom I've talked with about it often express a kind of melancholy or nostalgia that suggests that the older Mexican tournaments held a special kind of value that is now out of reach. Others are unsettled by the change. If softball is not as central to everyday life as it once was in Mexican American communities contained by segregation, the intensity of affective investment among those who carry on the fastpitch tradition speaks to the place it holds in collective memory. The commitment of those who continue to come out for tournaments, look forward to playing in them, and put in unpaid hours of work to make them happen all provide evidence that maintaining and recognizing a connection to the specific history these events come out of is a priority.

To some, the open format also improved the level of the game. Ambitious tournament directors sought out the best competition regardless of ethnicity to make their events more exciting. Beyond recruiting entire teams, this became a question of pitching. Men's fastpitch in most instances is a nonprofessional game, but at a certain level of competition, it becomes a high-dollar endeavor as team owners and sponsors pay dearly for bragging rights. Pitching is the main position for which players can get compensated if their skill and strength are rare enough. Fastpitch is a pitching game. Having a player with not only the power but the technique to stymie batters is vital, and aficionados of the sport reminisce about glory days when games would often be decided by a single run.

Again, given the sparse and diffuse men's fastpitch scene currently, truly capable pitchers are few and far between. Those who make a name for themselves in major tournaments, especially in the International Softball Congress world tournament, have the opportunity to travel and get picked up by teams around the country and across national boundaries. For this, they can get paid.

Israel Rey in Austin noted the financial angle on this in our interview, saying teams with money buy the best. For his own team, the Reys, Israel relies on family connections, reaching back to his home in El Paso. "We can't afford two-three thousand for a pitcher. My brother invites his friends for a little gas money." The drive is eight and a half hours from El Paso to Austin without stops. The investment of time and travel compensates for a lack of funds, because the Reys know a lot of good players in El Paso and Juarez who are willing to make the trip to join a competitive team.

Others are of the opinion that bringing in pitchers for hire "killed" fastpitch. Local pitchers could not compete with the world-class ringers, which hurt local interest in the game. Tony Castillo notes the Jokers followed a different policy, "Play with what you got. Dance with the one that brung you," and rode their ace Big John Limon for years. Coach Castillo maintains that to spend thousands of dollars to "win a twenty-dollar trophy" is an overall detriment to the game.

As teams got better and social constraints loosened somewhat, local champions began to travel farther afield to compete not only in "Mexican" tournaments, but to represent their barrios and cities, their communities, in larger sanctioned tournaments. When I attended my first Latin, spending much of the weekend with David Rios, he told me about how his dad's team, the Glowworm, traveled to Kansas, California, Nevada, Missouri, and a few other places. "If it wasn't for my dad, I never would have gotten out of San Antonio." A bigger world is part of what softball did for him.

John Limon Jr., the son of "Big John" of the Austin Jokers, has devoted a substantial part of his life to softball as a player, manager, tournament director, representative for softball associations, and, most recently, a pitching coach especially for young girls. Reflecting on the racial tradition of Mexican American fastpitch, he seemed mildly bemused about why Mexican teams and leagues kept within the identity framework after the segregation that more or less required it began to loosen. He told me,

> Kinda funny, cause you're dealing with, you know, the Hispanic . . . culture in fastpitch softball. I don't know why, but our culture was so close-minded to where, you know, at one point we actually had a Butler softball complex in downtown Austin, and then we had Pan Am. And unfortunately, Butler was known as the white-boy league, and Pan Am was known as the Mexican league. Now that was the way that our fathers, on both sides—cause trust me, I knew kids who I went to high school with that their dads played over at Butler but wouldn't play at Pan Am. And all, "the Eastside was dangerous." And we were like, "Aw, we ain't playing with the white boys," you know—my dad, you know, and that group. And it's funny, cause little by little they were at 10 to 12 teams, . . . then we're like at 8 teams, and then we're at 4 teams over there, for—and I was one of the ones who finally went to one of the dads over there and said, "Hey, dude—four teams on your league and four teams—for what? Cause you don't want to play over here, we don't want to play over there? That's ridiculous. You know, let's do something about this. So we started getting the programs together, and we started playing more and more with each other.

At the Newton tournament, Bob "Güero" Sandoval introduced me to Marlon Decker, from the small nearby town of Burns, Kansas. Güero and Marlon worked together in a factory, and once when their conversation turned to playing ball, Marlon mentioned that he "used to chuck a little." Güero brought a pair of gloves the next day, and Marlon threw hard enough playing catch on break that Güero recruited him to join the Newton team for an all-Mexican tournament. The team augmented Marlon's Dutch-origin name, calling him "Decker Lopez," and won the tournament. The story of Decker Lopez resonated with that of Charlie Porfirio, an Italian American member of the Austin Jokers team in the same era. Charlie had grown up on the Eastside and played fastpitch in Comal Park. He attended St. Edward's high school, taking part in a summer work program to pay tuition, and said the Catholic school was integrated, unlike Austin's public schools in the 1950s. Joining the Jokers at the age of twenty-one,

Charlie played with the otherwise Mexican American team in the league at Pan Am Park, as well as traveling to tournaments. Former teammates recalled to me that when questions arose about the white boy on the field, they would say, "Oh, that's Santos." Charlie told me he was sometimes called "Chale," the word for "no" in the hybrid language of *caló*, popular in Mexican American street culture at the time.

Part of navigating segregation in sport was striking a balance between assembling a team from the community and picking up players who might help you win. This juggling act was complicated when players like Decker Lopez or Santos Porfirio were not exactly outsiders but part of the everyday life of neighborhood, school, and work, despite being ethnic outliers. It is easy to speculate that Anglos had less difficulty crossing those boundaries than the nonwhite groups would have. Eventually the presence of one or two Anglos would be codified into the Newton tournament's rules, but before other tournaments opened up, it could be a point of contention, especially when an Anglo guest came in as a particularly strong ringer.

The tradition of designated-Mexican tournaments not only eventually attracted players from outside the community, but produced homegrown teams and players skilled enough to be competitive beyond their home neighborhoods. In the 1980s, contractor Ignacio "Nacho" Hernandez sought to build a tournament-winning team by assembling the Houston Nine, which played throughout the Mexican American fastpitch circuit, but also in tournaments sanctioned by the Amateur Softball Association at the "major" level and the International Softball Congress, which hosts the annual world tournament (Solis 2018). Around the same time, Gil Solis made a similar effort by recruiting members of Newton's Holy Name team and the next generation of players that he scouted from seven states around the Midwest and Texas to join his club, the Metros. The Metros faced the Nine at Newton and the Latin, and both teams then campaigned to qualify for even bigger competition ("Metros Cover the Midwest" 1999). Several Mexican teams have won national trophies in open competition, including the Argentine Eagles in 1988, competing in ASA class B, and the Emporia Brown Express competing in the ASA master's division in 1995 (Santillán et al. 2018). In 2009 the Kansas City Angels won championships at both the Newton tournament and the North American Fastpitch Association class A world series, held in Minnesota (Solis 2018).

Players coming out of the Mexican American fastpitch tradition have also been picked up by national teams. One of the most recent was Caden Luna from the Kansas City area, whose family was long connected to the Newton tournament. In 2019, Luna was selected to play for Team USA in the U-17 Pan American Championship. Members of the fastpitch family raised funds to support his travel to the tryout in Michigan and competition in Guatemala, and then watched and shared the games on Facebook Live. This kind of path also has long precedent. Frank del Toro recounted to me that in the 1981 world championship tournament, he and four other teammates from El Paso All-Sports, the dominant Mexican American team in that city at the time, played for Mexico.

Both the move to expand a tournament by opening up to outsiders and the decision by a player or team to compete beyond the community-based tournaments were ambivalent, representing gains and losses. It is easy to assume in a sports context that a larger scale of competition is an improvement: a move from the margins to a more central location and greater visibility, taking a turn in the mainstream, and competing with all available opponents for a chance to be the best. And yet such "progress" in the level and status of barrio fastpitch was not an unmitigated good. The nostalgic scene of neighborhood games, narrated for my benefit again and again, represented a conviviality that is partly lost despite efforts to keep the tradition going. Some of the people raised in close-knit communities moved on, and public support for socially embedded recreation waned. But where tournaments continued, they offered a chance to remember and revisit that shared vernacular space around a ball field.

4

BALLPLAYERS IN BARRIO LIFE

AS ONE OF THE STORIED TEAMS to form during the heyday of soft-ball from the 1960s to the 1980s, the Austin Jokers worked hard to recruit the best players and made a name for themselves around the region, traveling to Kansas City to compete and regularly placing at the Latin, though they never won it. According to former manager Tony Castillo, the early Jokers as a matter of principle did not bring in pitching, but "rode" their ace, Big John Limon. When John died in 2013, his friend Ernest Nieto wrote a tribute, which included the following observations:

> Goodbye to John Limon from Austin's Eastside: In every barrio of Latinos there are those people with reputations that others privately admire and respect, the ones who break the stereotypes of having cracked the barriers that hold us back from pursuing and achieving dreams. We admire and respect them even more when they show us that they never forget, that old friends remain old friends, that camaradas of old remain camaradas til the end. . . .
> There are John Limon's [sic] throughout our nation, in almost every place imaginable where raza lives, whether in Austin, Houston, San Antonio, East LA, Kansas City, Albuquerque, Phoenix, El Paso, Baytown, or even Beeville, Texas. Among all carnales there are individuals who are strong and show all of us the way without ever having to lower our dignity or self respect.[1] We rely on their strength of character and capacities to dare the odds. They hit the home run when we've all but lose the game or strike out the most menacing batter

of the opposition when we imagine seeing the ball sailing over the left field to once again face defeat.

One feature of this eulogy is that "every place imaginable where raza lives" actually reads a little more like a list of places that have sent fastpitch teams to Texas tournaments (with the possible exception of East LA). The portrait Nieto paints of a role model of self-accomplishment and relationship, a kind of hero of everyday life, complements another portrayal that is typical when people on the fastpitch circuit speak of a former player as accomplished in the sport as a John Limon: *He was one hell of a ballplayer.*

The stature of ballplayers in Mexican American fastpitch-playing communities is not just a function of talent and athletic achievement. Their role in the community and in the webs of relationships around the sport are part of what keeps people connected to their fastpitch home, even if athleticism takes them further. Mario Garcia of Newton was a ballplayer, but his first love was basketball, and he turned down offers from two professional baseball organizations to play hoops in college. After graduation, he continued to play semiprofessional baseball and softball, competing with former major leaguers. Not quite reaching stardom, this athletic career nevertheless allowed Mario to pursue his passion for sports and travel around the country. All the while, though, playing in the Newton Mexican American tournament remained a standard of achievement he had yet to meet. He said, "In the back of my mind, Fourth of July was always there." His chance to take part in the Mexican American tournament came when, on the road with the Wichita Boosters softball team, he received a call from home:

> Ray Arellano called and said, "When you're ready, you need to come out and try out for the Holy Name team." And I knew what that meant. You know, even—whatever it is I've done, that doesn't mean, automatic. No. Cause the guys that were playing were my idols and heroes. My uncle Jim was on first base, my uncle Curly was catcher. I mean, I had family members in there. What place am I going to take? I can't take their place at the table, let alone on the field!

Mario returned from the travels that his athleticism had afforded him to join the bench of the Holy Name team, and he gradually earned a position in the lineup, joining his elders as a ballplayer.

Gil Solis, a former tournament director and manager from Newton, shared a similar comment as I left his home in a Kansas City–area suburb, having just barely scratched the surface of his vast collection of photographs, news clippings, programs, and other memorabilia from decades of fastpitch softball in Mexican American communities. Gil told me, "You have to understand, when I was younger, my heroes weren't Mickey Mantle or one of those major leaguers. My heroes were Johnny Boy Torrez! Rocket Rocha! Blanco Gomez!" The softball pitchers he named were well known in their day along the corridor between Topeka, Kansas, and Kansas City and in railroad towns around that state. "I looked up to them not just for how they threw but how they carried themselves, the kind of men they were."

Further corroborating this view of ballplayers, Tony Castillo explained to me that the original Jokers team held a place of prestige within the East Austin community:

> Because we—you know, we weren't hot dogs. We were pretty good guys. We really were. You can count it on one hand the number of guys that, you know, that didn't pan out well. . . . We were the leaders of the community, to be honest with you.

As the previous chapters suggest, many players and fans cherish Mexican American fastpitch as a source of identity grounded in everyday life. But the identity at play in fastpitch was not only expressed in team names (for example, the Aztecs, Amigos, and Mestizos), or in the cuisine sold at concession stands, or the music played from press boxes and at tournament dances. Within the Mexican American sphere, there was also a more specific identity that emerged from the fastpitch scene: the ballplayer.

In this chapter, I unpack the figure of the ballplayer as a particular identity produced through participation in fastpitch softball. On top of the vernacular institutions that communities have built in order to make and maintain the Mexican American fastpitch tradition—teams, tournaments, clubs, ball fields, halls of fame—the sport has also produced a certain character type. There are running conversations affirming favored characteristics among ballplayers and debating who the best examples are. The associations with being recognized as a ballplayer also vary with historical context. Without proposing that it is softball alone that produces a certain kind of person or, on the contrary, that people come fully formed to softball without being changed by it, I argue that fastpitch provides Mexican American communities with a means akin to what Michel Foucault (1980) termed a "technology of the self" (Rose 1999), for developing, embodying, and promoting a certain kind of subjectivity. Such projects always take place on ground prepared by historical relations of power, but constructing a self can also happen in tension with those relations and what they seem to have in store for the subjects confronting them. The particular subjectivity of a barrio ballplayer was not primarily a plea for recognition from a larger power structure so much as a constitutive enactment of relationships and channeling of efforts within fastpitch. People seen to be doing this well occupy a valorized position in the community.

The self-making power of softball is something that proponents of the sport widely believed in. But the kind of character building associated with bat-and-base games in general gains specificity against the backdrop of negative constructions of Mexican identity and subjectivity, which developed within the historical contexts of military conquest, racial government, and the management of labor. In this chapter, I show how fastpitch constructions of the ballplayer engage a complex intersection of race, gender, and citizenship in ways that counter specific racist narratives about Mexicans. Some of those narratives provided an alibi for exclusion by casting Mexicans as being incapable of or indisposed to athleticism. To become a ballplayer and remain unabashedly Mexican in the United States was to disprove some of the racist tropes about Mexicans. Moreover, since an intrinsic part of the racialization of Mexican America was the ascription of a class position confined to certain sectors of the labor force, the meaning and value of certain work was also in play, and fastpitch held appeal for the ways that it valorized and aestheticized certain attributes of that work.

Part of this appeal was that softball, in the historical context of Mexican American fastpitch, provided access to a means of masculinity that held some allure for subjects for whom gender was part of a colonial structure of exclusion and containment. That is not to say that softball offered a clear or simple path to normative, gendered claims to full citizenship. Indeed, it becomes clear at times in the sport that navigating the field of dominant and subaltern masculinities can lead in multiple, conflicting directions, with ethical and political consequences always subject to vigorous debate. The complexity and messiness of real life has prompted some critics to counsel caution in the tendency of Mexican American studies to focus on heroic cultural figures such as the protagonists of corridos (Rodriguez 2010). Sport studies can easily fall prey to this due to a tendency in modern sport to highlight exceptional and successful individuals. Those devoted to the illusio of a particular sport also like their heroes. On the vernacular scale, however, the spectacular feats of legends and the social activity of ballplayers—some perhaps more admirable than others—all take place in close social quarters, and I propose that this intimate scale is where much of the value of self-making can be found.

THE MEANS OF MASCULINITY

Fastpitch without a doubt was first culturally articulated with masculinity in U.S. society, as nearly all competitive team sports have been, despite the fact that women had more access to softball from the beginning than to many other sports. Yet in the current sex-segregated athletic landscape, fastpitch is mostly played by women, a fact that leads Erica Westly to characterize it as a "women's sport without a male counterpart" (2016, 177). This is an incomplete character-ization, not only because of the Mexican American tradition but also in other contexts, like the Native American communities that maintain the game and come together in the annual All-Indian tournament in Oklahoma, which in-cludes both men's and women's divisions and has run since 1952. There also is still enough undesignated men's fastpitch to support multiple associations and state, national, and world tournaments. Nevertheless, Westly's general point is well taken: broadly speaking, men's fastpitch in the United States today is a niche sport, and the mainstream of fastpitch is undeniably the women's game, which draws girls from an early age to develop their skills and possibly cultivate dreams of high school, college, and even professional or Olympic play.[2]

From its explosion as a national participatory and spectator sport in the 1930s, fastpitch has favored and rewarded strength, power, speed, and fierce competition that belies its names (besides softball, the sport was earlier called "kittenball" and "playground ball" among other names). The scaled-down field and duration of games made softball accessible to people of various athletic abil-ities and in various spaces, but in its most competitive form, the close quarters of the game amplified rather than diminished its intensity. Given the importance of base running on the compact field, bunting and short hits are a key part of the game's strategy: when a situation suggests that a player might bunt, the pitcher, first-base, and third-base fielders all may move in close to prepare for a short ball. This creates a situation where a player may also swing the bat as hard as he or she can and drive the ball—which is less dense than a baseball but not in any sense actually "soft"—directly at the fielding players at a distance of only thirty feet or less. The scale of softball thus introduces a degree of danger that ironically enhances the "hardness" of the game. Youth players concerned about safety sometimes wear protective masks in the infield, not unlike a catcher's or umpire's mask but much lighter and less obtrusive. I have seen only two people wear this equipment in the men's game: a shortstop who is a highly accomplished player in the Mexican tournaments as well as on a national scale, and a young pitcher from Canada competing in a North American tournament. The excitement, difficulty, and danger of fastpitch is a point of pride for many players of various gender identities. Men who play fastpitch, though, often actively interpret the sport's intensity as gendered, and I have heard more than one person call slowpitch "sissy ball" by way of distinction.

In his ethnography *Desi Hoop Dreams* (2015), Stanley Thangaraj unpacks how gender, race, and citizenship intersect in the cultural dynamics of pickup basketball played by South Asian Americans. As a participant observer in this other vernacular sporting practice, Thangaraj notes that players emphasize "manning up" and other performative signals that masculinity is at stake in the self-making accomplished through athletic activity. He connects this to "white homosociality" (120), citing the historical example of the *Bhagat Singh Thind* (1923) case to explain how notions of citizenship in the United States have been tied to race and gender. Thind was an Indian American who had successfully petitioned for citizenship on the basis of now-discredited scientific theories about the geographical origins of human races, which he argued qualified him as "white," as required at the time by naturalization law. Despite the fact that courts had previously referred to the same racial science to deny Takao Ozawa's bid for citizenship in another case (on the basis that as a Japanese American, he was not "scientifically" white), the appeal of *U.S. v. Baghat Singh Thind* ultimately defined whiteness for legal purposes as being a quality that the "common white man" would recognize, rescinding Thind's citizenship (Thangaraj 2015, 120).

Mexicans, having been legally defined as white, would not have to appeal to courts for citizenship in quite the same way as Ozawa and Thind did but the ruling that race would be officially defined in the eye of the "common white man" was an explicit statement of a practical reality for many Mexicans: regardless of legal status, they would "commonly" be recognized as something other than white. As Natalia Molina argues, after the *Ozawa* and *Thind* cases, nativists who wanted to exclude Mexicans from the privileges of whiteness, if not its legal definition, drew support for this position from the commonsense notion of whiteness affirmed in *Thind* (2014, 6). Since Mexicans did work that was essential to U.S. economic growth, however, including those recruited by the railroad, the focus for restricting access to "white" citizenship was less on exclusion than producing manageable labor (2). Molina notes that the early twentieth century posed a dilemma for the Anglo state: expanding American capitalism needed Mexican labor, but there was a national-cultural investment in racial and cultural homogeneity (20), which in "common sense" would not include Mexicans. A prominent answer to this Mexican question was to construct Mexicans as a precarious, shiftless labor force.

As Jeffrey Garcilazo (2012) reports in his history of *traqueros*, Mexican railroad laborers in the Midwest, the managers who recruited immigrants to do labor such as railroad track work often held infantilizing views of their workforce in the early twentieth century. Garcilazo quotes one from an industry publication:

> The peon is very much like a child. He likes brightly-colored things and will spend his last cent to get some trivial ornament. He has no thought of the morrow and little does he care as long as his wants for the present are satisfied.

Another said:

> Constant reiteration of rules and orders is absolutely necessary in handling Mexicans. Like children, they soon forget. When properly handled they are willing to do a great deal for a man, often working for ridiculously low wages or giving the very best of service for common wages. (2012, 66)

But like the widespread and official use of misnomers like "unskilled labor" today, the paternalist discourse of managers about the traqueros was far from factual. While their pay reflected the low prestige of "common" labor, the traqueros were required to master a wide range of tasks and responsibilities. Garcilazo gives a sense of the variety and complexity of the work required of so-called common laborers:

> Among other things, they dug ditches, shoveled rock, graded road bed, lifted and laid ties and rails, and drove spikes. Traqueros replaced ties, rails, fastenings, frogs (switches) and ballast. Track workers cut the overgrowth of grass and weeds on banks, handled new and old materials, kept ditches open, adjusted fastenings, and maintained gauge (distance between rails) by re-spiking, adzing (trimming ties), raising joints, and ballasting. Then, in addition to all this, traqueros removed snow and ice and repaired the damage constantly being done by water and weather. (59)

This responsibility for maintaining a piece of ground and the infrastructure of the railroad resonates with countless stories I have been told about the improvisation and bricolage that goes into carrying off a local softball tournament.

Every locale has its repertoire of tales about when the rains came and the fields were too wet. In the old days, it was not uncommon to dump gasoline on the ground and burn the fields dry, but this fell out of favor. At least once a resourceful host dumped cat litter on the infield. According to an oft-retold story, another called in a favor with someone in the air national guard, who flew a helicopter to hover low over the rain-soaked field and blow it dry. One tournament director discovered that they were short on lime for lining the fields after the supply stores had closed for the weekend and confessed to me that he ran to an all-night grocery for sacks of flour to ensure the fields would be ready for an early start.

Besides cultivating the ingenuity to make things work, being a traquero had an athletic side. Garcilazo reports on an industry magazine's account of an Anglo college athlete who worked as a track hand in 1915 and spoke of the skill he had witnessed on the line:

> The regular hands laughed at me because I could do only half as much work as they could and the result of my labor was remarkably rough. . . . [He recounts that he had trouble hitting spikes.] Time and again I have seen regular laborers drive spikes with the "pointed end" of the spike maul, which has a diameter of only five-eighths of an inch or thereabouts. And these laborers take a full, free swing with all the recklessness and abandon of a Ty Cobb at the bat. (2012, 62)

This observer's reference to a legendary professional ballplayer in order to underscore the physical skill and precision of the track workers gives lie to the idea of childlike, "common" labor and also suggests how social prestige may become attached to channeling and aestheticizing specific physical skill into games, and particularly baseball.

In Kansas, one of the legends to emerge in the 1960s era of consolidated Mexican tournaments was "Johnny Boy" Torrez, brother to Mike Torrez, who played eighteen years in major league baseball (Iber 2016). In lawn chairs around the ball field at a tournament in Topeka, Johnny Boy told me he had been the first Mexican to play baseball for Topeka High in the late 1950s, but he later injured his arm playing football and had to stick to softball. This was an option, he said, since the underhand pitch puts less strain on the arm than a baseball pitch does. But that is not to say he took it easy on his arm. While working for the railroad, he used to take a sixteen-pound ball bearing and swing it around to work out. Sometimes he would slip into an empty boxcar and pitch the shot-put-sized bearing against a wall with a huge crash.

Not all Mexican Americans who took up softball have done the same kind of work, though the way that the fastpitch circuits in mid-América follow the skeleton of the railroad is also not accidental. Many of the communities that ended up cultivating a significant fastpitch tradition consisted of people who drew their livelihood from industrial logistics, having found work on the docks in Houston, in meatpacking and locomotive maintenance in Kansas City, and in track work throughout Kansas. Part of the social embeddedness of fastpitch in these communities lies in how this particular recreation afforded chances to aestheticize, celebrate, and take advantage of skills and capabilities related to work.

By asserting themselves into popular sporting space, Mexican Americans not only pushed against devaluations of their work and physical capabilities, but also against a powerful discourse of racial pseudoscience that justified their exclusion from athletics by underestimating both their potential and their will to compete. Iber, Regalado, Alamillo, and de León, coauthors of the textbook *Latinos in U.S. Sport*, recount how racial theories that were widely held in the early twentieth century led to assessments like that of scholar and coach Elmer D. Mitchell, who in 1922 posited a hierarchy of "the races" according to their physical attributes. Mitchell argued that

> the South American has not the physique, environment, or disposition which makes for a champion athlete. In build he is of medium height and weight, and not rugged. . . . [He] has inherited an undisciplined nature. The Indian in him chafes at discipline and sustained effort, while the Spanish half is proud to a fault. . . . [His] disposition makes team play difficult . . . the steady grind and the competition involved in winning a place on the Varsity has no attraction for them. (Mitchell 1922, cited in Iber et al. 2011, 75)

The reference to "the South American" indicates that Miller was a bit overly ambitious in his generalization, not to mention essentialism, as he goes on to speak more about mestizo racialization than precise geographic origin. But such racist pseudoscience provided intellectual cover for excluding Latinos and Latinas from opportunities to compete athletically. The idea that mestizo heritage somehow prevented Mexican Americans even from wanting to play varsity sports or pursue athletic success was the kind of proposition accepted at face value by much of society without ever being exposed to the test of evidence. Thus, it justified keeping Mexican Americans off high school teams, for example, a damaging underestimation that was repeated in other aspects of education. By extension, such essentialist narratives also painted Mexicans as unworthy of self-government and in need of administration.

This was part of the cultural-political context for Mexican American base-ball teams in the 1920s. Through the entirely mainstream idiom of sport, Mexican Americans challenged the racist ideology of their own physical and mental inferiority. Newton's Cuauhtemoc club, followed by Los Rayos, was matched by clubs named Los Aztecas in Kansas City, Wichita, and Houston and by Mexican baseball leagues in Austin's Parque Zaragoza, the Spanish American League in San Antonio, and the international leagues in Houston. By the time softball trended nationally in the interwar period, Mexican American communities had embraced sports as both a self-organized field of activity in everyday bar-rio life and a public stage on which Mexicans might claim a chance, however, limited, to represent themselves and their families and barrios in a cultural environment all too prone to disparage them.

For Mexican American men, being interpellated equally as docile, common laborers at their jobs and undisciplined natives in their bodies, masculinity would have been one part of the normative complex of race-citizenship-gender that they could influence for themselves by developing physical and mental capacities that would serve them well on the playing field. Like the Desi bas-ketball players Thangaraj worked and played with, Mexican Americans took on this project in the field of sport, playing for normativity by performing the preferred characteristics that had been promoted as Americanism by cultural movements such as Muscular Christianity, an ideal based on "the convergence of masculinity, physical activity, asceticism, racial purity, and the white man's burden" (Besnier, Brownell, and Carter 2018, 45). Indeed, the YMCA was instrumental in promoting softball in the early part of the century, advocating for it as an alternative to other sports, including baseball, which according to the Y was tainted by associations with gambling and drinking (Westly 2016, 26). The race-specific purity and temperance that reformers thought would be promoted in softball would not stand the test of time, but the sport did reward courage, strength, and skill at a time when society at large culturally coded these as masculine traits. Size and brute strength were also not absolutely required, as Morris Bealle had observed that "the small wiry player with instantaneous reflexes and quick get-away is the star of softball" (Morris Bealle, cited in Westly 2016, 32). In these and other ways, softball afforded resources to rearticulate gender, race, and physicality in concrete, visible forms.

John Limón Jr., the son of "Big John," the Jokers' pitcher, told me a story to illustrate how ballplayers turned the underestimation of Mexican players' capabilities and will to play against unsuspecting Anglo opponents:

> Now I remember my dad actually playing a team, he always talks about this, Stevens Transporters. . . . And they had big-time pitchers and players. They went to the world tournament, ok? They went to the world tournament, finished third in the world, came back to Austin, played in the Austin tournament, and . . . Little Louie Murillo, the original Joker? Well Louie's always been 4 foot 9, ok, he don't grow more than that, right? Well . . . my dad goes to pitch against that team. First pitch, boom! Guy hits a home run off of him. So Tony Castillo, the manager, comes up and says, "You know, Big John," he says, ". . . I know you're our ace. But let's mess with them a little bit. Let's throw Louie."
>
> So they bring Louie in. Louie just strikes them out, Ben! With just little change-ups and junk ball and curve ball. His fast ball, guy's like, "That his curve ball? That his change?" Catcher's like, "That's his fast ball!" you know? Funny story, true story. . . . Louie beat 'em 2 to 1.

For the Jokers and their fans, neighbors, and families, there is a vast archive of stories of triumph and tragedy, with some of the favorite tales recounting victory over unsuspecting Anglos, presumed to be the dominant team whether because of physical size, superior resources, or the idea that Mexicans lacked the discipline or strategic intellect necessary to succeed at this highly competitive and fast-paced game. In the segregated midcentury and the decades of its aftermath, self-styled Mexican teams loved to prove these stereotypes wrong. David "Wheel" Acosta told me about playing with the Baytown Hawks: "We didn't have the better pitchers, we didn't have the home run hitters, but we had the speed and we had the cunning. So we did a lot of double steals. Stole home. We did a lot of bunting. We did a lot of sacrifice, you know."

• • •

A team that I recognized from league night in Armourdale and that appeared to me to have numerous Anglo players was in a hard-fought game in the Newton tournament. The hometown team they were playing had come from behind and gone ahead by one run. From the bleachers, I heard a ruckus and saw an animated conversation converging around home plate. Two tournament committee members near the press box said something about "a lot of güeros on the field." The tournament director joined the conference, then strode back around the backstop fence, shaking his head and saying, "It's not my call." The umpire called the ball game. The team that had just taken the lead had lodged a complaint against the visitors: too many Anglo players. The tournament rules allow two on the field at a time. The arguments spilled off the field into the stands as the players returned to the benches and packed up their gear. A coach from the sanctioned team approached the tournament bracket, posted on paper below the press box, and wrote over the name of the opposing team: "Crybabies." A younger teammate looked at it and muttered a curse. The coach turned on him: "Hey! Watch what you say." He then turned back to contemplate the bracket again, "But I can't believe they would do that." A committee member remarked, "He had the right, but in our time that wouldn't have happened." The tournament director answered, "I don't disagree with you." Rules were rules, but he hadn't gone out of his way to enforce them. "We never would have back in our day."

Although sports provide the clarity of winning and losing, what it means to be a ballplayer is not always cut and dried. Fastpitch is competitive, and people want to win. Umpires are imperfect but must arbitrate the game. These factors ensure that there are disagreements, and the same intense commitment to the illusio of the game that produces exciting play can produce controversy. In this case, it was not merely a dispute over who would win the game but an ethical dilemma that exposed a duality embedded deep in the particular tradition of Mexican American fastpitch. On one hand was an ethos valuing concrete performance over abstractions, suggesting that the best way to decide a winner is to "let them play." The outcome should be settled on the field. On the other hand was an ethos of responsible adherence to rules, suggesting that the established tournament guidelines were known to all before the game, so it was fair play for one team to lodge a complaint when the other team didn't follow them. But the rules were somewhat gray as well. Not everyone with Mexican heritage carried an obviously Spanish surname, such as the highly sought-after pitcher Ray Foster. Before opening up, it was not uncommon for tournaments to require birth certificates from players. At Newton, the last closed Mexican tournament, most of the players and their families were known. Controversy over the identity requirement was not common in my experience at the Newton tournament, but in this rare event, the dilemma between concrete results—"Let them play it out"—and adherence to an organized structure—"Rules are rules" highlighted how a ballplayer's ethos bears a complicated relationship to socially and historically defined values.   What is accomplished on the field, including what is decided there, is considered to be concrete fact. This is one reason why securing the opportunity to play became so ethically weighted in the age of de facto segregation. The value of concrete results is related to the articulation of masculinity with hard labor, coming out of the historical context of the traqueros. But the value of rule-governed organization also has a place within softball, which, like baseball, is a relatively legalistic sport. Having established rules is one of the features that affords a sport the status of being "official," and running a tournament in strict accordance with them is a mark of responsibility, a trait affirmed in certain class-associated versions of masculinity. In turn, knowing the rules inside and out is one of the ways players and managers conduct their tactics, making decisions based on a precise understanding of the situation the team is in, which may lead them to try to end a game when they hold a slight advantage.

The let-them-play ethos is of profound importance to the tradition of Mexican American fastpitch, given the arbitrary exclusions of Mexicans in earlier eras. When athletes didn't get a chance to play, it didn't always mean that they had been found lacking, but often that they had been shut out due to untested assumptions. In light of this, the chance to show what players could do concretely and determine who was the better team in direct competition held great prestige. But at the same time, once the tradition of Mexican tournaments had been established, the question was not just who can physically play but also who can run a good tournament. Consistency and follow-through on one's professed word were the kinds of characteristics that demonstrated a capacity for responsibility. Moreover, softball's baseball-derived rules have a fine grain, with detailed specifications on matters such as stepping in and out of the batter's box, running on a dropped third strike, holding back a swing on a ball outside the strike zone, and others that turn on inches and split-seconds. The ethos of running a well-officiated game and tournament resembled what Ralph Cintron (1997) termed "discourses of measurement" that perform a rule-governed responsibility, articulated by implication with class- and gender-associated qualities of effective management, a kind of bourgeois masculinity.

Thus, sport has historically offered participants the chance to achieve and perform different gendered forms of worthiness. In fastpitch, these articulate with masculinity in ways that can be inconsistent, even contradictory. The path to being a celebrated ballplayer may lead someone in different directions at once. Whether specific players leaned more to performances of rule-governed responsibility or concrete results on the field, engaging and displaying these qualities fashioned their public selves as ballplayers, and the whole self-making process occurred within a community of practice formed around softball. Linguistic anthropologist Norma Mendoza-Denton notes that certain subjects emerge within a community of practice as "iconic speakers." These exemplary figures are "not necessarily the *sources* of innovation, but they are the ones who put together a style that is salient, identifiable, and indeed recognizable and prone to imitation by others" (Mendoza-Denton 2008, 211–212). Recalling the eulogy for Big John Limon, we may conceive of an iconic ballplayer: a ballplayer who does not necessarily resolve the tensions of cultural citizenship or normative masculinity, but thrives in the process of engaging them within the socially embedded milieu of the vernacular fastpitch tradition (Figure 14).

LEGENDS

Sitting under a tarp stretched for shade over the bleachers in Houston's Memorial Park, I find myself in the middle of a historical debate. Two tall Mexican American men in their sixties are rehashing games from thirty years ago or more that took place on the field in front of us.

"Did you know we have a record?" one of them asks as he leans back on the bench in front of me and catches my eye while also making sure his former rival can overhear. "Most second-places in this tournament. Because *somebody* always brought in outside pitching!"

The man to my right, whose team had taken the championship in many of the years being discussed, replies, "Hey! Why didn't you walk me? I always got a hit off you guys in the final."

When I told people later that I had found a seat at the Latin between Frank del Toro of the El Paso All-Sports and Rick Lopez of the Baytown Hawks, they would laugh knowingly: "Oh, those guys used to really go after each other! A couple of legends."

When I attended fastpitch tournaments, the names of ballplayers—sometimes only the nicknames (among them, Manuel "the kid" Navarro, Linga Hernandez, Chopper, Tree, Cobra, Cheddy Boy, Boom Boom, Sparkle, Boosty, Stretch, Fancy, Champ) drifted around the park as spectators and former players reminisced:

"Rocket Rocha was the daytime pitcher. He could go all day in the sun. Then
    Blanco Gomez took over at night—he could hurt you."
"The best pitcher around here was Charlie Salazer, the Loose Goose. He was a

FIGURE 14 David "Who Dat" Rios, after the day's games at the Latin, Houston Memorial Park. Photo by the author.

      farmer, and he wore bib overalls, short socks, and a hat cocked to the side. He
      drank whiskey from a flask, but they couldn't hurt him."
  "There were no time limits in those days. One year Paulie and them came down
      from Kansas City, and they went twenty-two innings, with a final score of 1–0."

The list of nicknames is seemingly endless. I asked one old-timer about his nickname, and before he told me the story of how he got it, he said, "There are people who I don't even know their real name." As ball tournaments become reunions, you sometimes see aging men greet each other and ask, "What was your nickname?" The sense of celebration and nostalgia at these reunions makes it clear that strong, lasting bonds of friendship come out of these events.

The fastpitch family does get specific in recognizing some of its iconic players in the halls of fame maintained by several clubs throughout the region. The induction ceremonies and sometimes publication in a souvenir program provide opportunities for the selection committee or friends of the inductees to sing their praises. In one such ceremony, inducting the brothers Andy and Gilbert Martinez to the Rusk Athletic Club Hall of Fame at the club's final tournament in Houston, David "Wheel" Acosta spoke emotionally about the mentoring role that iconic ballplayers play, referring to his recently deceased brother, Alan Acosta, as he addressed the crowd.

> Y'all remember Alan, right? [cheers] The day after my brother Alan died, I got a phone call from one of these guys that I'm going to introduce today. I hadn't talked to anybody that day outside my family. And he called me, and he said—and he was crying. And I started crying, I didn't know why I was crying. . . . He said, "Look, man, I gotta tell you about your brother Alan. You might not know this. But when I was playing with the Hawks, I had many talks with him in the dugout. And he would come over there and start telling me, about . . . teaching me about things."
>
> And I said, "Oh yeah, he was teaching you how to bunt, he was teaching you how to do all that—" He goes, "No! He was teaching me about *life*. And how to *live*." That's what goes beyond softball." And this whole Rusk Athletic thing goes beyond softball. It's about familia. It's about friends. It's about family. It's about God. And it's about all of us being together, against all odds. [applause]

Wheel's collection of memorabilia and statistics that he shared with me shows him to be an enthusiastic historian of Mexican American athletics in the Houston area. Nevertheless, he emphasized personal traits and background when inducting these athletes who had certainly put up their share of numbers and trophy-winning performances:

> Andy and Gilbert, they grew up across Mason Park. Anybody played in Mason Park before? [cheers] It gets flooded during the hurricanes out there. Well, they were lucky that they played there because they got the—they knew what it was like to be a kid and play ball down there. Just like when we were in Baytown, we played at de Zavala, and Guadalupe Park and all that. If you're taught early in life about how to get all dirty, it doesn't bother you later on. And I'll tell you what: all of us have been dirty at one time or another, plenty of times.

Finally, the official induction came:

> For their over forty years plus of participation, outstanding play, helping the
> Rusk Athletic Club, the love of the game, and building a new generation of
> fastpitch softball players, I am proud to announce the new inductees to the
> Rusk Athletic Club Hall of Fame, Andy and Gilbert Martinez.

As Wheel's induction of the Martinez brothers suggests, mentorship joins
physical and mental traits as well as camaraderie as favored qualities of an
iconic ballplayer. When I interviewed Louie Aguayo, the pitcher and beloved
coach, at the San Antonio Glowworm tournament, he recounted how Chilolo
Rios had taken him in as a young pitcher:

> And I used to play in commercial leagues. . . . They weren't strong, but
> they would go out there and have fun. But then, finally Glowworm,
> Mr. Chilolo—you've heard that name before. He asked me if I wanted to play
> competitive ball. I said, "Sure, why not?" . . . So I started playing for him. First
> tournament he threw me in was against the Jokers, up in Austin. . . . So he
> said, it's going to be your baby. You want to play competitively, there's a time
> to start, so . . . They eight-run ruled me.[3] I told him, "You want to put someone
> in there?" He said, "No, you stay there." He said, "You want to play competi-
> tive, learn." I tell you, from that day, I grew up. I thought I knew everything
> about fastpitch, but from him, he gave me that confidence. He said, "You're
> going to face them again." And I did. I faced them again here in San Antonio,
> I beat 'em one to nothing. See what I told you? He says—right there where they
> build your confidence, that's when [you] turn things around. So, and from
> there on I just stayed with them. You know, like I say, I wasn't overpowering,
> I was just competitive. And that's what you need—hey, this kid's got to learn
> how to be competitive. You know, be up there. Don't beat yourself by saying,
> "Oh, they're big boys, they do—they've got this kind of uniform, they look like
> a million dollars." I say that don't mean nothing. I said, it's how much you put
> into—effort into the game.

Each tournament hosted by a club that maintains a hall of fame features
similar ceremonies of recognition, and participants in the fastpitch family
highly value induction. While the typical induction recognizes a retired player
after a long career, communities sometimes make use of these events to express
shared, public emotion in times of loss. One such circumstance was when Arturo "Tury" Garcia Jr. was inducted into the hall of fame at the Kansas City

Angels' tournament shortly before he passed away with a cancer diagnosis at the age of forty-six in 2012. Tury was part of the closely knit Garcia family and their team, the Kansas City Indios, which in its third generation was always a formidable contender in the Kansas City area throughout the time of my fieldwork. Tury has been further honored with an annual sportsmanship award that the Indios make at their own tournament, recognizing a player for exemplifying "the characteristics that Tury had on and off the softball field" (G. Chávez 2015). The plaque for the Arturo "Tury" Garcia award reads, "To the Player Who Demonstrates Sportsmanship, Generosity of Time, Knowledge, Friendship, Dedication and Love of the Game. Kansas City Indios."

BALLPLAYERS BEYOND THE FIELD

On my first trip to Houston to attend the Latin for fieldwork, I wore a T-shirt from the Newton tournament, which became my routine in the multi-sited research space. By picking a shirt from another town but within the fastpitch tradition, I presented myself as a somewhat initiated outsider. Right away I was approached in the crowd.

"Newton, Kansas? Do you know Gil Solis?"

Gil Solis, Sr. is not only known throughout the fastpitch scene as a player, manager, and former tournament director; his name linked to Newton Holy Name, the Metros, and the Mexican American tournament, but also for occasionally hosting an entire team from Texas in his home in greater Kansas City. In the early 1990s, it was the Houston Nine. More recently, San Antonio Glowworm enjoyed the Solis hospitality. Gene Chávez's video documentary captures Gil making a statement he did frequently in person as well, describing a network of support developed over decades of specific communities playing ball:

> For me it was more than a sport. It was more than; the tournaments were more than just gatherings. You know, they were family reunions. . . . And it was more than just playing softball. And I know today that I can go anywhere in those communities . . . and have a place to stay the night, something to eat tonight, and if I was down on my luck and I needed some money, I'd have that as well. Just because of playing fastpitch softball. (G. Chávez 2015)[4]

One occasion when Gil reiterated this view was in 2015, as part of a series of sports-related public humanities events sponsored by the Smithsonian Institution and state humanities councils. Collaborating with the Kauffman Museum in North Newton, Kansas, to collect and present material on the Mexican American fastpitch tournament to the public, I conducted a kind of

group interview before a small audience in a college auditorium.[5] Mario Garcia was another of the former players to speak. Around halfway through the
evening's proceedings, I asked a question about friendships that participants
had developed out of playing fastpitch, and Mario took his turn. He announced
his story with a reference to an earlier statement he had made to explain the
importance of the identity requirement of the Newton tournament—*mi raza*, he
said, *es mi orgullo*. My race (my people) is my pride. When I asked the panelists
to talk about friendship, Mario's voice quickly thickened with emotion, and his
narration took on a slow, deliberate rhythm that lent gravity to what he said:

> Ben, I'm going to go a little different route. It fits in with the friendship and
> it fits in with *mi raza es mi orgullo*. In 1990 my wife passed away from cancer
> in Kansas City. . . . And Gil's brother, Joe Solis, who was a former ballplayer,
> played for many teams—he took me in. "You're not staying at any motel, you're
> not doing anything, you're staying with me."

Mario paused as his voice tightened. The room grew still as he drew his audience in:

> I'm going to try to do this without getting emotional. I lived with that man
> for three months while my wife battled cancer. When she had her victory, Joe
> said, "Come on. I'm taking you to Mora's." Mora's was a Mexican American
> bar, a drinking establishment. Not the place I wanted to go right after my wife
> died. The furthest thing from my mind did I want to go anywhere and do that.
> But he made me go, and when I got there—

He paused again and swallowed:

> It was this *mass* of former ballplayers. They had all given blood, hoping that
> their platelets would help. And they had donated tons of money. And they
> hugged me and they loved me. And when we finished at that location he took
> me to another spot, and we did it again, and again, and again, for three days he
> took me to a location, and each time I received the same thing. We take care of
> each other. I will never, ever forget that.
>
>   Do I have friends? You better believe it. Some I know very closely, some I
> don't know very well at all. But I know what they did for me and my loved ones.
>
>   Oh, yeah. Ballplayers.

⚾ 5 ⚾

MEN AND WOMEN IN
GENDERED FASTPITCH

THE CATCHER WAS A BIG, barrel-chested man with a screen-idol mustache. He crouched without protective pads other than a face mask, and when a foul tip slammed into the center of his chest, he fell back and took a moment to recover. When the opposing team took a couple of runs, he swore loudly at the end of the inning, heading back to the bench, and after his team's at-bat, he pulled his teammates together for an impromptu cheer before they took the field. He remained grave, all business, as the team battled back to the lead and won the game. Afterward, in a victorious mood, a younger, skinnier teammate danced around the catcher, play-boxing at him as if to coax him out of his game-face deadpan. After a couple of jabs, the catcher lunged at him with faux aggression, chin jutting out, and the boxer dodged away. "Yeah, hit and run!" jeered the catcher. "That's all you do! Just like a little girl."

At a tournament in another city, two games were running simultaneously in the Memorial Day weekend heat. Two women who sat in camp chairs just behind the backstop fence at one field shouted regular encouragement to the young man at bat, who wore colors that matched theirs. "Come on, kid, get you one! Good cut, good cut! Wait for your pitch now. Don't let that crow-hopper scare you."

One of them took a phone call without substantially altering the volume of her voice: "Yeah, I'm out at Del Valle." Her tone changed to suggest an eye roll. "Watching some guys who *think* they can play fastpitch."

• • •

Though the tournament titles do not always say so explicitly, the softball tournaments that make up the tradition of Mexican American fastpitch are usually, effectively "men's softball." In a way, this makes them anachronistic. Indeed, the way that Mexican American fastpitch is gendered is part of what makes the tournaments represent continuity and connection with the past. In the archival newspaper coverage of earlier days of Mexican teams and tournaments, when reports said "softball," they often did not designate that the game was played by men or that it was the fastpitch variety. Both characteristics were normative. Today things are different.

In much of the country, if men play softball recreationally, it can usually be assumed to be slowpitch. The regulations placed on pitching in this variety of the game maximize the batter's chances of hitting fairly, dialing down the intensity of the confrontation with the pitcher. This allows for the game to reproduce ordinary tactics of fielding and base running—though the legality of stealing bases varies among governing associations—without requiring the same level of skill and effort to put the ball in play, a point that fastpitch players frequently emphasized to me. Slow-pitch softball is the version that in the eye of the general public produces the stereotype of a relaxed, sociable game, amenable to a "beer league" atmosphere. It is also in many places co-recreational, allowing or even requiring participation by men and women together.

In contrast, if a woman or a young girl is identified as a competitive softball player, she most likely plays fastpitch. Erica Westly's characterization of fastpitch as effectively "a women's sport without a male counterpart" (2016, 177) is, as noted in the previous chapter, incomplete but not far off the mark given that fastpitch is overwhelmingly played by women today. In telling the important story of women's continuous participation in fastpitch from the 1930s on and the changing landscape of gendered opportunity that these athletes weathered, Westly does not focus on the niches where a men's game endures. But Westly's insights about the competitive nature of fastpitch and gender-regulated opportunities to develop and express athleticism also illuminate the condition of Mexican American fastpitch today as well.

Where fastpitch does get played by men in the United States, it tends to be in specific communities that stubbornly maintain the game as an aspect of local identity. Many of these corners in the overall national sporting landscape are midsized industrial cities such as Appleton, Wisconsin, or Ashland, Ohio, a scene documented by New York artist Jeremy Spear's immersive documentary film project, *Fastpitch* (2000). In these locales, where men's fastpitch inevitably carries some connotations of nostalgia as a throwback or hanging-on sport identified with more prosperous days in the rust belt, ambitious sponsors also bring in players from other countries where the men's game enjoys more support than it does here, such as Canada and New Zealand.

The upshot of this broad historical context is that if "Mexican American fastpitch" refers to the tournaments and teams most supported over generations by Mexican American communities, then it largely refers to a game played by men. Historical pressure to reproduce gender roles has had its impact on this tradition. My decision to use tournaments as a primary point of access has allowed me a broad, multisited perspective, but it also has limitations: tournaments do not provide a comprehensive slice of Mexican American society and culture as much as a sustained dive into the fastpitch family's sense of itself.[1] By the same token, the Mexican American fastpitch tournaments do not provide a comprehensive account of "Mexican Americans *in* fastpitch," which includes substantial numbers of Mexican American women who have seen opportunities open up outside the racial tradition maintained in their communities, spanning levels of competition from junior traveling teams, through school-sponsored varsity, to scholarship-granting college sports, and even to a small professional league. A bit of evidence of the Mexican American presence in competitive women's softball is the fact that of fifteen players selected for international competition on the Mexican national team in 2019, twelve were born in the United States (Gomez 2019).

The facts that there are more opportunities for girls than for boys in mainstream youth fastpitch and that the tournaments identified in the Mexican American tradition are mostly designated for men do not generally produce a sense of competition between them as much as mutual support. As in sports in general, the segregation of men's and women's competition is largely taken for granted, but not ironclad, as women periodically play in men's tournaments. In discussion of the gender boundary, though, people do tend to assume that sexual dimorphism produces predictable differences in bodies, such as in strength. This contrasts intriguingly with common references to a racial dimorphism by which Mexicans are stereotyped as small in stature and whites represented as bigger and stronger. While there is abundant evidence to break up these residual stereotypes, they continue to produce lore about less massive Mexicans defeating their apparently dominant opponents through commitment, drive, and "cunning."

Mexican American fastpitch does not directly break down all gender scripts of the broader society, then, but the concrete features of athleticism do refract historical change in the sport in specific ways because of its social embeddedness. Even at the vernacular scale, sport as a public, leisure practice exists in a sphere of activity in which men have historically been more welcome and more celebrated. Within this historically gendered division of space and labor, women were interpellated as culture bearers in social reproduction, including activities such as food preparation, religious devotion, and the early socialization of children, while men were expected to carry the standard of identity into public arenas such as political and economic advocacy. The ritualized competition of organized sport falls into that favored, public arena (though without quite as much gravitas as business or politics). Just as racial ideologies developed to explain and rationalize the exclusion of Mexicans from opportunities to play sport, gendered boundaries between public and private spheres were reinforced by enduring ideas about women being in need of protection from the rigors and risks of certain sports. Again, these are normative stereotypes, not descriptions of reality.

Here I engage this historical dynamic in two ways: by recounting examples of women involved in the Mexican American fastpitch tradition, and not only in the generally invisible supportive labor that allows a sporting tradition to exist, but as participants both on and off the field. Also, I propose that a crucial aspect of the story of Mexican American fastpitch at this moment is the historical regendering of fastpitch over the past century, from being enforced like most competitive sports, as a presumed-male activity, to becoming virtually the preeminent arena for women's athleticism in the United States. Thus, Mexican American fastpitch began with communities building sporting institutions in an arena in which women were allowed to some extent but men were prioritized. From that foundation, Mexican American communities have accumulated cultural resources in a racial tradition. Today, though, and moving into the future, a great deal of the significance of those cultural resources lies in how they interact with and are channeled into the larger contemporary fastpitch scene. An important aspect of this is that women are taking their own experience with what is effectively their family's or community's sport and running with it in other fields of competition and opportunity.

• • •

At the final Rusk Athletic Club Latin American tournament, in 2019, the organizing committee made the unusual decision to induct one of their own members, who had not been a player or manager in the tournament, into the hall of fame. This decision was also unusual because Maricela Rodriguez Vasquez was the first woman inducted. Her father, Jumpin' Jess Rodriguez, noted while introducing her that before her service on the committee, Mari had played softball from the age of ten but also contributed volunteer hours "shagging foul balls" and selling concessions. Upon joining the committee, also worked on T-shirt designs and programs, organized and awarded scholarships, and made announcements and presentations at the tournament. As is the custom, Mari had the opportunity to speak when her induction was announced:

> I'm very proud to be amongst these men who have made an impact on this great game of fastpitch softball, and this tournament. There should have been plenty of women inducted before me, but I share [sighs] I share this recognition with all the women, wives, girlfriends and daughters who have ever volunteered, helped fundraise, play, coach and overall support these men, who get to play on these fields. It's the women—you guys are the real MVPs. [applause] I appreciate the hard work that the Rodriguez family has done over the years. My father was president of the Rusk for over ten years, so coming out to the Rusk as a little girl, I would help any way that I could. As I got older I wanted to help even more and grow this tournament, what it is today. . . . One of the best things about being part of the Rusk was the night that we call the Hall of Famers, when they have been inducted . . . and letting them know that they had made it. To hear these men cry, and be so excited and so honored, that was probably one of the best moments of every year of me serving on the Rusk board. That was truly my favorite. So receiving this honor as the first of a long line of deserving women, I am grateful and humbled by this opportunity to be part of the 2019 [she begins to weep] Hall of Fame Rusk inductees. [applause and cheers]

●   ●   ●

Historical exhibitions and self-published booklets about the Newton tournament, most of them collected and mounted by Ray Olais, usually include mention of a "Mexican girls' team" contemporary with the founding of the Newton tournament. The Newton City Cab team played against *mexicanas* from other towns like Wichita and Lyons, and hosted an all-women's tournament in the post–World War II period as well. Most intriguing, the *Evening Kansan Republican* reports that Mexican American women approached the city Parks and Recreation Department to request that a "girls' league" be founded alongside the popular men's league. The rest of the story remains untold somewhere in the cracks of documented archives, but given the importance of softball for women's athletics today, it is notable that in at least one locale, it was the daughters of immigrant laborers who initially agitated for opportunities for women ballplayers in general. Such fragments of a history of *mexicana* participation in sport disrupt commonsense narratives that tend to assume that assimilation in the United States provided progress from "traditional" exclusion to more "modern" integration.

In Newton, when I was interviewing veteran players of the Mexican American tournament, I asked about the women's team sponsored by Newton City Cab in the 1940s. Mario Garcia reminisced:

> My mom played a lot of baseball. When I ask my mom who all was on that team, I don't get a lot of names. I get nicknames. Like what we have here, only I'm like, you're not helping me, Mom. Name some of these girls that were on there. Trina Camargo, and Sally Hernandez, who was a great shortstop, by the way. She was a great athlete, even though she wore huge glasses. Sally Hernandez was fast, she had a stick, she could throw just like a guy, it's not a girl thing, it was like a guy thing. Her I remember distinctly because she was a shortstop and just, man she was really good.

Mario leaped ahead to sometime after 1963, when rancher Zennie Leonida bought out the coffee shop in the Newton train depot, which had until the late 1950s been a Harvey House chain restaurant:

> The Ladies of Leonida's, I remember that tag. Leonida's used to be the restaurant that was in the old railroad station. That's where they used to work, the trains going in and out, well they were the waitresses there. They had a softball team. They used to play.... Family picnics, and that kind of stuff in our household as well as others, I can attest to that, but especially ours, and our family's extremely large. When we would gather we would go to Sims park because it was the only place that could hold us all. Then we had summer baseball, softball, but men, women, kids, grandkids, all played. I mean, you didn't have a choice. I mean you played!

Margie Sandoval, whom I interviewed at the Newton tournament, remembered playing fastpitch in the park as a schoolgirl, though by that time, the early 1960s, there wasn't a women's team associated with the tournament anymore. In 1960 the tournament had moved to the lot behind Our Lady of Guadalupe church and was being directed by the Holy Name Society men's group, which was how the team was known for years. Margie's family moved into a house across the street from the park in 1961, and she remembered the tournament as part of ordinary life:

> MARGIE: Every year we'd be at the ballpark, from little kids on. We'd be out there, getting the foul balls, and 'cause that was before anybody would show up, we'd be out there early in the morning, you know? At that time I think they gave us a nickel. [laughs]
> VICKI TORRES: Yeah, right. You get a quarter now. [laughs]
> MARGIE: I played fastpitch, but they didn't have a women's team. . . . I mean, we all just grew up together. And everybody was friends, and all'd known each other. . . . It's like one big family.

Turning back to the excitement of tournament time, Margie recounted how women took on the substantial work involved in hosting guests from out of town:

> MARGIE: And my mother cooked, she'd always cook, and—
> BEN: For the tournament?
> MARGIE: Yeah, she would. She'd make food, and people would come, walk across the street, to eat. People would just come out in the yard to get under the shade to cool off, or wet themselves down with the garden hose, or whatever, you know? Just to survive the heat.

The women of Newton City Cab played a competitive team sport at a time when, as Westly (2016) notes, women were generally encouraged to keep physical activity less rigorous and more sociable than competitive (Figure 15). When there were opportunities for women to play sports, the motto tended to be, "Play for play's sake." Fastpitch was a lifeline to women for whom "being a top female athlete meant pushing hard when the other women around you were only half-trying and defying coaches who told you to slow down and take it easy" (11). Women's softball was hugely popular when fastpitch exploded as a spectator sport following the 1933 World's Fair. The Orange Lionettes, a women's team sponsored by the Lion's Club, won a Southern California championship in 1938 with twenty thousand people attending the final (53). That figure beats today's average attendance of the National Basketball Association, the National Hockey League, and Major League Soccer in the United States. Company teams like the Brakettes, sponsored by the Raybestos company out of Stratford, Connecticut,

FIGURE 15 Mexican American women's team, sponsored by Newton City Cab, 1947. Standing, left to right: Catherine Jaso, (unidentified), Frances Nunez, Fifi Sifuentez, Henrietta Rodriguez, Carol Martinez. Sitting: Maggie Gallardo, Alice Gallardo, (unidentified), Esperanza Terrones, Julia Jaso, Sally Hernandez, (unidentified), Loretta Gonzalez, Carmen Llamas, Lorenza Terrones. Photo courtesy of Raymond Olias.

which made brake linings for cars and tanks, provided opportunities for women to play competitive ball with a job at the company as part of the deal. Westly notes that "playing for a company softball team wasn't usually lucrative, but it was exciting, even glamorous, compared to what most women were doing for work in the thirties" (38).

Mexican American women in Kansas were part of the "Rosie the Riveter" mobilization of women's labor for the war effort, many going to work at Boeing in Wichita to literally rivet together military aircraft (Escobedo 2013). The fact that support for the City Cab team and the women's tournament dwindled after the war lines up with a general timeline that saw larger cultural efforts to redefine women's social roles domestically. As Westly tells it: "'We Can Do It!' posters that had encouraged women to enter the workforce during the war years were gone, and in their place were advertisements championing domestic life" (88–89). In her account of Mexican American women in this period, Elizabeth

Escobedo notes that women of color were particularly subject to being pushed back out of the labor force where they had gained a foothold in the postwar reconversion that included the ideological push for domesticity in order to regender high-paying jobs as "male" work (2013, 126–127).

Women's softball survived this cultural shift, but not without difficulty. Westly describes how women were competing in national softball champion- ships at the same time that Adlai Stevenson advised graduates of Smith College that supporting their husbands was their most important job—but women athletes were again playing against the grain of efforts to gender and regulate sport as a domain for men. This shifted for softball as men began to leave the sport and, later, as Title IX regulations created new opportunities for women to pursue higher-education athletic scholarships.

The passage of Title IX legislation in 1972, meant to eliminate sex-based discrimination in educational opportunities for men and women, opened a new era for women's college sports despite its ongoing contestation, such as Representative John Tower's early efforts to exempt athletics programs from regulation by the act. Clearly, opportunities for women to play team sports have greatly increased since the implementation of Title IX, and not only at the college level. This changing landscape of opportunity coincided with a decline in company-sponsored softball as other options for entertainment multiplied, especially with the proliferation of broadcast media. But athletic scholarships created new ways for women athletes to find social mobility through competitive sports. As part of larger historical shifts in both racial and gender barriers to playing sports and articulations of gender to softball, young women in Mexican American communities had more opportunities to play in school or in private clubs among the general public.

Vicki Torres was another of the spectators who stopped by my extra lawn chair and open microphone at the Newton tournament, and while telling me about her brothers who played, including eventual hall-of-famer Barney Torres, she mentioned that her niece Heather Torres had pitched in the tournament that year and the previous one:

> She was the first female to pitch for the Mexican American tournament. . . .
> Yes, she played fastpitch, uh-huh. Fastpitch in high school, she was a pitcher. . . . And so my brother took her up on his team last year, and, um he let her pitch, and stuff, so she was the first Mexican girl to play in the all-men Mexican softball tournament. I don't know what some men thought of it at the

time, when she struck 'em out, but [laughs] you know? [laughs] Now last year they actually had a couple other girls. . . . I forgot who they were, one of them wasn't from around here.

Other people mentioned offhand that there had been women who played in the tournament. A commemorative booklet for the fortieth annual tournament in Newton states that Brenda Cervantes was the first in 1980, playing left field for the Newton Fiesta '80 team.

Jerilyn Barranco played in the infield for Topeka in the 2014 Newton tournament. I had a chance to interview her and her dad, Juan Barranco, who has collected all-tourney honors at Newton since the late 1970s. Juan had been invited to the old-timers' game that opens the Newton tournament on Friday evening, but he was also still playing competitively and joined Team Topeka when they were short of players. He told Jerilyn to bring her gear and be ready to play, saying, "You never know; we might need you." The team was short several players, and the coach was about to forfeit when Jerilyn volunteered to play. Ordinarily she pitches or plays third base, but she covered second and shortstop for Topeka, positions she had never played before. Juan posted about the game on Facebook: "My weekend was a Field of dreams":[2]

The 4th inning I came into pitch. On the pitching mound as I looked to my right I saw Jerilyn playing shortstop. That is when it hit me. I have played in this tournament so many years. I saw many good teams and players. As a 6 year old I was a batboy for Harold's Price Package, who my Dad, (Sal) pitched for. Both Ryan and Jordan my sons have played in this tournament with me. I never thought I would be playing ball with my daughter Jerilyn in this prestigious tournament. The icing on the cake was she ripped a single to left field. After the game ended I told Jerilyn how proud I was of her. I told her not many girls have played in this tournament and also got a hit. I realize how very special this game was. We lost the game but I gained a special memory with my daughter Jerilyn.

Later when I spoke with them both, Juan elaborated:

JUAN: And of course I was proud of her, down in Newton, 'cause, uh, course my son played, and Jordan played and I was pitching. And then it just hit me. . . . I just realized I had all my kids playing with me at fastpitch. And you know, her playing at shortstop, and I just said wow. And of course when she got a hit, all the crowd was going, "What was that? Girl Power?"

JERILYN: Yeah. Not a lot of girls played in that tournament, and hardly any get a hit.

JUAN: I was telling Gilbert, I said, "I've seen one girl that pitched, you know, but I have never seen a girl hit the ball and she was one that—and she pulled it—she pulled it to the left field, so she's a righty and she pulled it. And of course the team we were playing, they were . . ."

JERILYN: They thought I came to pitch.

JUAN: She was warming up, I was thinking about it, but no, Better protect her. . . . The other team, she was jawing back with 'em, too. They were kind of surprised. And when she got a hit, oh my gosh. That was it. She was jawing at 'em."

JERILYN: It was a really great memory.

Jerilyn told me that she had grown up at the ballpark, watching her dad and brothers play. She started playing baseball while she was too young for softball, "playing up" with five- and six-year-old boys when she was four. Her dad coached her for much of her childhood, and whenever the family visited her grandfather, Sal Barranco, who is in the hall of fame at Newton, he told her to bring her glove and ball.

The idea of playing competitive softball as a family activity, as opposed to something that might take individual athletes away from family life, is one of the features of the Mexican American fastpitch tradition as a cultural resource. In one of the very few academic social or cultural studies of softball players, Katherine M. Jamieson (2005) interviewed Latinas who had played ball at the college level. Jamieson found that these past and present student-athletes used their opportunities to play and to study as chances to craft lives that interrupted stereotypical scripts laid out for them along race, class, and gender lines—not unlike the formation of ballplayers discussed in the previous chapter. In this endeavor, they often received moral support from their parents, but for women from immigrant or working-class backgrounds, it was still difficult to access educational institutions that were unfamiliar to those in their support networks and distant from their social experience. Jamieson found that "among the women interviewed, part of the strategy for gaining entrée to higher education and collegiate athletics required separating from families and class origins but simultaneously finding ways to stay connected to these vital resources" (144). Even when their talent and dedication opened doors, advancing athletically meant engaging with sport as part of educational institutions that were not hospitable or even accessible to them in many ways.

In contrast, where softball is a valued and enduring popular institution, it can actually be one of those "vital resources," suggesting that a community sporting tradition may make a difference in how women are able to access opportunities distributed through college sports. One example from San Antonio is suggestive about how the dense fabric of relationships through and around softball can function as a supportive community resource.

Jennifer "Bitty" Benavides Rios, whom I interviewed at the Glowworm tournament in 2012, began to play competitive softball at nine years old, and she understood even then that it would be her path to higher education and social mobility. Her parents had let her know that they would not be able to pay for college out of pocket, and her father had researched athletic scholarships. Bitty enjoyed playing lots of sports, but her father informed her that since she was not tall, volleyball was not a promising choice. She excelled at softball, and when her father learned that pitchers drew the best scholarships, she began to pitch. Bitty's grandfather, Emeterio Benavides, who had been a champion hardball player in the Mexican American leagues of San Antonio, brought her to the Glowworm tournament every year. She explained in our interview:

BITTY: He would take me to whoever was the top pitcher in the tournament, and go see how they held their rise ball or curve ball, just to get some pointers I guess.

BEN: And were they pretty interested in showing you how to do that?

BITTY: Oh, yes, they were always interested. I remember the players always being so kind. I guess 'cause I was a girl. And they were pretty fascinated that a girl could pitch. And I remember pitching on the side for them, to show them that I could pitch.

Her father started a traveling team when she was twelve, the San Antonio Heat, and Bitty pitched for Holmes High School for four years, earning All-American honors from the National Fastpitch Coaches Association as a senior. She told me she was the first Hispanic player in South Texas to win this prestigious award, and a scholarship to play at NCAA Division II University of Incarnate Word followed. Besides the traveling team, Bitty developed her skills with private pitching coaches, first Letty Morales, who taught her to throw a rise ball, a signature skill in fastpitch. Then she trained with Louie Aguayo, who had been recruited to competitive softball and the Glowworm team by Chilolo Rios many years before, and who, she said, "taught me the rest of my junk pitches, which were like my curve, my screw, and my drop."

Letty Morales-Bissaro grew up in California and learned pitching basics along with her father, who had never played ball before. Moving to San Antonio when she was twelve, Letty pitched for St. Gerard's High School, where she learned to throw a rise from pitching coach Jerry Meuth. At St. Gerard's, Letty won state championships in 1980, 1981, and 1982. She then played at St. Mary's University, where she was the team's MVP for all four years and a two-time National Association of Intercollegiate Athletics (NAIA) All-American. In 1986, St. Mary's won the NAIA national tournament, for which Letty pitched every inning of all eight games. Letty is in the San Antonio Sports Hall of Fame, as well as the National Hispanic Hall of Fame, and is the pitching coach at St. Mary's, where her daughter followed in her footsteps to play ball (San Antonio Sports Hall of Fame 2012)

When I interviewed Louie Aguayo at the Glowworm tournament in 2012, he told me that it was when St. Mary's was preparing for the 1986 national tournament that he volunteered to "throw some batting practice" for the team and met Letty. He became a pitching coach at the university, he said, for eight or nine years, which included multiple trips to the national tournament. That was where he got to know Herb Dudley, who was a fan of St. Mary's and liked to follow its postseason. Dudley was a multiyear ASA All-American who threw over one hundred no-hitters, for whom the pitching award at the ASA National Championship is named. Louie told me they always met for a meal and discussion of softball pitching at the NAIA national tournament and that "over the years, I've been teaching these kids the same philosophy he had." When Louie died in 2020, an obituary stated that he

> mentored thousands of young ladies in the art of fastpitch softball pitching and developed them into elite pitchers, players, students, and leaders. . . . Many of Coach Louie's student athletes developed into the finest and fiercest softball pitchers in Texas and went on to win many District, Bi-District, Area, Regional, State, and National Championships and honors. (Calderon 2020)

A protégé of both Letty and Louie, Bitty pitched at Oliver Wendell Holmes High School for four years. The team slumped in her junior year and didn't make the playoffs, losing five starters and then their coach. The new coach was Victor Castillo, a fastpitch player himself, unlike many men who coach women's softball. Bitty recognized him from the Glowworm tournament and instinctively respected his knowledge of the game. He had also followed her success. The respect was mutual. Since her teammates were not as familiar with the tournament, Bitty convinced them to trust their new coach. That year, the newspaper preseason poll ranked them last in the district. They ended up winning the district and going to state in what would be Bitty's All-American season. She recalled,

> So, for him to turn it around in just one year, . . . I really think it was because he started playing in these tournaments, to get on to his coaching career, and molded us and our work ethic into what he thought we could be. And so it showed me that it wasn't really about, you know, having the best talent in the world, it was kind of like just believing, and that's really what happened.

After that first year of coaching, Castillo invited the girls from Holmes, which today fields a varsity softball roster full of Spanish surnames, to watch him pitch at the Glowworm, and Bitty told me she still meets up with friends and teammates at the tournament.

After college, Bitty met David Rios Jr., one of Chilolo's grandsons, at a slowpitch tournament. When Bitty brought David home to meet her family, her grandfather Emeterio showed interest that he did not often grant to friends of hers after learning that David was from the Rios family that ran the Glowworm tournament. When the two began dating, Bitty suggested to David that his generation of the Rioses should start to play in the tournament rather than just watching, and he asked her to pitch. She did so for two years, winning one game in each, which as far as I know makes her the only woman pitcher to post wins in a Mexican American men's tournament. She said she earned the respect of opposing players:

> You know at first, they're—I guess 'cause of their egos, kinda like, "Oh, who's she?" and a lot of them didn't know of me because they were from out of town. If you're from in town, a lot of 'em do know me. But you know other than that, when they got up to the plate, I guess because I had a lot of junk, they had a lot of respect for me. . . . After the game they always shook my hand and treated me really well.

Bitty stopped playing in the Glowworm tournament after getting hit with a line drive to the elbow. She told me it was a routine injury and that she had been hit before, but tournament organizers in both San Antonio and Austin were concerned that it was risky for women to play against men in the all-out competition of fastpitch. She said, "I guess just us playing against men, um, I think they just decided . . . and just said, 'We don't really want them to get hurt and us be a liability.'" I asked if she agreed that she was in more danger of getting hurt than men who pitched:

> Yes and no because I know that they're stronger than me, their reflexes might be better than mine . . . yeah. They're probably . . . I think maybe they can take a ball more than I could, probably. Remember, I'm five foot. So I think if a ball hit me in the chest I would be knocked out. I've seen a guy get hit in the chest here, and he picked up the ball and threw it to first, so.

Still, when we discussed how many players claim that men's fastpitch is a dying sport since boys do not learn to pitch, I asked whether she thought she would see any more women playing in the men's tournaments. She replied:

> I really wish, because I come from a family where we're all pitchers. My sisters, I have younger ones, played through college as well. . . . I know if I brought them out here, I have a nineteen-year-old, she's a real good pitcher and hitter. She just got Offensive Player of the Year for the Heartland conference as a freshman, so I want to. I told David, I said, "We should bring her out and she should hit for your team because, you know, she's hitting the ball and she's hitting home runs where she's at. I know she could hit off these pitchers." So I really wish they would let girls, even if it wasn't just to pitch.

Bitty said at the time that she had suggested that the Glowworm run a women's division at their tournament, but she thought they wanted to keep things as unchanged from the time of Chilolo's death as possible for the sake of tradition. Two years later, the Latin in Houston would add a women's division to its tournament schedule.

After college, Bitty went to work in finance, struggling to carve out time to give pitching lessons in the evenings. A friend she had played with was coaching high school and called Bitty when there was an assistant coach opening, with a faculty position in business education. Bitty leaped at the chance and started with a provisional teaching certificate. I asked if she thought her players viewed softball as a means of mobility. She said:

> Oh, definitely, because I coach in the South Side. . . . you know it's not one of the wealthiest areas. So, a lot of our kids don't even think they're going to college. So, it's really important as a teacher and as a coach, since I was there at one point, is that they know they can do it, and they will do it. . . . And our team, we actually were district champs, and . . . out of my four years we were district champs two. And we made it to playoffs every single year. And so we

have a very good program, but we always tell them you are a student first, and you're an athlete second.

The idea that sport provides opportunities and pathways to social mobility to those willing to put in the work to develop their talent and physical capability is a stock narrative in the American mythos of meritocracy. Indeed, this idea feeds the vast entertainment industry of big-college and professional sports by producing a reserve army of would-be athletes, vying for their chance to pursue a dream. But in stories like Bitty's, there is even more going on than the channeling of substantial talent, potential, and work. The network of kinship, friendship, and larger community relationships among people captivated by the illusio of softball, who then cultivated it in turn, formed a social base on which promising players could seek their chance in higher education. In addition to general, normative values like hard work and commitment, though, the specific craft techniques of playing softball like the "junk" of technical pitches formed an archive of vernacular knowledge that was accessible to Bitty and players like her through those very social networks.

The Rusk Athletic Club introduced a girls' under-18 division in the last few years of running the Latin tournament, which was extended to an under-23 women's division in order to let college athletes play. One year that I attended, the winning team, Elite 9, was a select club based in Settegast Park in the Second Ward barrio that is also the original home of the Rusk Athletic Club. Their coach, Lauren Bautista, was the recipient of a tournament-sponsored scholarship in 2008 that supported her studies at the University of Houston, and she also played as a senior in high school. In our email correspondence following the tournament, Bautista recited a kind of genealogy:

> My father is Richard Bautista who played for many years in the Latin Tournament and was a part of the Latin Legends team along with my godfather Earnest Shepherd. I grew up watching these guys play softball since I was a little girl. My little brother now plays in the Latin tournament.

Bautista goes on to report on her budding career as a middle school physical education teacher and coach not only for softball but for baseball, volleyball, and soccer. She also lists some players she has brought to the attention of college recruiters. She concludes:

> I believe that I am where I am today because I grew up around watching all these guys play fastpitch with my dad. I owe everything I have to him and this

organization and it was an amazing feeling to come back and win a tournament that I once played in . . . but now as a coach.

• • •

Through the serendipity of social media, I noticed that a Mexican American
fastpitch pitcher whom I had met at tournaments posted a link with a caption
apparently addressed to his fellow men: "Hey all you slow-pitch players, come
and play a man's game." Somewhat in tension with this gendered characterization, the video depicted professional softball pitcher and Olympic gold medal-
ist Jennie Finch, the dominant player of her time, striking out Albert Pujols,
a star in his own right as a major league baseball hitter. The video presented
the confrontation, which apparently took place at an exhibition softball event,
in a battle-of-the-sexes format, feeding its viral character. The ordinary confrontation of pitcher and batter, though, was complex in this case, and the
significance of two sports facing off and represented by a man and a woman
spurred effusive comments.

At six feet in height, Jennie Finch has commented publicly about how her
experience as a "big and strong girl" at times rendered gender norms challenging for her when she was younger, which was part of the value of finding softball
as a place to channel her physical capabilities in ways that would be recognized
and rewarded. As her successes on the collegiate, Olympic, and professional
fields built her renown, media lost no opportunity to gender her, as comments
on her "beauty and charm" accompanied accounts of her fearsome power as a
player. In the video facing Pujols, himself an image of masculine strength and
skill at not only hitting major league fastballs but driving them past the outfield
in home runs, Finch utterly disarms the major leaguer with her rise ball—a
softball pitch that breaks sharply upward, at times reaching the catcher's mitt
well above head level. It is a pitch for which hardball players, accustomed to
overarm throws, are completely unprepared. Finch's long stride, even without
the "crow-hop" that is common in international men's fastpitch but forbidden
in the U.S. women's game, placed her well inside forty feet from home plate
when she released the ball, which she was capable of doing at nearly 70 miles
per hour. This means that Finch's pitch required a reaction time comparable to
a baseball thrown at 90 mph but from 66 feet, 6 inches, the regulated distance
from a baseball pitcher's mound to home plate. And despite being substantially
larger than a baseball, the softball was veering in a direction that the batter
never swung for otherwise.

Comments on the video revealed a fascinating range of perspectives on sport and its capacity either to explode or affirm dualistic gendered thinking on questions of athletic ability and strength in particular. Viewers who celebrated Finch's athleticism were answered by others who basically retorted, "Not so fast on the girl power," presenting convoluted arguments to downplay her achievement in striking out the professional slugger. Many commentators denied the implication that Finch had defeated Pujols in a head-to-head athletic matchup, taking for granted that Pujols had held back, most likely out of kindness to Finch, since if he had applied his true big league swing, the resulting drive would have "destroyed" her. This interpretation was clearly ignorant of other softball-baseball matchups, including the precedent set by Joan Joyce, who struck out both Ted Williams and Hank Aaron in exhibitions (see Westly 2016, 123–124).[3]

Others disputed the significance of the showdown, pointing out that softball and baseball are distinct games with distinct skill sets. Assuming that Finch would never be able to hit a major league fastball, these critics proposed that given a little practice, Pujols would obviously master Finch's rise ball, so the matchup of two different sports was basically invalid and unfair. This position is intriguing for the way it particularizes the distinct sports, baseball and softball, also gendering them as the normative arenas for male and female athleticism, respectively. Commentators paradoxically pointed out that a contest between a softball and a baseball player was arbitrary, a mismatch of skills that belonged to separate arenas but at the same time ranked those activities comparatively. However arbitrary and specific the skills of baseball are (in this case, being oriented toward hitting overhand pitches, which cannot rise the way a softball can), they were presumed to be valid and accurate as a test of strength and coordination, whereas softball skills were implicitly specialized and unfair. So the contradiction was that Pujols's failure at softball was arbitrary, but his established success at baseball was an expression of physical superiority.

This event, which had nothing directly to do with Mexican American fastpitch in particular, condensed many of the cultural dynamics that structure the gendered social field of sports in general, and base games in particular. The Mexican American pitcher who shared the video on social media referred to fastpitch as a "man's game" in distinction to slowpitch, claiming masculinity for his own discipline of the sport as opposed to the version that is more widely played by men. The fact that it was a woman demonstrating the essential characteristic of fastpitch in the video, the enormous challenge of hitting a fastpitched softball, demonstrates that however Mexican American fastpitch traffics in gendered notions of sport and athleticism, it does so in complex ways. The comments on the video reinforced a general anthropological observation of hierarchical gender systems in which "male and female are sociocultural constructs forming a cherished binary opposition that must be maintained and defended against threats" (Besnier et al. 2018, 157), even as it became evident how the concrete acts of the sport itself break up the ascription of gendered qualities and sexed bodies to a clear-cut binary. The pitcher who shared the video to identify a "man's game" was performing a gendered act of distinction, but he did so in specific-sport solidarity with Finch.

It is worth noting that the gendering of baseball was historically unstable and required active regulation, partly because softball's greater openness to women provided them with opportunities to develop skills that were transferable to other sports. Women were officially banned from "organized baseball"— essentially, the professional game— only after Eleanor Engle signed to a minor league team in Harrisburg, Pennsylvania, as a shortstop in 1952. Prior to Engle, the most famous woman to play baseball against men was probably Jackie Mitchell, who pitched for the AA Chattanooga Lookouts in an exhibition game with the New York Yankees in 1931. In that game, Mitchell struck out Babe Ruth looking, followed by Lou Gehrig in three straight swings. Whether the men were really trying to hit the ball remains the subject of debate, but commissioner Kenesaw Mountain Landis evidently voided the pitcher's contract and Mitchell was left to play out her career in barnstorming teams like the House of David, with which she reportedly beat the St. Louis Cardinals in another exhibition (Horwitz 2013).

Twenty years later, Engle was signed on as a shortstop with the minor league Harrisburg Senators in a move that the team president insisted was motivated by her ability but that others assumed to be a publicity stunt for a team that had seen attendance at their games flag to below five hundred people. The team's manager refused to play her, and in the first game she warmed up for, both the opposing manager and the umpire threatened to quit if she played. The next day, league officials issued a ban on signing women. Engle maintained that she was a serious athlete, not a gimmick, saying, "I think baseball is making a big mistake. . . . I still feel I can bat a ball just as far as any of those fellows" (Preston 2009). She was offered a tryout with the All-American Girls Professional Baseball League, known for its fictional representation in the film *A League of Their Own*, but she declined and the league folded two years later. Blogger J. G.

Preston pulled an editorial on Engle from the *Sporting News* as evidence of the rationale behind the ban she inspired:

The reasons should be readily apparent. Opposing players would be reluctant to slide into a base guarded by a girl infielder, pitchers would hesitate to throw too close to a feminine batter, tagging would be a problem, baseball could not afford to take a chance of injury to a women [sic] in a game played for keeps by men. Dugout language is too sulphuric for the ears of ladylike performers, special dressing rooms would have to be provided, and there always would be the risk of insulting remarks hurled by smart-aleck fans. . . . THE SPORTING NEWS hopes this is the last time it will ever find it necessary, as a matter of news coverage, to print the picture of a woman ball player on a men's team. Woman's place may not be altogether in the home, and feminine athletes have won distinction in many sports in which they can compete against others of their sex. But as far as Organized Baseball is concerned, woman's place always will be in the grandstand. (Preston 2009)

The ban on women in professional baseball was rescinded in the 1990s, and women have competed in baseball at high school, college, and minor league levels. In work that would reinforce Mario Gomez's and Margie Sandoval's personal accounts, leading authority on women in baseball Jennifer Ring argues that women and girls have played ball on the vernacular scale for as long as anyone else and that it was the professionalization of baseball that led to their exclusion. She also notes parallels with the exclusion of nonwhite men, as the privileged identity of Anglo, Christian masculinity constructed around the "official" sport was solidified in institutions: "The manliness of baseball as well as the early Whiteness of the game was limited to organized professional baseball" (2009a, 376). Ring has collected abundant evidence of women who have continued to play baseball in what she calls an "underground," struggling to persist in the game they love and biding their time for opportunities.

Summarizing other research on ways that nineteenth-century baseball consolidated an emergent, modern form of American masculinity, Ring argues that "the masculinity reconstituted on the ball field or in the bleachers was a masculinity that reinforced the unequal distribution of power based on class, race, and gender" (2009a, 381). Exclusions along the axis of race have proven less tenable than gender as organized baseball has integrated, but Ring shows that the masculinity of baseball has continually been actively defended from social change at critical moments brought on by events such as the passage of

Title IX. Immediately following that act, a series of lawsuits aimed to make the Little League Baseball organization accept girls who already played on teams that were facing sanction or exclusion from the league for including them. The moment produced volumes of contorted arguments as the organization and its supporters were forced to articulate previously unspoken assumptions that baseball was the prerogative of boys. Arguments about physical risk and protection, essential character traits, boys' emotional vulnerability in competing with girls, and even the inviolable tradition of coaches congratulating boys by patting them on the butt came up. In the end, the Title IX standard of equality was addressed with a separate Little League Softball division for girls, which Ring notes was the slowpitch variety (2009a, 386).

In further elaboration of this work, Ring again draws a compelling connection between gender segregation and professional organization, arguing that even when girls earn a place on a Little League team, playing time gets treated as a boy's entitlement, given that there are more realistic avenues for them to pursue future participation in baseball at higher levels. In other words, girls may get benched regardless of their ability, when for them to take the field is interpreted as taking a place away from a boy who may develop enough skill to reach the big leagues (2009b). Ring (2018) has gone on to document the experiences of women who have continued to play hardball including on the U.S. Women's National Team, currently managed by Veronica Alvarez. Many more women and girls have refused to accept the status of softball as a lesser, "consolation" sport, pushing to advance the level of athleticism in fastpitch.

The gendered history of softball reveals the uneven and shifting ground on which the particular racial tradition of Mexican American fastpitch has laid a path. An ideological continuum of the presumed characteristics, capacities, and vulnerabilities of bodies ascribed to be male and female maps onto an equally constructed and contested continuum between the comparative rigor, excitement, and difficulty of different sports. Softball occupies not only a complicated position in the spectrum of gender, but also bears a complex relationship to baseball. As Ring's work compellingly proposes, many of the stakes and dynamics of these various sortings of sports and athletes into defendable categories are the result of the professional organization of sport, when there are material stakes involved beyond just the chance to play. Despite its sometimes folksy resonance as "America's pastime," baseball is deeply embedded in bureaucracy, a feature performed in the term *organized baseball* to refer to the sport's multiple levels of professional leagues and the grand title "commissioner of baseball" bestowed on that organization's executive. In contrast, softball exists in multiple forms with various rules, competing associations, and opportunities for professional competition that are far from stable or enduring.

Women, Mexican Americans, and people with various other identities have found athletic expression of their own in softball partly because of its status as an auxiliary to baseball. A substantial number of men with whom I've spoken in the fastpitch scene related that baseball was their first love and describe softball as the best available substitute after opportunities to play dry up after high school or college ball and maybe a bit of semiprofessional or minor league play. But softball has a unique illusio all its own and draws devotees to the quick, tactical dynamics of the game once called "lightning ball." The crafts of pitching and batting differ from baseball, and fastpitch players enjoy telling me about how surprising it is for a hardball player who struggles to make the transition. Involvement and proximity to the Mexican American fastpitch tradition cultivates considerable devotion to that specific game, which I noticed one afternoon between interview appointments. I had stopped in an Eastside barrio sports bar a few blocks from Pan Am Park in Austin for lunch and noticed that all the TV screens were playing the NCAA women's national fastpitch tournament.

Despite occasional moments as a televised spectacle, though, the secondary status of softball is one of the features that has allowed or even caused it to remain a deeply vernacular game. That is, over more than a century of its existence, softball has always been played extensively on the vernacular scale. This is what has allowed people who were excluded from more organized sport the opportunity to claim space in softball, a phenomenon that repeats far beyond the example of the Mexican American game under study here. Of particular note is the Native softball played by teams that sometimes take part in Mexican tournaments and convene annually in Oklahoma's massive All-Indian Softball Tournament, as well as the long and rich history of softball as the "lesbian national pastime," offering a space for women to both socialize and compete hard without having to confront harassment for their gender performances or perceived sexuality (Zipter 1988; Westly 2016, 166).

• • •

The game is called for time, and the teams line up to shake hands. A young girl, maybe nine years old, lines up behind the crowd of men in white uniforms giving the opponents five. She and another one (maybe twelve years old and maybe her sister) put their hands into the huddle for the final cheer.

In the stands, a Joker and a 76er chat about one's eight-year-old grand-daughter, an All-Star in her second year out of T-ball. "Le digo, you wanna play? She went to that tournament at la Round Rock y a la Cedar Park. One of them teams was like Amazons."

As the players file off the dirt diamond, a cluster of kids, boys and girls, run on, immediately beginning to mime a game at a frenetic, exaggerated pace: pitch, swing, throw, catch, run. Their game with imagined gear carries on in the summer night under electric lights as the adults gather in clusters to talk.

· · ·

Articulations of gender and softball have shifted throughout the sport's history, from its relatively open origins to the wartime period, when it was a means of national masculinity for those seeking to solidify their citizenship, but also accessible to more people because of temporarily relaxed gender boundaries. Now in the present and near past, the game has been partly characterized as one of the few default avenues for women's athleticism. These changes reveal the contested relationship between sport and gender. One feature of this story that stands out is that while there are always narratives close at hand about the essential characteristics and capacities of differently sexed bodies, what determines participation in sport most directly is the uneven distribution of opportunity. In softball, without an extensive, lasting professional apparatus comparable to baseball, this is also a result of how sport is funded. Men's fastpitch, which so many participants tell me is a "dying sport," is anachronistic because it is rooted in a time of massive investment in public parks and playgrounds, including public programs to provide equipment, coaches, and leagues to develop the game. Today such public resources pale in comparison to the investment in school sports, where football and basketball generally command more support. Opportunities to participate in athletics at school are also carefully doled out in a gendered distribution.

Although the public impact of Title IX achieved some redistribution of athletic opportunity, softball also became predominantly a women's sport during a time when public investment in recreation was in decline and youth sports in particular became more universally associated with "pay-to-play," private clubs and leagues. This ironically coincided with the proliferation of athletic scholarships. So just as opportunities opened up for working-class women to potentially access social mobility through higher education by developing their bodies and performance as athletes, opportunity was paradoxically being restricted at the front end by the high cost of youth participation in the game. The fastpitch tradition, then, which historian Gene Chávez theorizes as *herencia*, or heritage (2015), became in a very direct and material sense a form of cultural capital (Trueba 2002).

Without playground leagues, it has become increasingly rare for boys to learn the specific skill of softball pitching unless they do so expressly to join a Mexican team. Some family-based teams, such as the Indios (Garcias) of Kansas City, make a point of training younger generations of boys to continue the game. Certain teams, with the benefit of sponsors who are fully invested in the illusio of winning a Mexican tournament, commit the funds and the recruitment efforts to bring in pitchers from abroad. But in some corners of the Mexican American fastpitch world, elder players see young girls as the obvious heirs for the wisdom of their experience. Watching the final of the first women's division tournament at the Latin, Rudy "Chato" Velasquez, the head scorekeeper and self-described "somewhat historian" for the Rusk Athletic Club, expressed his admiration for the players and their devotion to the game. Nobody had

FIGURE 16   Rusk Athletic Club Latin tournament 2019 Most Valuable Players. Photo by the author.

to pay them to play. Maybe it was time, he suggested, to turn it over to them. Four teams competed that year, with substantial sponsorship from one of the members of the Rusk committee.

The women's division was more extensive at the seventieth, and last, Rusk tournament. Some of the spectators (men and women) I spoke with while the men's bracket was being played out told me that they weren't interested in watching "the girls." At the fields for the women's division games, it was a different crowd, mainly parents of the players in these elite traveling club teams. The teams appeared more extensively multiracial, presumably not all from a particular neighborhood, though chatting with spectators informed me that one team was based in the Second Ward's Settegast Park, the home field of the Rusk Athletic Club. Before a game, I saw a player from the men's tournament warming up the girls on one team, fungoing balls for them to field as they ran through drills with energy and precision.

One way the effective herencia of the fastpitch tradition comes into view is at the end of a tournament, when families and generations gather for the ceremony for awarding all-tournament honors. At the last Rusk tournament, the Most Valuable Player for the men's open division was Peter Rodriguez, who had been a standout player throughout the time I have been involved in this research, and I have seen him holding more than a few trophies. The MVP for the women's side was LeAnna Limón. The MVPs posed together for photographs as families milled about the field and teams and fans packed up to head home (Figure 16). Both wearing uniforms marked by the dust of a long weekend of hard play, the two seemed to represent the past, present, and future of Mexican American fastpitch.

6

BETWEEN THE LINES

Softball as Utopian Form

IN A WIDELY READ CHAPTER of his ethnography *Learning Capitalist Culture* (2010), Douglas Foley writes about the "Great American Football Ritual." Since high school was one of the primary sites of Foley's inquiry into race, class, and gender in South Texas, football provided a rich repertoire of cultural practices and meanings to unpack. This ethnographic analysis of a particular genre of sport that is a familiar feature of ordinary life in many American communities is a model that has influenced my own take on vernacular sport: what makes high school football in "North Town" interesting for Foley is not its exceptionality but its typicality. The main story is not of athletes who distinguished themselves through unbeatable performances but of denizens of a town who learn, reproduce, and sometimes contest social mores through athletics. Foley's arguments about football in the historically particular (but pseudonymous) setting of "North Town," which at the time of his fieldwork was a community undergoing political restructuring in the relations between Mexicans and Anglos in particular, rely partly on readers' familiarity with the sport and its ritualistic role in high school and civic life.

That role for football, according to Foley, is to socialize youth "to carry on a number of traditional cultural practices governing class, race, and gender relations" (2010, 28). In other words, Foley sees in football the power of ideology, functioning in a way reminiscent of Paul Willis's (1981) take on working-class culture in Britain, in which the oppositional expressive practices of the "lads" in a working-class community situated them all the more firmly in a relatively stable class structure. In Foley's account, the masculine posing and verbal art that Willis describes among the lads is joined by routine practices carried on by athletes, cheerleaders, band kids, and others involved in football. Foley is more attentive than Willis, though, to how race, gender, and involvement in political movements make a difference and complicate the actual vernacular landscapes on which social reproduction is at stake.

Foley's work on sport is paradigmatic for the way it frames sport as embedded in everyday life. This ethnography, joined more recently by work by Levi (2008), Rand (2012), Robideaux (2012), Thangaraj (2015), and Willms (2017), among others, reflects ethnographic priorities by centering the practice of a sport itself within the field of meaning that it constitutes for those who take part in it. This is a departure from sport studies that answer the triviality question by emphasizing the large scale of spectacle, evident in the size of audiences or investments, or by focusing on "firsts" and "greats," standout athletes who burst into the history of sport and drive it forward. Instead, these ethnographies of sport prioritize communities of practice on the vernacular scale, perhaps reflecting more of a deep than a broad contextualization. A rationale for such an approach is that if sport is important to a particular population, it should be important to someone seeking to understand the lives and circumstances of that population. That "importance," or symbolic power, is a mixture of the specific illusio of a particular sport and the articulations that people craft and feel historically, between the narrative drama of games and the concerns and priorities of their ordinary lives.

In this chapter, I consider softball itself on a formal level in order to map particular resonances between the historical forms of Mexican American experience and the aestheticized, embodied forms of playing fastpitch. A clear understanding of this relationship requires some attention to the particularities of softball but also an effort not to accept too readily a certain humanist idea that baseball and its derivative game hold a mythical, universal appeal. Within the specific stream of a racial tradition in sport, I propose that we can see something other than an unchanging essence at work, but also something other than ideological instruction. Rather, the home space constructed in the Mexican tournaments and playgrounds through many seasons of ball games becomes a bounded, temporary world offering utopian flashes of a preferred existence, even while ongoing social structures never let the participants mistake it for the rest of ordinary life. To make this case, I lay out how my take on fastpitch fits within an interpretation of sport as cultural contestation. This is distinct from an approach that identifies baseball with humanist universality, as well as others that treat sport as characterized by more general features of American nationalism or global capitalism. Instead, I follow Foley's take on sport as a space of contestation over meaning and power, in accord with C. L. R. James ([1963] 2013) and others taking a critical approach (Carrington 2013). This informs an analysis akin to Américo Paredes's framing of cultural poetics as being embedded in conflictual historical relations, forming a resource by which people engage with entrenched and compelling social questions in their ordinary lives (see Limón 2012). Taking some cues from the symbolic interactionist analysis of Robert Perinbanayagam (2006), I trace here how some of the specific features of softball intersect with some of the historical experiences and conditions of Mexican American life.

BASEBALL HUMANISM

Writers and scholars of many stripes have taken various approaches to render sport as a serious topic. For baseball in particular, articulated as a modern tradition of U.S. nationalism, literary representations frequently present sport as a unifying feature of human life at various scales of community. This kind of humanism is exemplified in an apparently sincere essay that Philip Roth (1973b) published in the *New York Times* in the same year as the release of his more typically sardonic work, *The Great American Novel*, which satirizes the articulation of baseball with "America" and imperialism in accounts of the "Patriot League." In the *Times*, Roth credits baseball for instilling him with patriotism as a child of immigrants otherwise unmoved by nationalist ritual. For Roth, the appeal of baseball was more in its "mythic and esthetic dimension" than even in the fun of playing. Baseball was "a kind of secular church that reached into every class and region of the nation and bound us together in common concerns, loyalties, rituals, enthusiasms, and antagonisms." Roth compares the impact of baseball on his life as a boy to that of his discovery of literature as a college student, but he hastens to assert that the appeal of baseball is more general than that of letters:

> To sing the National Anthem in school auditorium every week, even during the worst of the war years, generally left me cold . . . in the end just another school exercise. But on Sundays out at Ruppert Stadium (a green wedge of pasture miraculously walled in among the factories, warehouses and truck depots

of Newark's industrial "Ironbound" section), waiting for the Newark Bears
to take on the enemy from across the marshes, the hated Jersey City Giants
(within our church the schisms are profound), it would have seemed to me
an emotional thrill forsaken, if we had not to rise first to our feet (my father,
my brother, and me—together with our inimical countrymen, Newark's Irish-
men, Germans, Italians, Poles, and out in the Africa of the bleachers, Newark's
Negroes) to celebrate the America that had given to this disparate collection of
men and boys a game so grand and beautiful.

Roth describes the greatness of "America" as seen in the diverse multitudes
of people drawn to baseball, and notably in the process, constructing a multi-
ethnic, national masculinity. Even with its occasional hyperbolic spice, Roth's
lyrical aesthetic appreciation remains about as ineffable as discussions of the
canonical greatness of a Shakespeare or a Beethoven. For Roth the essayist, the
beauty and grandeur of baseball is self-evident and something that everybody
can potentially appreciate, as is evident in the tossed-salad demographics of
American baseball fans. This is a note of patriotism in that the greatness of
America is defined by its capacity to produce such a beautiful game. Roth concludes, "Baseball made me understand what patriotism was about, at its best."

Roth's image of baseball as a more pure distillation of American ideals
than the "secular" nationalism of school resonates with certain historiographi-
cal narratives that situate sport within a progressive timeline of evolutionary
improvement in race relations. Critical sociologist Ben Carrington makes this
point about A. S. Young's *Negro Firsts in Sports*, a book he selects as representative of a "functionalist-evolutionary" paradigm in the socially oriented study
of sport, and compares it unfavorably with C. L. R. James's *Beyond a Boundary*,
published in the same year, 1963 (2013, 383). The functionalist approach looks for
ways that sport plays a compensatory or peacekeeping role in society riven by
inequality. Carrington attributes this to Young's celebratory narrative, focusing
on exceptional African American athletes as role models transcending racism.
Sport allows space for the promised features of Americanism that are deferred
or denied to racialized citizens off the field. Victory within this rarified space
inspires the oppressed and dominant alike and drives progress forward. "As
American sport evolves," sums up Carrington, "racism dissolves" (2013, 383).

The affirmative optimism of humanist or functionalist paradigms does not
age well as inequality off the field stubbornly endures. Still, writers continue to
update and recharge the optimistic case. For example, Michael Chabon, in his

young-adult-oriented fantasy novel *Summerland* (2002), appeals not to a diverse urban public so much as a shared, primordial, folkloric culture in which the myths of numerous discrete groups meet on an otherworldly, multiculturalist baseball field. In Chabon's book, baseball provides a kind of lingua franca in a land of all myths, where the protagonists of American tall tales and Native American tricksters alike go to bat in between epic battles over the survival of the Tree of Life. No doubt there is a bit of postmodern, ironic play here, but assembling all cultures under the big tent of baseball also comes off as a gesture to modern multiculturalism: Can't we all get along since we all love baseball?[1]

PLAYING BALL: AN ECUMENE

In their programmatic statement for an anthropology of sport, Bresnier, Brownell, and Carter (2017) counter such affirmative culturalism by insisting on the "global sport system" as an important context for analysis to consider. This take proposes that planetary-scale systems of power and networks of capital articulate in various ways with localized sporting phenomena to shape how difference comes together unevenly on the playing field. Drawing on the important contributions of world systems theory, these authors advocate for anthropological inquiry that does not fall prey to the fallacy of an imagined world of discrete cultural mosaic pieces each with their own games (Gupta and Ferguson 1992), let alone one in which finding common ground at play resolves social rifts and hierarchies. Against such essentializing notions, attention to the global sport system tracks the ways that sports practiced in many specific contexts are interconnected through layered political economy and cultural media, both subject to the influence of the global system and capable of shifting it, however slightly, through some effective change in the way that sport is played.

Sport as an entertainment industry, employing people both on the playing field and off and as a mass media spectacle reaching far beyond the local, is clearly entangled in the political economy, functioning as both production and product. It can definitely obscure things to overemphasize "culture" when explaining specific sporting phenomena in such a situation—for example, by arguing that the simple reason that there are so many Dominican ballplayers in the American major leagues is that Dominican people have a special knack for baseball, as opposed to considering long-running colonial relations between the United States and the Dominican Republic, the dynamics of professional baseball as a business, and trends of offshoring and global labor sourcing. Alan Klein (1991, 2006, 2013, 2014) has made substantial contributions in this direction. The global approach is necessary, then, for an adequate understanding of baseball—or any other sport—as an industry, one involving actors on the sides of labor and capital who are as responsive to historical conditions as anyone in any other industry. Such an approach resolves the triviality problem of mounting serious inquiry into games by showing their imbrication with global capitalism and power.

But for the vast majority of those who play sports, being in an industry and engaging in athletics as compensated labor and broadcasted performance is only aspirational. Using the global sport system as a framework for the social understanding of sport in contemporary life and in the past directs attention and priority to the elite levels of sport—that is, sites of formally organized sport, played for financial compensation or within the patronage of some kind of representative affiliation, as in the competition of national teams in the Olympic Games or world championships under another aegis. While vernacular sports are not insulated from world systems in terms of capital, power, or symbolic meaning, they do tend to fall off the radar when global reach is what provides the rationale for study and contemplation. The point is not that either a humanist/multiculturalist or a global/systemic framing is wrong. It is more that vernacular sport embedded in a long-running history of social struggle occupies a position of contestation in all of these relevant contexts. However much playing ball may be a kind of transnational cultural ecumene, an extensive, border-crossing sphere of some common understanding or idiom of practice, it is brought down to earth in the specific sites of vernacular play.

It is important to note that playing ball as a cultural ecumene coincided with movements for Muscular Christianity, play reform, and welfare capitalism, which were directed toward immigrant communities in the United States as a means of Americanization and social control. As I have described, social reform projects played into what would become fastpitch-playing communities, driving programs at the Pan Am Center in Austin, the Rusk Settlement House in Houston, and others. But it would be a mischaracterization to suggest that softball was essentially Anglo culture imposed on immigrant laborers. The dynamic engagement of Mexican Americans with fastpitch resonates with what Adrian Burgos (2007) discovered in his research on Latinos in professional baseball. Indeed this influential historian of the game characterized his earlier "flawed working hypothesis" as being "that baseball's popularity among Caribbean Latinos was primarily an outgrowth of U.S. imperialism." Rather, a more complicated and multilayered process of exchange and cultural co-constitution was at work as Latin Americans encountered and adapted "America's game." Through processes of migration and professional play, Burgos argues that for Latinos, "baseball also became a site for building community, making citizens out of colonial subjects, teaching appropriate class behavior, and displaying masculinity" (xiii).

So to tell the story of fastpitch as "America's game, played by Mexicans" is not quite right. The rise of softball as a participatory national pastime in the interwar period was far from being Mexican Americans' introduction to bat and base games. Before Mexican American fastpitch, there was Mexican American baseball, and Mexican baseball before that, history that generated a matrix of cultural articulations and hybrid meanings that carried over into softball, affecting the social contexts of both sports. Historian José Alamillo frames his discussion of the importance of baseball to early-twentieth-century farmworkers in California partly with the observation that whatever national meanings have been actively articulated to baseball, the sport has been transnational and hemispheric for much of its organized history.[2] Alamillo argues that Cubans in the Yucatán brought baseball to Mexico in the 1860s, and its growth was promoted throughout the Republic alongside U.S. railroad and mining concerns that came with foreign investment during the Porfiriato. Alamillo notes that "American investors and Porfirian liberals recognized the game's potential of introducing modern industrial values such as teamwork and self-discipline to the Mexican lower classes. . . . [Thus] U.S. companies subsidized baseball teams on both sides of the Rio Grande to increase worker productivity and foster company loyalty" (2008, 100–101).[3] However much certain North Americans may have wanted for baseball to be a channel for promoting U.S.-Americanism, though, its imbrication throughout the hemisphere and cultural hybridization has been long underway.

CULTURAL CONTESTATION ON THE FIELD

Arguing for a critical sociology of race and sport, Carrington looks to historian C. L. R. James's 1963 work on Trinidadian cricket as a model that masterfully blends both world-historical power dynamics and cultural specificity in analyzing the complexity of a sport practiced passionately within and against colonial histories. James situates sport as a field of cultural contestation, the space of "meanings, aesthetics, and practices" informed but not wholly determined by political economic forces (Carrington 2013, 382). As cultural forms in societies shaped by struggles of power that themselves take place partly in the cultural domain, sports can be seen to constitute space in which "classed and raced antagonisms" are played out (381). This focus places James at the forefront of a critical approach that anticipated cultural-studies-informed work by anthropologists like Foley that I have cited here.

The cultural dynamic of baseball/softball, then, is not the expression of a nationalist essence or universal human values, but what, in the vein of Stuart Hall, we might call unstable articulations, meanings that were saddled to the sport but that, like any other cultural theme, were subject to the shifting historical-political tides of hegemonic process and therefore subject to contestation. Hall defines articulation as a linkage between form and value or meaning that is ultimately revealed to be "not necessary, determined, absolute, and essential for all times; it is not necessarily given in all cases as a law or a fact of life" (2016, 121). The historical character of articulations makes them malleable. Sometimes articulations are pushed off base by social and cultural activity that runs counter to their claims. Sometimes they go unstable under the weight of contradictions in their own ideological justification. In sport, the concreteness of embodied practice that would seem to underwrite ideological power in fact is what opens up the form to historical revision.

One vector of instability in the articulation of baseball with U.S. nationalism, besides its long history beyond the borders of the United States, was that the sport in the early twentieth century carried a strong class connotation as well as a national identity. As Alamillo recounts in his history of the leisure lives of lemon pickers in California, immigrant workers encountered baseball in the Corona area as an activity of the wealthy growers. The Lemon Men's Club, a business organization of landowners, included a baseball game in their annual field day in the 1920s, an event that built solidarity among the growers and fostered an image of themselves as successful, self-made men. The Mexican laborers who picked their orchards would have experienced such events only as spectators. Yet if baseball was an elite activity among the growers, it soon was promoted to the working class as part of a paternalist welfare capitalism (Alamillo 2008, 25). According to this approach to managing a stratified political economy, leisure and the fun of recreational sports were not only luxuries earned by those who successfully accumulated capital, but could be part of an overall quality of life that would promote labor peace by instilling contentment and even gratitude among laborers. Organizing industrial baseball leagues and giving workers permission to play at lunch were examples of this form of management, going along with other recreational offerings, promoting marriage and family life among workers, providing housing, and other measures of welfare capitalism.

Offering baseball as part of a packaged "good life" provided to placate workers was further supported by "play reformers" who sought to promote both Americanization and moral uplift among immigrant workers. For such proponents of baseball, immigrants were prone to "unwholesome" recreation and needed to be "Americanized" in the interest of their own health and morality. Alamillo characterizes this in the site of his research, Corona, California:

> The associated male leisure activities of public drinking and gambling in saloons and pool halls along North Main Street threatened the moral and social order of the community. Play reformers targeted immigrant children in schools, playgrounds, churches, and settlement houses to mold them into a submissive working class with middle-class Anglo Protestant values. (2008, 102)

Citing James, Alamillo points out that despite these efforts, sport proved to be an unreliable technology of control, as Mexican American ballplayers put baseball to their own uses, in his words, "to promote ethnic consciousness, build community solidarity, and sharpen their organizing and leadership skills. . . . In doing so, they transformed the ball clubs into a political forum from which to launch wider forms of collective action" (2008, 100). Mobilizations for civil rights that followed in the mid-twentieth century attest that this was more than the play reformers and welfare capitalists had bargained for.

Presented with baseball as a valued symbol of the good life and a pedagogical exercise in character development, Mexican Americans took up the pleasures and drama of team competition with their own agenda. In Alamillo's words, "In the context of economic exploitation, racial discrimination, and resurgent nativist attacks aimed at the Mexican population, second-generation Mexican Americans used baseball to proclaim their equality through athletic competition without fear of reprisal and to publicly demonstrate community solidarity and strength" (2008, 99–100).

This is similar to the ways that Arjun Appadurai has discussed how cricket, presented as a "means of modernity" to people colonized by the British Empire, became an "emblem of Indian nationhood" through a process of indigenization (1996, 112). Appadurai calls this a "hijacking" of a modern, standardized, rule-bound sport thought to be a "hard cultural form," or a stable articulation, meaning one that "changes those who are socialized into it more readily than it is itself changed" (90). By "tightly yoking value, meaning, and embodied practice" (111) the sport seemed to promise a pedagogical effect to inculcate Britishness as it was spread and popularized throughout the occupied country in print and, later, broadcast media. A funny thing happened on the way to the pitch, though. The pedagogical dissemination of the sport led to its vernacularization and, as Appadurai notes, the "appropriation of agonistic bodily skills" by colonized subjects (111). In other words, people began to play. Within this imposed practice, the pleasure, passion, and purpose afforded by the game apparently opened up the hard cultural form to revision. For one thing, the illusio of the sport provided an anchor of commitment that could animate human effort for its own sake but was not as tightly yoked to specific nationality as it seemed. The complaint "that's not cricket" could retain profound significance even as it gradually ceased to mean "that's not British." Moreover, the actual practice of the sport in the acts of raced, material bodies created an idiom of realist representation in which the highly elaborated ideology of empire, which turned on the sorting of races and extensive knowledge about what "they are like," was subject to being disproved and rewritten in broad daylight and real time.

Moving from understanding sport as a hard cultural form to a site of unstable articulations, taking vernacular form on uneven and shifting fields of packed dirt, brings together the questions of how sport functions in society and why a particular form of sport is especially important to Mexican Americans. In the case of fastpitch softball, this derives not so much from the sport's position in the global sport system (which could be called marginal), but follows instead from prioritizing the specific forms that Mexican Americans found available and chose to engage while navigating their historical social circumstances.

THE NARRATIVES OF BASE GAMES

Eric Dunning, a leading proponent of the sociology of sport, argues that the broad appeal of sport cannot be reduced to a social or metaphorical function:

> Sport, like every social field, generates its own *illusio* but this level of interest rests on sport being a "real" game, not a metaphor or a window onto another social milieu. In this sense, the sportive illusion is paradoxical because it is a belief based on the idea that sport is played for its own sake rather than for material rewards, that sport represents freedom and fun, that it is an essentially superficial activity played for pleasure, for beauty, and so on. . . . One might say that we take part in sport simply for sport's sake. (2001, 165)

The widespread enthusiasm for sport in modern Western society seems to justify itself. Typically sports fans are not asked to explain or rationalize their commitments. But those who study sport within the context of contested social and cultural history often justify their work by viewing it through a lens that refracts connections between the playing field and larger social fields—hence, the prominent role that segregation plays in the history of Mexican American fastpitch. If sport were, as Leon Trotsky had it, truly an "alternative to politics" (cited in Carrington 2013, 381) then why would so much political energy be channeled into its organization, especially in efforts by those in a dominant social position to keep others off the field? It is probably true that sports teams like the Mexican Catholics or their African American counterparts, the Wolverines, in Newton, Kansas, found some opportunities on the playing field because it was "only softball" and not the city council or school board. But it is also true that when the gates of segregation shut hard, their enforcers made it clear that even the institutions of fun were not just a game when it came to enforcing the boundaries and hierarchies of the social order.

The cultural contestation that Carrington, James, Foley, Appadurai, and others identified in sport reveals that more than being just a set of formalized and rationalized physical contests, sport is an idiom and field of cultural performance rich with meanings and drama.[4] Sociologist Robert Perinbanayagam (2006) argues as much—that sports and games are forms of narrative. Softball has provided a repertoire and space of performance for Mexican Americans to use in narrating their own community identity, its valued qualities, and its relation to the larger society. Again, this resource was available in times and places coincident with Mexican American identity formation partly because softball was so widely promoted by social reformers, managers of labor, and other members of society who believed that baseball-derived games were effective ideological training for producing docile, reliable, and fully Americanized workers. Perinbanayagam (2006, 231), however, draws on Karl Mannheim's social theory to distinguish such ideological functions from other possibilities latent in sport as narrative form; here I will follow that line of analysis to consider sport as a narrative not of universal ideology but utopian particularity. We need not travel too far with Mannheim, as his concern with the role and function of intellectuals is not the focus here, but the contrast between ideological and utopian modes of articulation will be useful for representing Mexican Americans' particular relationship to several cultural narratives embedded in the form of softball.

According to Perinbanayagam (2006), a game functions ideologically if it presents a particular narrative as universal, smoothing over the discontinuities (such as those marked by race, class, and gender) that are actually salient. This is how sport may stage, for example, certain Protestant or Puritan values as universal, which James noted in the cricket of his youth, but truly understood in their cultural specificity only when he saw the Puritan values of reticence and stoicism violated in a baseball game in the United States ([1963] 2013, 43). If ideological narratives connote universality, Perinbanayagam interprets Mannheim's notion of utopia as being more particular and by definition limited in their application to the real world. Indeed, while ideology represents a specific social order as natural and therefore beyond question or alternative, utopia is defined in sharp contrast to ordinary life. While participants in Mexican American fastpitch affirm and celebrate forms of meritocracy that are structured into the sport, I argue that this is not entirely ideological in the sense of asserting that meritocracy exists naturally, everywhere. On the contrary, in the Mexican American tradition, meritocratic sport occurs in a delimited space and time and carries value not as a representation of a natural and universal order but by its sharp contrast from the social world that participants in the game have experienced. The constant awareness of this contrast is what rules against the functionalist paradigm that Carrington critiques. Rather than serving an ideological function, the racial tradition of fastpitch carries on in a utopian mode.

The concept of utopia blends "the good place" and "no place," and my use here emphasizes the second sense. So the utopics of softball do not necessarily or successfully assert a perfect order, but rather are characterized primarily by a formal and aestheticized separation from ordinary life. This may seem contradictory to my insistence that Mexican American fastpitch is embedded in a social base of vernacular interaction, but that is precisely why the game should be understood as an active cultural production. Between the foul lines and fences that mark out the playing field, the constituents of Mexican American fastpitch construct a temporary and highly meaningful departure from the social experiences they know as ordinary, even though in the process of a game, they select certain relations and qualities from that ordinary life to prioritize, perform, and highlight. The departure is not necessarily from the social relations with their neighbors. Rather, they move together within those relations to break out of larger, routine exclusions of ordinary life. It is the selective engagement with modernity (García-Canclini 1995), in the form of normative, modern sport, that makes this a Mexican American cultural poetics.

It is important to emphasize that I am describing a utopian thread running through fastpitch, not suggesting that the game constructs a successful or complete utopia on the field. The narrative content of the sport and any particular game remains emergent and contested, much in the way of the ethical argument between strict adherence to rules and letting things play out in physical contests, described in Chapter 4. Thus, the utopian narrative is by no means mutually exclusive with ideological ones. For example, we should not celebrate sport as a perfected utopia, "the good place," as long as it also reproduces hierarchies within the insidiously gender-ordered world of sport. As Mexican men struggled for recognition as full citizens of modern U.S. society, they based their claims in part on valued forms of masculinity, and this creates its own material contingencies for meritocracy, throwing up its own restrictions on who gets to step on the field.

Within such limitations, though, fastpitch has provided opportunities to engage on a vernacular scale with what Perinbanayagam references as Georg Simmel's notion of adventure—the appeal of games as "dropping out of the continuity of ordinary life" (2014, 87). Sport presents adventure in a series of relatively balanced chances of overcoming and being defeated by obstacles formally imposed by the characteristic structure of a given sport. In fastpitch, these obstacles include the challenges of hitting or catching a ball, but also challenges embodied in opponents trying to stop you or throw you out. The adventure of agonistic competition is a kind of dialogue, with players "speaking" back and forth through their physical actions (and also in actual speech, "jawing at" each other, as Juan Barranco put it). Perinbanayagam suggests that the dialogic and agonistic character of sport forms the means for players to put "the self into play" on the field (2006, 18). The forms and genres through which these dialogues take place characterize specific games. In what follows, I consider the characteristic narratives about individuality, opportunity, and meritocracy that have contributed to Mexican American cultural investment in softball.

Individuals

The Diamantes are facing the Reys. The Reys are from Austin, kind of. Israel Rey lives there now, but his family is from El Paso/Ciudad Juarez, and many of the players make that long road trip to play for his team in the tournament. The Diamantes are from Mexico and are accustomed to the international style of pitching, which allows jumping off the rubber before the ball is released. The

ASA requires contact with the ground until the ball is released, so pitchers under those rules usually drag the back foot as they step forward to throw. For their Memorial Day tournament, the Jokers are making an effort to follow ASA rules. The umpire summons the Diamantes into the pitching circle to explain. The pitcher, who along with the third baseman plays for the Mexican national team, has to practice not jumping. His windup includes a high, straightforward kick, like a Prussian soldier. The Diamantes' fans cheer loudly in Spanish—apparently family members who have come along on the trip, wearing Old Navy shirts emblazoned with U.S. flags.

The form of softball is a confrontation. Fastpitch players tell me it is all about the pitching. When the conversation goes to the recent decline in the game, it is because no one trains pitchers anymore. When a reason is needed to explain why a particular team has a dynasty of winning, supporters of other teams might say, "Well, they pay for pitchers." The pitcher, *lanzador* in Spanish, stands like a knight facing the opponent's bat. An opponent who can hit, who is said to be or to have a "stick," is capable of sending the ball back with formidable power, potentially right back at the pitcher. Facing the pitcher is the batter, who has stepped into the focal space of the batter's box through the ritual of taking turns. One at a time, in the sacred batting order, players step up to represent their team, community, and family. In a nonprofessional game, they may be playing to boost their reputation, but their role as representatives of the team is paramount. As individuals, they must do their best for the collective.[5]

Players who tell me stories of the pride that they gleaned from playing ball will sometimes break into an imaginary monologue: *Yeah, we showed up. It's like, "I faced him."* It is naturally boast-worthy to have gotten a hit or a run off a renowned pitcher, but merely to face one is nearly as good. Even when there is a trace of resentment about teams paying top dollar to pick up a pitcher, if that player is famous in fastpitch circles, maybe even world ranked, some of the prestige spills over to the batters who faced him. A whole genre of memories from segregated days involves quick turns from shame to pride when Mexican teams went from being excluded from competition in the mainstream of local recreation, or at least made to feel unwelcome, to holding their own as contenders in games against teams presumed to be dominant even though they had been isolated from competition up to that point. "We faced them" is a common refrain regardless, almost, of who brought the trophy home, though if the speaker's team was successful, the trophy will come up too.

Later, the Reys are warming up to play Rios, the next generation of the venerable Glowworm team. Rios will bat, so the Reys are following the typical routine to warm up the pitcher. He throws a number of pitches in before the catcher calls out, "Going down!" the signal that he will throw to second. After this, the infielders for the Reys pass the ball around as they slowly move in toward the pitcher—third base, shortstop, second, first—closing the short distance until all four players have converged in the circle and one flips the ball to the pitcher. He palms it in front of himself as his infielders turn and jog back to their stations. The pitcher makes the sign of the cross with the ball, perhaps in defense against the possibility of a line drive to the face, and steps to the rubber.

• • •

The confrontation of bat-and-base games is a feature shared by cricket and provides James with evidence to argue for the dramatic richness of sport:

> Cricket is first and foremost a dramatic spectacle. It belongs with the theatre, ballet, opera, and the dance. In a superficial sense all games are dramatic. . . . [Cricket's] quality as drama is more specific. It is so organized that at all times it is compelled to reproduce the central action which characterizes all good drama from the days of the Greeks to our own: two individuals are pitted against each other in a conflict that is strictly personal but no less strictly representative of a social group. One individual batsman faces one individual bowler. But each represents his side. The personal achievement may be of the utmost competence of brilliance. Its ultimate value is whether it assists the side to victory or staves off defeat. . . . The batsman facing the ball does not merely represent his side. For that moment, to all intents and purposes, he is his side. ([1963] 2013, 196–197)

Particularly in what Perinbanayagam calls "hit-and-run" games, this physical presentation of the self in confrontation between pitcher and batter resembles a heroic and sacrificial character in myth. James also calls it "primitive," meaning "as the battle between Hector and Achilles is primitive" ([1963] 2013, 8). In the agonistic face-off,

> an individual has to handle the situation as best as he or she can and the manner of handling it will confer esteem or dis-esteem on one and will be used to estimate his or her character. One can "cut and run." He or she can display cowardice and incompetence or he or she can "face up" to the challenge, dis-

> play courage, and confidence in the handling of the adversaries. (Perinbanaya-
> gam 2006, 125)

Being in the spotlight, the center of attention, is an opportunity for heroics and also to be the scapegoat who can be blamed for the team's loss. This is what seasoned player Bobby Alonso described to me as "the guy" nobody wants to be: the guy who loses the game with a costly error or missed opportunity. Bobby told me that while of course ballplayers want to win, an even more crucial aim is not to be *that guy* who lets down a team.

The intensity of focus on individual capability and performance as the basis for collective achievement may be part of what supports the idea that a certain "Americanness" inheres in baseball and softball, namely, an individualist ideol-ogy. But the individualism embodied by the batter-versus-pitcher confronta-tion is tempered by a mutually constitutive relation between individual and team that also has a particular resonance with Mexican American identity. Mexican Americans have historically confronted a dominant Anglo culture that highly values and rewards competitive individualism and yet generalizes and stereotypes racialized subjects as primarily defined by their group. In this context, it makes sense that the turn-taking nature of softball, with the dramatic batting confrontation at its core, held appeal for those seeking to demonstrate and claim the capacity for fully recognized citizenship. This was salient in a specific way in the formative years of Mexican American fastpitch. But if the Mexican American communities of the World War II era have by now secured their belonging in the United States, recurrent forms of anti-Mexican racism continue to cycle through the U.S. political landscape in ways that specifically operate through modes of individual and collective subjectification. Certain high-profile developments in forms of anti-Mexican racism that became nation-ally prominent during the time of my fieldwork exemplify this general theme, in what we can now recognize as the unfolding logic of political Trumpism.[6]

Sandra K. Soto provides an indispensable perspective on these develop-ments in Arizona, namely Senate bill (SB) 1070 and House bill (HB) 2281, having been directly engaged with them as a critical ethnic studies scholar working in the state. These 2010 legislative acts, which mandated state policing of immigration status and banned K–12 ethnic studies educational programs, respectively, were part of a common political moment and a broad attempt by conservative whites in the state to reestablish a notion of American identity and history as racially white and culturally Anglo. Soto observes that the explicit aim of the SB 1070 "show your papers" law was "to make attrition through enforcement" the policy of all government agencies in the state (2011, 5). Thus, there were no bones to be made about this legislation's purpose: to wear down and weaken a targeted group of people. Politically justified as a measure against "illegal immigration," the law's provisions relied on forms of public visibility, including phenotype and language, that project a large target, encompassing Latina/o people in general. Proponents insisted that they were aiming at undocumented people and that their status was a question of individual responsibility, but the policies effectively targeted anyone deemed to look, sound, and *seem* Mexican.

At the same time that SB 1070 imposed attrition collectively on Mexican people, HB 2281 moved against ethnic studies education like that provided by Tucson's Mexican American studies program, which had been established in 1998 to support students and meet a federal court mandate to desegregate the public schools, already twenty years old (Soto 2012–2013). The bill explicitly mandates individualism in instruction, banning the concept of collective oppression, and requiring that teachers provide narratives of individuals acting as such, rather than recognizing the concept or historical reality of ethnic solidarity (Soto 2011, 2). Not all of this survived court review, but the two laws together crystallized a political moment, and with it a clear and forceful message to Mexicans and Latina/os in general: "You *must* understand your place in history and prospects in this society as those of a unique individual, with no relation to the oppression or achievements of others; and you *will* be treated on the street as an undifferentiated part of a suspect category of person." The focus of right-wing governance in Arizona was individualism as a mandate for inclusion, paired with collectivism for purposes of repressive surveillance.

If the project of attrition made unique strides in Arizona, these legislative acts presaged a more general movement to rearticulate U.S. citizenship as being Anglo with specific anti-Mexican features, which would become part of the national political zeitgeist with the election of Donald Trump to the presidency and the inclusion at various times of white nationalists such as Stephen Miller, Sebastian Gorka, and Steve Bannon on his White House team. In 2010, the coauthor of SB 1070 was Kansan Kris Kobach, who, after a pursuing an Ivy League education that included the mentorship of Samuel Huntington, built a career as a traveling anti-immigrant policy consultant even while holding public office in his home state. Most of the constituents of Mexican American fastpitch in mid-América were a generation or more post-immigration, and never mentioned being directly targeted by anti-immigrant policies in our conversations. There was certainly a diverse range of perspectives on these matters to be found in the fastpitch world. No doubt a handful of Trump supporters in the fastpitch family would take issue with my premise that the president's politics are anti-Mexican as opposed to anti-"illegal." The national racial climate did register at tournaments, however, mediated through jokes that marked the ambivalent position of Mexican Americans within it: "Hey, better not use that illegal bat—you'll get deported!" "But I'm legal!"

The point is not that the Arizona legislation had any direct influence on the softball traditions that began seventy years earlier under different conditions of segregation, but rather that a common double-bind dynamic can be found running consistently through Mexican American history, of being *expected* to act and think as individuals while being *treated* primarily as a group. Part of the pleasure and significance offered by softball to the communities that prioritize it is that the game offers a medium in which to perform a dynamic relation between individualism and collective identity and interests. Most important, it provides a chance to claim and practice authority over the nature of this relation.

Opportunity

The idea that a certain individual-collective dynamic plays out in baseball and softball differently than in other sports suggests that the historical malleability of sport does not make it entirely a blank stage or "empty form," as John Macaloon (1996) suggests in counterpoint to Appadurai's notion of a hard cultural form (1996). Beside the historical articulations that layer sports with meaning, the arbitrary features of different games, their particular illusio agreed to and accepted by all participants, constitute distinct forms. American football, for example, is a highly structured, technological, and specialized game in which even dedicated fans may not know all the arcane rules and certain players may spend only seconds on the field in roles that are nonetheless indispensable. This in many ways mirrors the modern organization of military and industrial institutions. Obedience and execution of a very specific role within the structure are keys to success on the gridiron. What the world knows as football, and Americans call soccer, is more improvisatory. Strategic intervention from the manager or coach may be limited to decisions about lineup and substitutions, but once the game is underway, players must shift positions and roles constantly to try to achieve the collective subjectivity of teamwork.

Bat-and-base games contrast with field games based on territory and possession in certain distinctive features: covering space in the infield and outfield is primarily a defensive concern while the offensive players move along a linear path, even though it is bent into a diamond shape. Perhaps most unusual, play begins with the ball in the possession of the defense. This small detail is remarkable in that it shows that the ball is not something to be won and kept like property, nor is it a primarily an instrument of space, marking out the territory that a team controls or concretizing their access to a goal (Perinbanaygam 2006, 53). When pitched and hit with a bat, the ball is a timing device. The position of the ball establishes the time frame that sets the scale of opportunity for the offense: the farther out of reach it gets hit, the more time to run. That scale begins as the split-second during which a pitched ball is within reach of the batter, a nearly imperceptible shard of time. The aim of the batter is to extend the time available for runners to advance by seizing the minuscule opportunity of the ball passing within reach to knock it out of the control of the defense, thereby introducing chaos and possibility into the positional order. A successful defense responds to these abruptly changing circumstances and reimposes order. A successful offense seizes whatever advantage they can in the moments provided between when a ball is hit and fielded.

All of this is mundane and obvious for those familiar with the game, but it offers significant cultural resonance with the historical experience of racialized immigrants and their successive generations, who, as the folklore has it that has been applied to various groups, "tried to make a dollar out of fifteen cents." Bat-and-ball games aestheticize and ritually repeat the experience of stepping forward with no resource other than what is offered by your body, your mind, and a simple tool (what amounts to a club!) to seize the slimmest of chances and extend it into an opportunity. The symbolic power of this is potentially enormous for anyone whose daily life is charged with the task of making the most of truncated chances.

The idea of softball as a formalized and aestheticized performance of compressed and stretched opportunity resonates with the appeal the game has held for other marginalized populations. Since I have begun this research project—motivated by an interest in Mexican American communities first rather than softball for its own sake—I have learned of Japanese American softball in internment camps, African American softball in Chicago, Micronesian immigrant softball in Kansas City, and the list continues to grow. Situated between my Kansas and Texas field sites is the annual All-Indian fastpitch tournament in Oklahoma, which in 2020 celebrated its sixty-eighth year. Any of these sporting histories is worthy of its own project and books. No doubt part of the appeal of the game to marginalized people is circumstantial: recall that as a focal point for the social reform efforts and pedagogical function ascribed to sport, softball was widely promoted as a playground and recreational activity and believed to be effective ideological training. But it is also reasonable to conclude that the game holds some special appeal for the way its form provides chances to break open possibility rather than locking options down.

Opportunity seized and extended against opposition is one of the themes that softball in Mexican American communities dramatizes and that resonates with Mexican American historical experience. But this articulation is not always congruent—that is, the historical experience has not always resembled the structural patterns of the game. In this way, the articulation of Mexican American fastpitch is utopian, not ideological. Similarly, the cultural form that Mexican Americans produce through softball as a practice of cultural poetics—a form of meritocracy and rigorous but fair competition—is more aspirational than is it representative of how the world always works.

Meritocracy

Through highly specific rules of competition, including fair turn-taking, rationalized scoring, and clarity of results, sport constructs a meritocracy internal to itself, in which success is earned. When victory is tainted by arbitrary or accidental events, it may be viewed as less authentic. If we see sport as a vehicle of ideology, this would appear as a pageant that naturalizes a general claim that meritocracy reigns in society. This, certainly, has promoted the historical dissemination of base games in U.S. society, including substantial public investment to support them in specific times and places. Ideologically speaking, to proclaim that meritocracy is the way of the world implies that social inequalities are just and permanent, and those whose lives are hampered by unequal structures simply have to compete harder for their share of the winnings.

In contrast, utopian distinction from normal life is marked by the festival-like tone of the annual Mexican American fastpitch events, as well as in nostalgia for times when, unlike the present, fastpitch filled the weekday calendar with regular, but heightened, exciting games. This is how Mexican Americans have articulated the symbolic form of softball to their historical experience, as a better chance at meritocracy than what they usually got. This interpretation resonates strongly with narratives I have collected in interviews, in which participants recounted experiences, as racialized minorities, of being persistently underestimated in their potential for various kinds of competition and success. Sports have appealed to minoritized and immigrant groups in the United States for their promise of an actual, if narrowly bounded and impermanent, meritocracy.

Among many experiences that caused Mexican Americans to doubt the ubiquity of meritocracy in U.S. society is the story of the all-Mexican, state-winning basketball team of Lanier High School in San Antonio in the 1930s and 1940s. This history is recounted in Ignacio García's book *When Mexicans Could Play Ball* (2014). Lanier was established for Mexican children and was the only high school on the city's West side. It had a vocational curriculum, which was appealing for families that did not envision that academic study would provide much opportunity for their children to advance socially. The school also emphasized assimilation, as one alumnus recounts: "Every Monday, the school would issue you a ribbon that said 'I speak English. I'm an American'" (Hassenfield 2017).

Lanier also built a winning basketball program led by coach William "Nemo" Herrera. Despite the team's dominating presence in San Antonio and numerous championship seasons, combining assimilation in school with victory on the ball court was not enough for the Mexican players to win full recognition of their equal citizenship. García recounts how fans attacked the Lanier players after a particularly dramatic victory over rival Brackenridge for the city championship in 1939. When Lanier won the state championship in 1943, their victory was not widely celebrated in public, and in fact there were grumblings in the press and beyond about their having "stolen" the trophy in Austin. A particularly dramatic event that García narrates occurred when a local school board president publicly speculated that Lanier was violating eligibility requirements by playing boys who were too old. This led to a feud with Lanier's principal over whether board members were subjecting a working-class Mexican school to unbalanced scrutiny. García writes that such hardline questioning of Lanier students' ages

> showed the length to which these school officials and their supporters were
> willing to go to prove that Lanier students cheated. . . . The spying on Lanier
> players revealed a deep-rooted suspicion that Mexicans simply did not play
> fair, and that suspicion fed off the old stereotype that Mexicans were treacher-
> ous backstabbers who sought to circumvent the rules. These perceptions had

been used for decades to question the integrity of the Mexican population and as a way to underscore their "inability" to play by American rules.

> To believe otherwise was to accept that Mexicans could maintain their ethnic identity, culture, and social-religious ways and still succeed in the American games of football and basketball. American sports' triumph and the legends that made those victories possible were canonized with a virtuous, follow-the-rule, oh-shucks character that exhibited a not totally unique American perception of itself that was particular to whites in the United States. (2014, 71)

While the playing field artificially simplified and leveled competition, offering visible results, it was in contrast to ordinary social life, where prejudicial assumptions about potential may have been taken for granted as truth. The symbolic form of sport was well suited as a resource to correct for a felt lack of opportunities, including the chance to face adversity in public and prevail, thereby exceeding expectations. But the opportunity to do so was far from guaranteed and, in fact, often limited. By taking charge of their own sporting tradition, Mexican Americans ensured their access to that chance.

The participants in Mexican American fastpitch are not radical critics of meritocracy and do not hesitate to affirm their sport as conveying general values. Fastpitch ballplayers have extolled the virtues of their game to me, speaking of a wholesome family activity, where kids "grow up in the dugout" and play pickup games behind the bleachers. They present fastpitch as a declining but superior form of recreation to "all the video games these days" that, by contrast, develop little in the players but fast thumbs. In this enthusiasm for the game and the melancholic sense of modern decline from a previous virtue, fastpitch players may seem ready to endorse all of the normative features of an American mythos—meritocracy, sacrifice, austere masculinity, and the rest. But the tournaments that provide sites for these valorized qualities to be enacted on the field didn't just happen by themselves; they were the result of struggle to build and sustain institutions. This is why reverence for founders of the local tradition, and not just inherent qualities of the game, are part of the historical consciousness of Mexican American fastpitch.

Fastpitch establishes a dynamic field of play and physical performance within sweeping dialectics of "American" modernity. As a sport taken up by the children of immigrants, fastpitch fits into, and yet disturbs, the normative "ethnic" narrative by which a national culture, engaged in idioms such as favored sports, serves as a gateway and guide for subjects evolving toward Americanness to shed their cultural distinction and take on what have been claimed as the habits and values of the receiving nation. At least this has been a prominent narrative of ethnicity, and baseball has figured in the public imaginary that perpetuates it. But clearly, the perdurance of "Mexican" tournaments with deep barrio roots troubles that idea of shedding difference to achieve citizenship. It also complicates the "United-States-ness" of playing ball.

Given the roots of Mexican American fastpitch in localized communities, formed under specific class conditions and racialized, spatial management of populations, the cultural dialectics of migration and assimilation quiver roughly in time with those of origins and destinations. The dialectic of social mobility and retained connections to a specific home infuses the relations of belonging that are palpable in a reunion fastpitch tournament, and opens up gaps in the clarity of other narratives—for example, that moving on represents progress. Beyond the national referent of this story of movement there is a class one, in which success, assimilation, or other values are ascribed to getting up and getting out of bad situations. For some people, this is a story of growing into adulthood and moving to a "better" neighborhood than before. For the nation, this is a story of leaving behind "the times" of prejudice and discrimination and moving into a world of equal opportunity and fairness. Fastpitch smudges these clear trajectory lines as well. The continuing Mexican tournaments offer a connection across history to the barrio-ized and segregated roots of the community and are embraced as such by some of those who have "gotten out."

As a racial tradition that began about the time that Jackie Robinson dramatized a breach in the most famous color line in American sport, Mexican American fastpitch embodies the ambivalences of integration. No one would choose exclusion willingly, and fastpitch ballplayers celebrate the changes in their sport that have led them to compete across lines of social identity. At the same time, something built as a home space and collective resource to resist the containment and isolation of segregation accumulates its own value over time, and the prospect of seeing its decline is not welcomed as progress.

Through repetitive practice and the assertion of cultural authority over fastpitch, Mexican Americans partially disrupt the ideological content of "playing ball" and rearticulate it to a utopian idea of meritocracy that contrasts with their particular historical experience. In some cases, players and fans built up athletic status that overlapped with social status in the community, replacing the degraded status afforded by society at large. Taking charge of their own sporting tradition to construct a space and time of fair play ensured Mexican American men of their access to that chance. In this way, the symbolic form of sport was well suited as a resource to negotiate a felt lack of opportunities, seizing the chance to face adversity in public and prevail, thereby exceeding expectations and cultivating their own.

⚾ CONCLUSION ⚾

PATRIOTIC, BUT WE LOVE
OUR CULTURE TOO

WATCHING THE STATELINE LOCOS' fiftieth annual fastpitch tournament in Shawnee Park, Armourdale, Kansas, I listened to old-timers reminisce about teams, tournaments, and road trips gone by. "Oh, we used to do it good here," one of them said. "We had a guy out to play the national anthem on the bugle. See, we're pretty patriotic." He nodded. "Pretty patriotic. But we love our culture too."

The distinction between patriotism and love of culture signals an understanding of culture often expressed in and around Mexican American fastpitch. Many participants have said to me, in different ways and under different circumstances, *"This is our culture."* The designation of softball as "our" culture, specifically contrasted with U.S. patriotism, reveals that despite the formal and historical ties with "America's game," for this speaker, softball is not exactly a unified "national-popular" phenomenon in Antonio Gramsci's sense (Rowe 2003). Therefore "patriotic" doesn't refer to the incorporation of Mexican Americans into an undifferentiated "American" ideological whole. The "we" who possess the culture of softball in this brief but rich statement refers not to the United States as a whole but to Mexican Americans.

• • •

The former player they call Cocoa told me that in his day, playing ball in Kansas City meant three nights a week and weekends, between the city league, the

Mexican American Softball Association, and tournaments. I ask Cocoa whether the Stateline Locos took their green and gold colors from the Kansas City Athletics, and he says yes but then notes that the Locos were the older team, since 1947. The Kansas City Amigos also chose that color scheme.

We're in lawn chairs behind his truck with a camper top and a bike on top of that. "I'm Loco Cocoa," he tells me. "Good at being bad." He introduces me to Princess, his short-haired dog. "She drinks too." He offers me a Tecate bottle, expressing his disdain for lite beer. Accepting his invitation to take a lime from his cooler, I notice provisions inside: hot dogs, tortillas. He is set for the weekend. "You're doing this in style," I say. "Style?" he responds indignantly. "This is culture." He takes a long drink. "You've got to take big swigs to taste this beer."

Some younger players stroll by and he calls out to them, gesturing to me. "See here? *National Geographic!*" The players laugh and call back, "You're going to be on TV?" I hasten to correct him. No, just a professor, I say, just a research project. After they move on, Cocoa scolds me, "You've got to learn to lie!"

Taking a pull on his Tecate, Cocoa gazes off toward the ball field as he drinks. "I used to run like Ricky Henderson . . ."

•   •   •

Ralph Ponce, from Chanute, another railroad town with a long history of ballplayers and an annual Mexican fiesta that has been running over one hundred years, tells me he slept only two hours after work as a paramedic before heading to Newton. He is a dedicated fan and there to support his son playing. "Are you going to Bambiland tonight?" he asks. This is the party hosted by Tony Sandate, known as "Bambi," who built a bandstand in his backyard for live entertainment. Ponce finds me again at the party and tells me stories about Decker Lopez and Jesse Arellano, who played with four sons. He talks about how his father was recruited from Guanajuato to work in Chanute and how six of his eleven siblings played ball—all but one of the brothers. Then without a pause: "Isn't this a nice night? Everybody drinking a beer, a band . . ." We both look around at the backyard transformed by not much more than amplified staccato sounds of Tejano music, some Christmas lights, and company. "That's our culture . . ."

•   •   •

After a long day in the sun at the Latin, sustained by the occasional brisket sandwich, sunflower seeds, and beer, a group of friends repair to the air-conditioning of a Houston Mexican restaurant, brightly decorated with *papel cortado*. The table of former players, umpires, and their families includes David and Yvonne Rios of San Antonio, who have taken it upon themselves to look after me. David is gregarious, basking in the festive atmosphere of the restaurant as if it is the culmination of what he's been telling me all day about the significance of fastpitch in his life. He sweeps one hand magnanimously over the table, drawing my attention to the colorful decorations. "You see, Ben? Our culture! Can you imagine? On a boat . . . ," and in his mind he may be drifting along in Xochimilco, without a care in the world. But as he explained earlier, softball tournaments are his destinations of choice.

· · ·

It is commonplace among academics who traffic in highly elaborated and critically tempered concepts to assume that "everyday" notions of culture and identity are essentialist constructions that require sophisticated theory to properly problematize and complicate them. I propose this is not necessarily the case, and that a trope of "our culture" that circulates in the fastpitch family is not an innocent illusion of wholeness or purity, but an active claim of space and legitimacy that responds in sophisticated ways to the stakes of cultural politics in a diverse and unequal society. The underestimation of popular theorizing owes partly to different discursive expectations. The purpose of academic concepts is often to lend precision to discourse, to pinpoint in a sentence an entire conversation or a range of phenomena held together with specific, enduring characteristics. In academic theorizing, concepts are also often like trophies of analysis, a point of arrival after considering sufficient information, racking up points of evidence and covering all the angles to support confident claims about placing the things of the world into "abstractable logics and structures" (Stewart 2017, 192–193). What I think was going on in that conversation behind third base at Shawnee Park, though, was a kind of theorizing where precision was not so much the product of rigorous logic or erudition, but a strong connection to the material and historical specificity of the phenomenon, buttressed with its own robust archives of evidence drawn from experience, if not reading. The concept, in this sort of nonacademic yet theoretical discourse, can be usefully loose, spoken not necessarily in an authoritative way but as a gesture—culture not as an intricately elaborated framework of arguments but an icon of a collective social experience that marks its distinction from others.

To invoke fastpitch as Mexican American culture speaks to economies of legitimacy. The term becomes a tool to situate a racial tradition in vernacular sporting space as a center of meaning, as opposed to being marginal to the "mainstream" of sport. To distinguish "our culture" from patriotism, or the practices and feelings of national identity, is a particularly interesting intervention in that it performs cultural citizenship. The conversation and bearing of some old-timers in the fastpitch scene suggested that military service in the 1940s and 1950s was a significant context for their formation of identities as citizens and ballplayers, and for them patriotism was an idiom of broad belonging and recognition. If wars and military service set the tone for these subjects to perform their duty and worthiness to the larger nation in a patriotic mode (Ramos-Zayas 2004), then building a tradition of Mexican teams and tournaments was a project of difference, carving out a piece of American life as something that was "ours." As invoked in an urban park in 2010s mid-América, "culture" asserted multicultural pluralism and claimed a local site of authority based on specific people's love of a game, the longevity of a tournament tradition, and even seemingly banal events like informal parties after a day's play, when opponents gather to drink beer in the backyard of a player from the hosting team. This version of the culture concept is a rhetorical move to qualify assimilation and, in the words of Juan Flores, avoid getting "lost in the sauce" (1997b, 176). It also functions to open up, rather than foreclose, complex repertoires of identity in the present. Thus, sport is not only the hard cultural form of an imposed, dominant modernity, but a cultural practice akin to those of the borderlands, in which lived experience continually troubles homogenizing nationalist discourses, even restructuring them (Madrid 2008, cited in Chávez 2017, 51).

• • •

"The thing to know about my family," says a woman, maybe a few years older than me and sitting on a portable folding chair under a shade tree in July, "is that my ancestors rode with Pancho Villa." This would form a refrain that I heard several times over the course of the weekend in Athletic Park, just west of downtown and the rail yards of Newton. The invocation of Villista relatives took me by surprise the first time. I expected to hear of exploits on the ball field, how Uncle Fulanito was a crack third baseman, not afraid to creep up the line toward home to intimidate a batter, or how Abuelita's *menudo* got hung-over ballplayers back on their feet on Sunday morning to begin the long day's slog through the loser's bracket. But several people in Newton first wanted to connect to the famous revolutionary.

I don't think they brought him up to emphasize that it was Villa who led the last military incursion across a border of the contiguous United States, into Columbus, New Mexico, and that it was this event, among others, that inspired the founding of the Border Patrol. Indeed, while there was uniform pride in Mexican heritage at every fastpitch tournament I've attended, that didn't mean there was any particular political consensus, even around questions of crossing the national border without permission. Those who tied their family history to the revolution were not establishing a rebellious heritage so much as a continuous connection with known historical events, situating their ancestors as active participants. There are variations of this personal tie to the historical. Gil Solis tells of how his father was born on the roof of a train as his grandparents fled the revolution out of Mexico City. Mario Garcia recounts his family history something in the vein of the biography of an athlete getting picked up by various teams:

> My Grandfather was a bullfighter and he got gored in his knee later in life. But my grandfather also fought in the revolutionary war. And he was on both sides. He started out, they kidnapped him from his farm if you will, three boys walking back to their farm, and my grandfather was one of them. We can only estimate he was 12 or 13 at the time. No records of course. And—"Which side are you on?" So they snatched him and put him in a uniform and gave him a rifle. . . . The *federales* got him first. And then he got injured. And when he come back out, he was on Pancho Villa's side.

Despite these references to revolutionary heritage, taking part in this tournament was not something that required an outright stance of "resistance," as scholars of minoritized vernaculars sometimes look for. When tournaments begin with a performance of the "Star-Spangled Banner," attended by a color guard bearing the U.S. flag, it is part and parcel of what my interlocutor in Armourdale had called "doing it pretty good." This custom of opening sporting events with the national anthem only became ubiquitous in the United States around the same time that Mexican American fastpitch tournaments were forming, in the postwar 1940s. And the Mexican national tricolor that appears amid many stars and stripes around the ball field in Newton is one sign that this event is steeped in local knowledge that to be Mexican in this small Kansas town was itself a political act of sorts. It was to bear witness to a history in which Mexican labor made the town to a great extent, at first in the service of the Santa Fe railroad and as time went on, in other industries.

Mexican families, though grateful for the company housing provided by the railroad, also could not help but notice that its location contained them on the south end of downtown, near the rail yards.

Mario had other ways of weaving an epic narrative, and at our panel discussion in Newton, he announced that as a child, his grandmother had walked him "hand in hand" from his home to the first Mexican American tournament. He then leaped forward in time to his playing days:

> Now we're at Our Lady of Guadalupe park and we're playing the Kansas City Pirates. And the pitcher's name was Garcia, like mine. We were in the bottom of the seventh inning, in the championship ball game, and I came up to bat, and I had a distinct ritual that I followed every time. And my grandmother sat in the bleachers, about the third row up. Never said a word, but she stayed there constantly. And I glanced up and looked at her, and I heard her voice over everybody that was there. And all she said was, *"Pégale, mijo. Pégale,"* which is, "Hit it, son. Hit it." And I nailed a home run over the centerfield fence. And when I got to second base, I busted out crying. When I got to home plate, I looked at her. She wasn't even clapping. She wasn't even smiling. She just said, "Told you."

Gil Solis asserted a similar articulation, tying softball to a specific life experience grounded in relationships, when interviewed in 1999 by a community newspaper about his work managing the Newton Metros. "For the Hispanic community, softball is more than softball," he is quoted as saying. "It's part of our culture. It's part of our family. It's part of what we're all about" ("Metros" 1999).

There have certainly been other claims to culture for related sports, such as the universalizing baseball humanism discussed in the previous chapter. In a different way, Choctaw writer and scholar Leanne Howe's work on Native ball playing presents what is perhaps a more conventional meaning of culture and tradition as being rooted in the premodern historical background. In articles, the novel *Miko Kings: An Indian Baseball Story* (2007), and a documentary short film with James Fortier, *Playing Pastime: American Indians, Softball, and Survival* (2015), Howe draws connections between Indigenous stickball games, groundworks such as mound building, and ritual events that include counterclockwise movement among other formal similarities to playing baseball and softball. For Howe, ongoing Native investments in ball playing such as the fastpitch tournament at the seventy-year-old annual Labor Day festival hosted by the Choctaw Nation in Oklahoma are part of a cultural continuity over centuries. As a scholar of stories and storytelling, Howe relates instances of ball playing in this oral literature, such as a story of when the animals challenged the birds to a game, providing a setting for ruminations like how the strength of Bear matched up against the speed of Eagle and Hawk. The story concludes with the observation that Bat can play for both teams (Howe 2014, 78). The traditional resonances of Howe's account resemble Chabon's affectionately ironic, mythopoetic fiction in *Summerland*, except the latter seems to be projecting baseball into a multicultural fantasy world of all folklores, whereas Howe is arguing for ball playing as a specific practice within a specific history not only longer than "baseball" as we know it but also older than "America" itself, tying together intriguing threads such as Lewis and Clark encountering a Nez Perce ball game in the Northwest that the people called "base" (Fortier and Howe 2015).

The fact that Native people continue to host fastpitch tournaments among other sports on tribal ground (the Choctaw festival also includes Native stickball, 3-on-3 basketball, volleyball, golf, and horseshoes as well as a 5K race) speaks to play as a place-making practice, part of an affective, embodied, and grounded mode of cultural poetics that resonates with Mexican American attachments to particular urban playground ball fields. Howe highlights the material dimension of life marked as cultural through ceremonial practices and meanings: shaping the ground into a field and moving on it; orienting practice according to geometric shapes and cardinal directions; and working with meaning-imbued positions within the field, such as the pitcher's circle, which she links to the central pole of Native ball games or the spot of return called "home." Howe notes formal homologies between the counterclockwise movement of running bases, southeastern Indigenous dances, tornado winds, and water flow (2014, 77). Such formal and meaningful resonances of play that cross temporal and geographic passages joined by memory and physical repetition constitute a rich historicity. They do not necessarily produce a tidy historiographic progression of cause and effect, laid out, as Walter Benjamin memorably put it, as a "sequence of events like the beads of a rosary" (1940, thesis XVIII). Rather, Howe's telling draws a constellation that outlines a topography of shared feelings, sense, and obligations something like kinship and deeply tied to place (2014, 90). Howe writes, "I do not suggest the Americans 'stole' baseball from Indians. Rather, I'm saying that if the land taught Natives how to play ball, it just might have taught non-Natives as well" (2014, 77).

This is a very different framing from work premised on sport as the product and synecdoche of modernity (Gutmann 2004). The sentence "fastpitch is our culture" invokes some of the sense of culture and tradition that signals continuity with a primordial or ancient existence and is part of the statement's affective power. But of course fastpitch is barely over a century old. The fact of fastpitch's modern provenance does not contradict or invalidate that rhetorical move to imbue the sport with a sense of longevity and importance. Instead the invocation of "culture" traditionalizes more recent, directly experienced pasts and shared ties to them (Bauman and Briggs 1990, 77–78).[1] That referent of culture, shared experience, is importantly relational and formed in social space fenced by operations of power, including ongoing racialization and class relations.

Mexican American fastpitch players could conceivably have embraced a position like Howe's, claiming fastpitch as cultural heritage through ties to indigeneity. Certainly, reference to being Indigenous has an extensive history in Chicana/o/x cultural and political mobilization, as well as in the racist pseudoscientific justifications for Mexican Americans' marginalization. Instances of Mexican American ballplayers signifying indigeneity, as in the many teams from the 1920s to the 1940s that went by "Aztecas" or Newton's "Cuauhtemoc" team, engaged less with the deep past than with the semiotic-political order that framed their own racialization in Kansas City, Houston, or elsewhere.

The Kansas City Garcia family's team name, Indios, harkens back to the Indios of Ciudad Juárez, the family's hometown. The Juárez Indios were a minor league baseball team that played from 1946 to 1984, reportedly named to honor the Indigenous Mexican statesman Benito Juárez. The complex and relatively recent history of such references suggests that there are many tributaries that feed into team names, which then also become legible to interpreters completely innocent of the broader historical resonance, who may only know of the appropriative and caricaturing modern tradition of U.S. sports team mascots. Thus, the Indios may appear to baseball fans as an ethnic version or parody of the Cleveland Indians, just as another significant Kansas City fastpitch club, the Bravos, may remind some in the bleachers of the Atlanta Braves. Neither Indigenous history nor the dynamic of parodying the big leagues is normative in these names, though, as they are used in everyday life. Instead, the Bravos, for example, signifies an experienced history of neighbors, rivals, league nights, and tournaments.

Mexican American ballplayers in mid-América have built bonds with Native players without necessarily thinking about the deeply rooted cultural practices Howe writes about, but through shared idioms and experiences of fastpitch,

segregation, and racialization. Invitations and travel to participate in one another's tournaments were part of a long-repeated exchange based on shared
Mexican and Native love of the game. In days of explicit but not de jure segregation, Mexican players were sometimes picked up by Native teams, like one
Newton player who related to me that he was recruited by a Wichita team to
come play with them with the rejoinder, "just shave real good and then come
down," suggesting the phenotypical dimension of qualifying for a game reserved
or restricted to Native players. Now that the racial boundaries of fastpitch are
less regulated, members of the Kansas City Mexican American fastpitch community participate in the tournament that is part of nearby Haskell Indian
Nations University's annual graduation ceremonies. The Newton tournament
opened up partially in 2020 to invite three Native teams, one of which took
the first-place trophy.

Articulating identity and tradition to a sport that is not primordial but
attributable to a specific span of recent history is to accept that such identifica-
tions are contingent, while insisting at the same time that contingency does
not make them trivial. The attribution of culture to softball chimes with a
conversation between Mexican and Native ball-playing families that I joined
at a tournament in Texas. Talking about food and swapping cooking tips as we
contemplated walking over to the pits for lunch, the adult daughter of a Native
pitcher well known at the Latin tournament commented that it was interesting that "all the different races have their way of cooking beans." The quality
that a casual reference to "races" conveys in this discourse is not primordial-
ism or essentialism, but collective difference and the specificity of long-term
implication in a common history. "Softball is our culture" in this context ties
the game to a "race" in the same sense. To invoke culture is to assert that the
community's commitment to the game is specific and valid. It projects that
claim into the broader national ecumene in which culture may legitimize one
or another kind of claim, on space, rights, and authority over priorities and
practice (Flores and Benmayor 1998).

Ballplayers' and fans' claim to "our culture" tempers the sheen of integration
without undermining a historical desire to break out of imposed social limits
and compete. It matters that this claim to cultural citizenship happens on a
vernacular scale of sport, which is less imbricated with the money and attention
of a mass-spectacle industry and remains close to what José Limón describes as
"the poetics of everyday life—understood as democratically constructed and
emergent, free-flowing performance either in language or in material craft or

a combination of both" (2012, 104). To link fastpitch to Mexican American cultural poetics in this way does not make it timeless, but situates the sport within the history of being excluded from school or Little League teams, run off from the park, turned away at the legion hall, or in myriad other ways having their capabilities routinely underestimated. Keeping the memory alive of these identity-targeted social barriers produces a racial sporting tradition as a project of what Sujey Vega calls "ethnic belonging" (2012).

Notions of culture and tradition were articulated to sport in Mexican American experience to move against notions of race that supported exclusion. The racial pseudoscience that raised alarms about the tendencies of "Indian blood" in mestizo populations may no longer be quite as admissible in court anymore. Today, exclusionary racial theories are reproduced out of a backlash to the multiculturalization of U.S. citizenship, in a context where public billboards occasionally appear bearing slogans like "Diversity Is White Genocide." Culture as difference and "the races" as groups that may legitimately cook, eat, play, dance, and speak differently from one another pose a threat to the resurgent white nationalism of the Trump era as restrictionist political moves in immigration, visa enforcement, and asylum and naturalization procedures join Twitter wars, debates over public memorials, street protests, and other clashes in which newly vocal or visible nationalists agitate for a white (European-derived) "America." White nationalists want "American" to be an ethnicity, and they want it to be white, a category that bears no specific origins or heritage but has been defined in the negative against the descendants of non-European populations deemed enslavable or removable in the half-millennium process of conquest.

The articulation of whiteness with power over the course of U.S. history has allowed for a racist imaginary to equate whiteness with American nationality, despite the fact that U.S. military adventures and economic trajectories have forced people without European ancestry into American society from the very beginning. This is the dynamic that brought on the contemporary situation, in which whiteness enjoys the status of being an "unmarked" category, while nonwhite identities carry the burden of being "marked." As Alex Chávez (2015) explains, U.S. ethnoracial politics operates within a "markedness structure" that sorts and ranks phenotypical, linguistic, and other cultural and material characteristics in such a way that situates Mexican people in contradistinction to a certain normative imaginary of a white U.S. nation (167). He shows how culture-as-difference in a colonial discourse marks presumed unruliness and disorder because it stands in contrast to unmarked citizenship as a feature of modernity, a "theoretical universality" situated in undifferentiated national space and "homogeneous empty time" (cf. Anderson 1983). This is despite the fact that it is that very modernity, what is sometimes referenced as the "mainstream" or "dominant" social formation of the United States, that has produced the effects of exclusion and marginalization. Chávez tracks how such structures and procedures work to dehumanize undocumented Mexican migrants as foreign others despite their thorough integration into a hemispheric (not to mention global) economy and often substantial Indigenous heritage on the unified continent now called America. Markedness structures also have kept open the possibility of calling into question the citizenship of U.S. Latinas/os (A. Chávez 2015, 154).

The markedness structure and ideology of a white U.S. nation runs throughout the entire history of exclusion, displacement, segregation, violence, and other experiences that Mexican Americans know well. Historical efforts to desegregate, that is, to enter and join public, normative social formations, is a clear rebellion against the structural hierarchy imposed by the ideology of unmarked and marked citizenship. But by building and maintaining institutions like Mexican American fastpitch, people are not simply rejecting the notion of marked citizenship; they are refunctioning an apparatus of cultural production that it uses (Benjamin [1934] 1998), that of differentiated identity. This is the project of cultural citizenship, claiming not only inclusion and rights but also space, such as the space on a ball field in a park (Flores and Benmayor 1998). At stake is the space to be a community for which the experience of markedness is común. The right to space also conveys a measure of authority, the right to define and inscribe meaning in repertoires of vernacular cultural production. Authority is being claimed when softball gets invoked as *our* culture" and exercised when social stakes and value are inverted in the process of marking something as "Mexican." The marked becomes what is desired and worthy of continuing.

This is how Mexican American fastpitch contests structures of meaning and power as participants and audiences at tournaments place a great emphasis on memorializing and renarrating the past. The annual reunion events reestablish and deepen ongoing, palpable ties to specific historical events as well as people and places. The message, in part, is that "we have been here a long time," and, what's more, "it has often not been easy for us." Even those in the fastpitch scene who are not eager to speak of discrimination as their own personal experience often want to make sure that their parents' experiences are not forgotten.

Why should anyone care about a nonprofessional sport that its own enthusiasts describe as somewhat archaic or "dying" as it is played in a particular community? What does it mean to highlight Mexican Americans "playing America's game" in the influential phrase of Adrian Burgos, even if it is a scaled-down, recreational version of that game? Researchers need to reassess the importance of informal and recreational organizations in Mexican American history and life, and consider their key role for surviving and thriving in a society that has sometimes made it difficult to do so. Even organizations devoted to fun and fellowship engage with this history of struggle in specific ways. When Mexican Americans have organized themselves, whether as a sports team, mutual aid society, fiesta committee, or however else, they have insisted on a blend of recognition and autonomy. By investing their efforts at both playing and organizing into a sport with wide national appeal, Mexican Americans registered their claim to be as worthy as any others, a claim to recognition. Yet by establishing the Mexican tournaments, they also asserted that their desire for full citizenship did not mean that they would surrender the autonomy to define their identities and interests, or to manage their own lives. In the packed brick dust of ball fields, nestled within the relationships and geographies of everyday life, they took the field and put cultural citizenship in play.

$\bigcirc$ E P I L O G U E $\bigcirc$

CALLED FOR TIME

THIS IS A RELATIVELY SHORT BOOK that took a relatively long time to produce. After the privilege of enjoying the hospitality of so many people in the fastpitch family, who gifted me with their memories, talk, and company over years, now I face the melancholic work of an ethnographer trying to find the back cover of a project. The whole premise of ethnography is that the world is bigger and richer than the books we have, and the cruel irony is that in order to make that case, we reduce it to another book. I have cut slices of Mexican American fastpitch to include in these pages with the hope of making it legible to readers and to try to deliver a taste of what is interesting and important about this sport for so many people who have kept it going long enough to call it tradition. Underlying everything I have written here about fastpitch is the general understanding that there should be more interviews, more writing, more collections, and just more attention across the board to the vernacular spaces and practices that mean so much in people's lives.

This book has not, and could not begin to, contain the historical material that exists in cardboard boxes and garages, and now on hard drives and contact lists, throughout fastpitch-playing mid-América. Even the finite lists of the halls of fame maintained in Kansas City, Newton, Austin, and Houston, among other places, proved to be too voluminous for me to add. So I offer this book with a plea for forgiveness from the uncountable players, managers, sponsors, fans, umpires, scorekeepers, groundskeepers, cooks, and child caregivers who are not adequately represented here, and with profound respect for all of the heroic games, the grinding loser-bracket Saturdays, the hustle for funds and permits, and so much more of the human relations and activity that are missing from the chapters but that all flow into the visible, concrete, ephemeral material of a game played. The work to make this knowledge available to those who want to learn from it is just beginning.

A project like this book is necessarily both general and specific—a little too much of each to represent its topic perfectly. The text has been guided by the arguments I have found embedded in fastpitch as a cross-generational, changing, and enduring milieu, including the implicit one: "We are here, and we have been here longer than you know." In the various sites of my research, this message projects in different directions. In Newton and Kansas City, it asserts the mid-Amércian presence of Mexicans before but not entirely separate from newsworthy "new" migrations and hemispheric entanglements of family, industry, and capital. Fastpitch preserves these stories also in places to which I have not followed it: Omaha, Grand Island, Pueblo, Chanute, Wichita, Emporia, Hutchinson, and East Chicago. In the cities of Texas, the refrain plays a little differently: fastpitch reinforces social ties that were born in barrios that have since been altered by gentrification and related forces that shape the urban landscape not unlike how infield dirt gets cultivated, smoothed, and then shoved around by slides and cleats dug in for acceleration. "We were here" is a subtext of ballplayers who wax nostalgic about neighborhood ball fields now surrounded by renovated homes, and the same nostalgia grounds the ethical and political imaginations of people who have moved on but come back for the tournament. The book is also necessarily partial in its coverage of fastpitch in the borderlands, notably neglecting El Paso and Brownsville but also corners of Greater Mexico in Arizona, New Mexico, and California, where "playing ball" has meant fastpitch. I am confident that their stories have been told frequently around the ballpark or while passing fading photographs from hand to hand. Many of them remain and deserve to be written.

NOTES

INTRODUCTION

1. This study draws from a wide range of field materials. The source material includes my experiences at fastpitch tournaments, recordings I made during interviews, and my handwritten notes.

2. *Grito* is a stylized, emotional shout that is part of Mexican performance tradition, interjecting joy or affirmation, often in response to music.

3. As an ethnographer, my practice is generally to use people's own names for themselves. My aim is to do the same with referenced material, using the terms of identity chosen by the author whose work I cite. Intervening in the politics surrounding Latina/o, Latinx, Latine, and other collective terms is not the priority of this project.

4. In the 2020 tournament, the long-time director, Manuel Jaso, was replaced in this role by Todd Zenner, who has played in the tournament for some twenty-five years. Zenner kept the identity rule with one expansion: predominantly Native American teams could now compete as well. In the first year with this rule, three Native teams competed, with one of them, Big Eagle Express, taking first place.

5. My thoughts on dirt are indebted to Steven Marston's dissertation on dirt-track auto racing in Kansas (2016, 119), part of which tracks working-class and gendered articulations of dirt with authenticity and agency in vernacular sport. One participant in that study observes, "Dirt's alive. So, it *changes*."

6. Recent ethnographies focused on different sports that take up a similar dynamic of asserting identities otherwise marginalized in national contexts include Michael Robidoux's *Stickhandling through the Margins* (2012) on Native hockey in Canada, Stanley Thangaraj's *Desi Hoops Dreams* (2015) on South Asian American pickup basketball, and Nicole Willms's *When Women Rule the Court* (2017) on Japanese American basketball. As I will discuss, studies focusing on vernacular spaces and practices of sport differ from the bulk of sport studies, which tend to focus more on professional or international sites, instances of sport that are self-evidently significant because of the scale and numbers of money, people, or fame involved. The work of Allen Klein, particularly in *Baseball on the Border* (1997), is notable as a rare ethnographic and transnational approach to baseball, and I share some of the key interests pursued in that essential work.

7. For historically oppressed communities, maintaining a racial tradition is a logical response to erasure. I certainly build on the invaluable work of historians who have sought to contest this erasure. Excellent published historical work has been done on Mexican American sport with a focus on a specific community (Alamillo 2003), a specific team (I. García 2014), or even a specific player (Iber 2016), each situated within broader histories of the relationships of Mexican American communities to athletic ambition and opportunity.

CHAPTER 1

1. George Sanchez argues that the notion of World War II as a watershed is misleading, as "much of the cultural identity and sense of self of the Mexican American second generation was already shaped before the war" (1995, 256). This account resonates with the history of Mexican American fastpitch in the sense that Mexican Americans were already organizing themselves to take part in softball as a ubiquitous feature of U.S. life, and building on longer experience playing hardball, when the war interrupted local league play. The war remains a significant landmark, however, of the context in which community softball thrived, especially because of the popularity of the sport within the armed services and in postwar civilian life.

2. In the 1942 Sleepy Lagoon case, the death of a young man near a Los Angeles area swimming hole led police to detain six hundred Mexican American youths, of whom twenty-four were indicted and twelve convicted collectively for murder.

3. People in Houston are divided on whether the neighborhood that includes the softball field at Settegast Park should be called East End or Second Ward. I follow the usage of the individuals I am quoting or representing in a given passage.

4. Isabel Wilkerson (2020) includes Newton as an example of midwestern segregation, describing the public machinations city commissioners used to open a whites-only swimming pool in 1934 without offering a "separate but equal" option for Black residents.

5. See Rosaldo (2019) for a poetic, ethnographic memoir on his own jacket club in Tucson, Arizona.

6. Conceptually speaking, my analysis of Mexican American fastpitch as a racial tradition of sport is closely aligned with that of Laura R. Barraclough on the subject of charros. For Barraclough, the competitions of *charrería*, which aestheticize and formalize historically Mexican practices and styles of horse riding and cattle herding, express participants' "attachment to Mexican culture while claiming rights and opportunity in the United States" (2019, 2).

CHAPTER 2

1. The seventieth Latin tournament was the last to be sponsored by the Rusk Athletic Club, which then disbanded. A local representative of USA Softball, formerly the Amateur Softball Association, promised to keep the tournament going and founded the Texas State Latin Club for that purpose, but the club's inaugural tournament was canceled in 2020 due to the COVID-19 pandemic.

2. Santillán has also made a massive contribution to Latina/o sports history, working with many collaborators on the Latino Baseball History Project to steadily publish photographic history books focusing on locations throughout Texas, California, and the Midwest. More than a dozen of these have been published by Arcadia Press, and I was a coauthor on *Mexican American Baseball in Kansas City*.

3. From the oral history collected by Gene Chávez in connection with the Kansas City Museum exhibition and documentary video *Mexican American Fastpitch: Connecting Communities across State Lines* (2015).

CHAPTER 3

1. *Compadrazgo* refers to the relation between the parents and godparents of a child, which takes the form of close friendship or spiritual kinship.

2. Tito Florencia had a probably unparalleled impact on fastpitch in Mexico as a member of the national team, founder of a pitching academy, and author of a pitching textbook. The star pitcher and his son, Tito Jr., also have the distinction of being the only father-son pair to be named Most Valuable Players at the same position, for the same team, in different eras of the Latin tournament. Tito Sr. earned the award for the Baytown Hawks in 1973 and 1977, and Tito Jr. won the same honor for the Hawks in 1998. This information, along with other "Tournament Milestones," appears in the 1999 commemorative program booklet for the fiftieth anniversary Rusk Latin tournament. I am grateful to have received a copy from Rusk board member and tournament historian Rudy "Chato" Velasquez. Tito Jr. pitched for a Monterrey team in the master's (over forty years old) division of the last Rusk-sponsored tournament in 2019.

CHAPTER 4

1. *Carnales*: brothers or close friends.

2. Prior to the disruption of the COVID-19 pandemic, softball was slated to be an Olympic sport in Tokyo 2020 for women only, alongside a men's baseball competition. This limited return of softball, which was included in the Olympic Games since 1996 but removed for 2012, is disappointing to men who play softball and women who play baseball but also reflects the strength of women's professional softball in Japan.

3. A "run rule" or "mercy rule" is a decision common in softball that puts a limit on how large a discrepancy in score can get between two mismatched teams. Louie's story of getting "eight-run ruled" suggests his game was declared a loss when his team was eight runs down at a designated point in the innings.

4. Gil Solis voiced the same perspective, nearly verbatim, when interviewed for a feature on his managing the Newton Metros fastpitch team for the *Kansas City Hispanic News* twenty years earlier ("Metros Cover the Midwest" 1999).

5. Rachel Epp Buller of Bethel College was the principal investigator of this "Hometown Teams," and made the panel discussion possible.

CHAPTER 5

1. This is a pitfall long critiqued by scholars working on other sports and music as

examples of gendered, identity-bearing activities (Herrera-Sobek 1990; Nájera-Ramírez 1994). Laura Barraclough's (2019) recent work on the riding and cattle-handling competitions in *charrería* shows how even a practice with specific gender connotations and cultural gravity as a Mexican national symbol can be a "flexible cultural formation" that various subjects, including women, have found ways to use (198). Generative work that critiques the gendered dynamics of identity and expressive racial traditions include Alarcón (1989), Pérez (1999), Ramírez (2009), and many others.

2. Acts and statements made in public carry some measure of assumed consent to be seen and heard, which is a rationale of photojournalism that carries over somewhat to ethnographic observation. Social media, as a quasi-public space, introduce complications to this already problematic idea, given the vast range of factors and determinants that affect who can see what. My practice here in relating a bit of discourse gleaned from social media is to protect subjects as follows: I do not quote or relate anything without permission if observing it required some kind of negotiation of gatekeeping such as registration and log-in. In this case, the post was "public," and visible to me without the gatekeeping of registration or login. Also, to offer subjects the option of deniability, I anonymize the attribution and context.

3. Joyce, currently the softball coach at Florida Atlantic University, is one of the most accomplished American athletes of all time. As a pitcher, she counts 150 no-hitters and 50 perfect games to her credit, along with numerous national championships and standing records. She also competed professionally or nationally, in basketball, volleyball, bowling, and golf.

CHAPTER 6

1. For a more detailed analysis of the novel, in conversation with the Roth's fiction, see Witcombe (2011).

2. Though it is too recent to be engaged at length here, Alamillo develops this line of inquiry in *Deportes* (2020).

3. Notably, baseball found its footing in Mexico well before the establishment of another game introduced by foreign workers, English association football (soccer), which was not supported by a Mexican national organization until 1927, but would later become the country's most popular sport, and its highest-profile foothold into the global sport system.

4. As Besnier et al. (2018) explain, the question of whether games constitute a "cultural performance" has been debated rigorously around the particular definition of that term that is part of the ritual theory elaborated by Victor Turner, (161). I am using a looser definition owing to my cultural poetics approach and thus not quite playing by Turner's rules here. The study of cultural poetics grounded in verbal art and vernacular practice emphasizes performance as a mode of quotidian cultural production (Rosaldo 1989, 217), rather than necessarily taking the heightened and transformative form connoted by "ritual" in a Turnerian sense. An inquiry into cultural poetics does not require a qualifying assessment in advance of how socially transformative a practice is in order to justify studying it. Instead, I take softball as a field of cultural production to be a site

in which and through which the social is engaged. In the vein of Stuart Hall, this is a cultural performance "without guarantees" (1986).

5. James (2013) makes a point of the batting confrontation to highlight the formal difference between cricket, with two batsmen on the pitch at a time, and baseball. That feature and others, such as the possibility of substitution and reentry in cricket, renders baseball a more rigidly structured form:

> The isolated events of which both games consist is in baseball rigidly limited. The batter is allowed choice of three balls. He must hit the third or he is out. If he hits he must run. The batter's place in the batting order is fixed—it cannot be changed. The pitcher must pitch until he is taken off and when he is taken off he is finished for that game. (The Americans obviously prefer it that way.) (2013, 198)

6. While Donald Trump's political fortune was made in large part on anti-immigrant rhetoric and policy, particularly aimed at the U.S.-Mexico border, the president did not invent this particular politics. Historian and sociologist David Montejano (2017) makes the convincing case that the politics represented by the Trump administration were developed in an earlier form under Governor Pete Wilson of California in the 1990s, a setting that would have been part of the formative milieu for Trump adviser and millennial nativist Stephen Miller.

CONCLUSION

1. Folklorist Dorothy Noyes proposes a sense of "tradition" that is apt for Mexican American fastpitch, and with starts with the Roman concept of traditio as

> the hand-to-hand transfer of—something. A practice, a body of knowledge, a genre, a song, anything sufficiently framed and internally structured to be entextualizable or objectified or named: in Urban's term, a cultural object. Let us agree that what is being transferred through the object is not in the first instance authority, which fetishizes the giver, nor property, which fetishizes the object while eventually debasing it into a commodity. Rather, the transfer is of responsibility. For many of us this term is tied to the famous Hymes-Bauman definition of performance as "the acceptance of responsibility to an audience for a display of communicative competence." More than that, it resonates with the awareness of every performer I've ever encountered that the tradition is not at bottom either a badge of pride or an inheritance to display but a job that must be done. (2009, 248)

REFERENCES

Abrahams, Roger. 1977. "Toward an Enactment-Centered Theory of Folklore." In *The Frontiers of Folklore*, edited by William Bascom, 79–120. Washington, DC: American Anthropological Association Series.

———. 2005. *Everyday Life: A Poetics of Vernacular Practices*. Philadelphia: University of Pennsylvania Press.

Abu Lughod, Lila. 1991. "Writing against Culture." In *Recapturing Anthropology: Working in the Present*, edited by Richard Fox, 137–162. Santa Fe, NM: School of American Research Press.

Alamillo, José. 2003. "*Peloteros* in Paradise: Mexican American Baseball and Oppositional Politics in Southern California, 1930–1950." *Western Historical Quarterly* 34 (2): 191–211.

———. 2020. *Deportes: The Making of a Sporting Mexican Diaspora*. New Brunswick: Rutgers University Press.

———. 2008. *Making Lemonade Out of Lemons: Mexican American Labor and Leisure in a California Town, 1880–1960*. Champaign: University of Illinois Press.

Alarcón, Norma. 1989. "*Traddutora, Traditora*: A Paradigmatic Figure of Chicana Feminism." *Cultural Critique* 13:57–87.

Anderson, Benedict. 1983. *Imagined Communities*. London: Verso.

Appadurai, Arjun. 1996. *Modernity at Large*. Minneapolis: University of Minnesota Press.

Barajas, Frank. 2006. "The Defense Committees of Sleepy Lagoon: A Convergent Struggle against Fascism, 1942–1944." *Aztlán* 31 (1): 33–62.

Barnes, Michael. 2014. "A Political Trailblazer—In 1970, Richard Moya Became Austin's First Hispanic Travis County Commissioner." *Austin American-Statesman*, October 19, D1.

Barraclough, Laura R. 2019. *Charros: How Mexican Cowboys Are Remapping Race and American Identity*. Berkeley: University of California Press.

Bauman, Richard, and Charles Briggs. 1990. "Poetics and Performance as Critical Perspectives on Language and Social Life." *Annual Review of Anthropology* 19:59–88.

Bealle, Morris. 1954. *The Softball Story: A Complete, Concise and Entertaining History of America's Greatest Participant and Spectator Sport, from Its Beginning in 1887 to Its World Tournaments in 1956.* Washington, DC: Columbia.

Benjamin, Walter. (1934). 1998. "The Author as Producer." In *Understanding Brecht.* Translated by Anna Bostock, 85–103. London: Verso.

———.(1940). 1968. "Theses on the Philosophy of History." In *Illuminations.* Translated by Harry Zohn, 253–264. New York: Schocken Books.

Berlant, Lauren. 2014. "Citizenship." In *Keywords for American Cultural Studies*, edited by Bruce Burgett and Glenn Handler, 41–45. New York: New York University Press.

Besnier, Niko, Susan Brownell, and Thomas F. Carter. 2018. *The Anthropology of Sport: Bodies, Borders, Biopolitics.* Berkeley: University of California Press.

Blevins, Cameron. 2014. "Space, Nation, and the Triumph of Region: A View of the World from Houston." *Journal of American History* 184:122–147.

Bourdieu, Pierre. 1988. "Program for a Sociology of Sport." *Sociology of Sport Journal* 5 (2): 153–161.

Bowman, Paul. 2019. *Deconstructing Martial Arts.* Cardiff, UK: Cardiff University Press.

Bretón, Marcos. 2019. "I Am Mexican American with No Hyphen and No Apologies—and Am Haunted by a History of Hate." *Sacramento Bee*, August 19. https://news.yahoo.com/am-mexican-american-no-hyphen-123000416.html.

Bryant, John. 1969. "Pan-Am's Cantu Has Seen Kids on Drugs . . . It Hurt." *Austin American-Statesman*, May 11.

Buchholz, Brad. 2004. "The Legacy of Mr. G." *Austin American Statesman*, October 17, A1.

Burgos, Adrian. 2007. *Playing America's Game: Baseball, Latinos, and the Color Line.* Berkeley: University of California Press.

Calderon, Ricardo. 2020. "Texas Legendary Fastpitch Softball Pitcher and Coach Louis 'El Diablo' Aguayo Passes Away at Age 83." *Eagle Pass Business Journal.* https://www.epbusinessjournal.com/2020/02/texas-legendary-fastpitch-softball-pitcher-and-coach-louis-el-diablo-aguayo-passes-away-at-age-83/

Carrington, Ben. 2013. "The Critical Sociology of Race and Sport: The First Fifty Years." *Annual Review of Sociology* 39:379–98.

Chabon, Michael. 2002. *Summerland.* Los Angeles: Miramax Books for Kids.

Chambers, Emily. 2015. "Fragas: A Hundred Years in the East End." *Houston History* 12 (3): 24–28.

Chappell, Ben. 2012. *Lowrider Space: Aesthetics and Politics of Mexican American Custom Cars.* Austin: University of Texas Press.

———. 2020. "Mexican American Fastpitch." In *Latinos and Latinas in American Sport: Stories beyond Peloteros*, edited by Jorge Iber, 127–148. Lubbock: Texas Tech University Press.

Chávez, Alex E. 2015. "So ¿te fuiste a Dallas? (So You Went to Dallas?/So You Got Screwed?): Language, Migration, and the Poetics of Transgression." *Journal of Linguistic Anthropology* 25 (2): 150–172.

———. 2017. *Sounds of Crossing: Music, Migration, and the Aural Poetics of Huapango Arribeño.* Durham, NC: Duke University Press.

Chávez, Ernesto. 2007. *The U.S. War with Mexico: A Brief History with Documents.* New York: Macmillan Higher Education.

Chávez, Gene. 2015. *Mexican American Fast Pitch Softball: Connecting Communities across State Lines.* https://www.youtube.com/watch?v=oY89Yz3aA4E.

Chávez-García, Miroslava. 2012. *States of Delinquency: Race and Science in the Making of California's Juvenile Justice System.* Berkeley: University of California Press.

Cintron, Ralph. 1997. *Angel's Town: Chero Ways, Gang Life, and Rhetorics of the Everyday.* Boston: Beacon Press.

Desjarlais, Robert. 2011. *Counterplay: An Anthropologist at the Chessboard.* Berkeley: University of California Press.

Dickson, Paul. 1994. *The Worth Book of Softball: A Celebration of America's True National Pastime.* New York: Facts on File.

Dunning, Eric. 2001. *Sport Matters: Sociological Studies of Sport, Violence, and Civilization.* London: Routledge.

Escobedo, Elizabeth. 2013. *From Coveralls to Zoot Suits: The Lives of Mexican American Women on the World War II Home Front.* Chapel Hill: University of North Carolina Press.

Fernández, Lilia. 2016. "Moving Beyond Aztlán: Disrupting Nationalism and Geographic Essentialism in Chicana/o History." In *A Promising Problem: The New Chicana/o History*, edited by Carlos Kevin Blanton, 59–81. Austin: University of Texas Press.

Flores, Juan. 1997a. "The Latino Imaginary: Dimensions of Community and Identity." In *Tropicalizations: Transcultural Representations of Latinidad*, edited by Frances Aparicio and Susana Chávez-Silverman, 183–193. Hanover, NH: University Press of New England.

———. 1997b. "Puerto Rican and Proud, Boyee!": Rap, Roots, and Amnesia." *Iberoamericana* 3/4 (67/68): 168–178.

Flores, Richard. 2002. *Remembering the Alamo: Memory, Modernity, and the Master Symbol.* Austin: University of Texas Press.

Flores, William V., and Rena Benmayor, eds. 1998. *Latino Cultural Citizenship: Claiming Identity, Space, and Rights.* Boston: Beacon Press.

Foley, Douglas. 2010. *Learning Capitalist Culture: Deep in the Heart of Tejas*, 2nd ed. Philadelphia: University of Pennsylvania Press.

Fortier, James, and Leanne Howe. 2015. *Playing Pastime: American Indians, Softball, and Survival.* Video. https://vimeo.com/122555481.

Foucault, Michel. 1980. "Two Lectures" In *Power/Knowledge: Selected Interviews and Other Writings*, edited by Colin Gordon, 78–108. New York: Pantheon.

Fraser, Nancy. 1990. "Rethinking the Public Sphere: A Contribution to the Critique of Actually Existing Democracy." *Social Text* 25/26:56–80.

Fuentes, Carlos. 1960. *Where the Air Is Clear.* New York: Ivan Obolensky.

García, Ignacio. 2002. *Hector P. García: In Relentless Pursuit of Justice*. Houston: Arte Público.

———. 2014. *When Mexicans Could Play Ball: Basketball, Race, and Identity in San Antonio, 1928–1945*. Austin: University of Texas Press.

García, Maria. 2015. "The History of Neighborhood House in Logan Heights: Los Chicanos, 1950s Social Club." *San Diego Free Press*, June 6. https://sandiegofreepress.org/2015/06/the-history-of-neighborhood-house-in-logan-heights-los-chicanos-1950s-social-club.

García-Canclini, Néstor. 1995. *Hybrid Cultures: Strategies for Entering and Leaving Modernity*. Minneapolis: University of Minnesota Press.

Garcilazo, Jeffrey Marcos. 2012. *Traqueros: Mexican Railroad Workers in the United States, 1870–1930*. Denton: University of North Texas Press.

Garrigou, Alain. 2008. "*Illusio* in Sport." In *Matters of Sport: Essays in Honour of Eric Dunning*, edited by Dominic Malcolm and Ivan Waddington, 163–171. London: Routledge.

Gaspar de Alba, Alicia. 1998. *Chicano Art inside/outside the Master's House: Cultural Politics and the CARA Exhibition*. Austin: University of Texas Press.

Gomez, Eric. 2019. "U.S.-Born Softball Players Keep Olympic Hopes Alive Playing for Mexico at Pan American Games." https://www.espn.com/olympics/story/_/id/27342181/us-born-softball-players-keep-olympic-hopes-alive-playing-mexico-pan-american-games.

Guadalupe Centers. 2019. "About Us." https://guadalupecenters.org/home/who-we-are/

Gupta, Akhil, and James Ferguson. 1992. "Beyond Culture: Space, Identity and the Politics of Difference." *Cultural Anthropology* 7 (1): 6–23.

Guttmann, Allen. 2004. *From Ritual to Record: The Nature of Modern Sports*. New York: Columbia University Press.

Hall, Stuart. 1986. "The Problem of Ideology: Marxism without Guarantees." *Journal of Communication Inquiry* 10:2 (28–44).

———. 2016. *Cultural Studies 1983: A Theoretical History*. Durham, NC: Duke University Press.

Haney-Lopez, Ian. 2006. *White by Law: The Legal Construction of Race*. New York: New York University Press.

Hassenfield, Noam. 2017. "Mexican-Americans Prove They Can Play Basketball—in 1939." *Only a Game*, WBUR, February 17. https://www.wbur.org/onlyagame/2017/02/17/lanier-basketball-ignacio-garcia.

Herrera-Sobek, María. 1990. *The Mexican Corrido: A Feminist Analysis*. Bloomington: Indiana University Press.

Horwitz, Tony. 2013. "The Woman Who (Maybe) Struck Out Babe Ruth and Lou Gehrig." *Smithsonian Magazine* (July). https://www.smithsonianmag.com/history/the-woman-who-maybe-struck-out-babe-ruth-and-lou-gehrig-4759182/.

Howe, Leanne. 2007. *Miko Kings: An Indian Baseball Story*. San Francisco: Aunt Lute Books.

———. 2014. "Embodied Tribalography: Mound Building, Ball Games, and Native Endurance in the Southeast." *Studies in American Indian Literatures* 26 (2): 75–93.

Iber, Jorge. 2016. *Mike Torrez: A Baseball Biography.* Jefferson, NC: McFarland.

Iber, Jorge, and Samuel Regalado, eds. 2006. *Mexican Americans and Sports: A Reader on Athletics and Barrio Life.* College Station: Texas A&M University Press.

Iber, Jorge, Samuel O. Regalado, José Alamillo, and Arnoldo de León. 2011. *Latinos in U.S Sport: A History of Isolation, Cultural Identity, and Acceptance.* Champaign, IL: Human Kinetics.

Innis-Jiménez, Michael. 2013. *Steel Barrio: The Great Mexican Migration to South Chicago, 1915–1940.* New York: New York University Press.

———. 2014. "Beyond the Baseball Diamond and the Basketball Court: Organized Leisure in Interwar Mexican South Chicago." In *More Than Just Peloteros: Sport and U.S. Latino Communities,* edited by Jorge Iber, 66–94. Lubbock: Texas Tech University Press.

James, C. L. R. (1963). 2013. *Beyond a Boundary.* 50th anniversary ed. Durham, NC: Duke University Press.

Jamieson, Katherine M. 2005. "'All My Hopes and Dreams': Families, Schools, and Subjectivities in Collegiate Softball." *Journal of Sport and Social Issues* 29 (2): 133–147.

Joseph, Miranda. 2002. *Against the Romance of Community.* Minneapolis: University of Minnesota Press.

Just, Arnie. 2017. "A Multi-Sport Athlete, Ray Evans Has Two Jerseys Retired at Kansas." *University Daily Kansan,* February 22. http://www.kansan.com/sports/retired_jerseys/a-multi-sport-athlete-ray-evans-has-two-jerseys-retired/article_cfba6326-f4a5-11e6-bf39-a7f87064e5a3.html.

Klein, Alan M. 1991. "Sport and Culture as Contested Terrain: Americanization in the Caribbean." *Sociology of Sport Journal* 8 (1): 79–85.

———. 1997. *Baseball on the Border: A Tale of Two Laredos.* Princeton: Princeton University Press.

———. 2006. *Growing the Game: The Globalization of Major League Baseball.* New Haven: Yale University Press.

———. 2013. "Transnationalism, Labour Migration and Latin American Baseball." In *The Global Sports Arena: Athletic Talent Migration in an Interdependent World,* edited by John Bale and Joseph Maguire, 183–205. New York: Routledge.

———. 2014. *Dominican Baseball: New Pride, Old Prejudice.* Philadelphia: Temple University Press.

Kreneck, Thomas H. 2012. *Del Pueblo: A History of Houston's Hispanic Community.* College Station: Texas A&M Press.

Levi, Heather. 2008. *The World of Lucha Libre: Secrets, Revelations, and Mexican National Identity.* Durham, NC: Duke University Press.

Leighninger, Jr., Robert D. 1996. "Cultural Infrastructure: The Legacy of New Deal Public Space." *Journal of Architectural Education* 49 (4): 226–236.

Limón, José E. 1994. *Dancing with the Devil: Society and Cultural Poetics in Mexican-American South Texas.* Madison: University of Wisconsin Press.

———. 2012. *Américo Paredes: Culture and Critique*. Austin: University of Texas Press.

Macaloon, John. 1996. "Humanism as Political Necessity? Reflections on the Pathos of Anthropological Science in Olympic Contexts." *Quest* 48:67–81.

Madrid, Alejandro L. 2008. Nor-tec Rifa! *Electronic Dance Music from Tijuana to the World*. Oxford: Oxford University Press.

Marston, Steve. 2016. "Intimate Collisions: Identity, Community, and Place in the Kansas Dirt-Track Auto Racing Sphere." PhD diss., University of Kansas.

Martinez, Ignacio. 1946. "No Mexicans Allowed." *Evening Kansan Republican*, August 19.

Mendoza-Denton, Norma. 2008. *Homegirls: Language and Cultural Practice among Latina Youth Gangs*. Malden, MA: Blackwell.

Mesa-Baines, Amalia. 1999. "'Domesticana': The Sensibility of Chicana Rasquache." *Aztlán* 24(2): 155–167.

"Metros Cover the Midwest to Be the Best at Fast-Pitch." 1999. *Kansas City Hispanic News*, June 3–16, 14.

Molina, Natalia. 2014. *How Race Is Made in America: Immigration, Citizenship, and the Historical Power of Racial Scripts*. Berkeley: University of California Press.

Montejano, David. 2017. "Explaining Trumpism and Border Walls." Paper presented at Siglo XXI: Mapping Latino Research, biennial conference of the Inter-University Program for Latino Research, San Antonio, May 19.

Najera, Jennifer. 2015. *The Borderlands of Race: Mexican Segregation in a South Texas Town*. Austin: University of Texas Press.

Nájera-Ramírez, Olga. 1994. "Engendering Nationalism: Identity, Discourse, and the Mexican Charro." *Anthropological Quarterly* 67 (1): 1–14.

Noyes, Dorothy. 2009. "Tradition: Three Traditions." *Journal of Folklore Research* 46 (3): 233–268.

Olais, Raymond. 2019. "A League of Our Own: Newton's Mexican-American Men's Fast-pitch Tournament, 1946–2019." Lecture at the Newton Public Library, Newton, KS, June 18.

———. N.d. *Our Lady of Guadalupe All Stars 1946–1970*. Self-published booklet compiled with Reynaldo Gonzalez.

O'Sullivan, John L. 1845. "The Mexican Question." *United States Magazine and Democratic Review* 16 (83): 419–428.

Paz, Octavio. 1961. *The Labyrinth of Solitude*. New York: Grove Press.

Paredes, Américo. 1958. *"With a Pistol in His Hand": A Border Ballad and Its Hero*. Austin: University of Texas Press.

———. 1995. *A Texas-Mexican Cancionero: Folksongs of the Lower Border*. Austin: University of Texas Press.

Pérez, Emma. 1999. *The Decolonial Imaginary: Writing Chicanas into History*. Bloomington: Indiana University Press.

Perinbanayagam, Robert. 2006. *Games and Sport in Everyday Life: Dialogues and Narratives of the Self*. Baltimore: Paradigm Press.

———. 2014. *Varieties of the Gaming Experience*. Piscataway, NJ: Transaction.

Pescador, Juan Javier. 2004. "¡Vamos Taximaroa! Mexican/Chicano Soccer Associations and Transnational/Translocal Communities, 1967–2002." *Latino Studies* 2:352–376.

"Pitched No-Hit Game and Lost: Estrada Won Duel with Ray Evans for Sox Super Service." 1947. *Evening Kansan Republican*, August 26.

Preston, J. G. 2009. "On Eleanor Engle, Who Wasn't Allowed to Play Shortstop for the Harrisburg Senators." *J. G. Preston Experience*. https://prestonjg.wordpress.com/2009/11/21/on-eleanor-engle-who-wasnt-allowed-to-play-shortstop-for-the-harrisburg-senators/

Pulido, Alberto, dir. 2014. *Everything Comes from the Streets*. San Diego: University of San Diego Department of Ethnic Studies.

Ramírez, Catherine. 2009. *The Woman in the Zoot Suit: Gender, Nationalism, and the Cultural Politics of Memory*. Durham, NC: Duke University Press.

Ramos-Zayas, Ana. 2004. "Delinquent Citizenship, National Performances: Racialization, Surveillance, and the Politics of 'Worthiness' in Puerto Rican Chicago." *Latino Studies* 2(1): 26–44.

Rand, Erica. 2012. *Red Nails, White Skates: Gender, Cash and Pleasure on and off the Ice*. Durham, NC: Duke University Press.

"Richard A. Moya Obituary." 2017. *Austin American Statesman*, February 19. https://www.legacy.com/obituaries/name/richard-moya-obituary

Ring, Jennifer. 2009a. "America's Baseball Underground." *Journal of Sport and Social Issues* 33 (4): 373–389.

———. 2009b. *Stolen Bases: Why American Girls Don't Play Baseball*. Champaign: University of Illinois Press.

———. 2018. *A Game of Their Own: Voices of Contemporary Women in Baseball*. Lincoln: University of Nebraska Press.

Rivera, John-Michael. 2004. "Embodying Greater Mexico: María Amparo Ruiz de Burton and the Reconstruction of the Mexican Question." In *Look Away! The U.S. South in New World Studies*, edited by Jon Smith and Deborah Cohn, 451–470. Durham, NC: Duke University Press.

———. 2006. *The Emergence of Mexican America: Recovering Stories of Mexican Peoplehood in U.S. Culture*. New York: New York University Press.

Robidoux, Michael. 2012. *Stickhandling through the Margins: First Nations Hockey in Canada*. Toronto: Toronto University Press.

Rodriguez, Ralph. 2010. "Chicano Studies and the Need to Not Know." *American Literary History* 22 (1): 180–190.

Rosaldo, Renato. 1989. *Culture and Truth: The Remaking of Social Analysis*. Boston: Beacon Press.

———. 1994. "Cultural Citizenship in San Jose, California." *PoLAR: Political and Legal Anthropology Review* 17 (2): 57–64.

———. 2019. *The Chasers*. Durham, NC: Duke University Press.

Rose, Nikolas. 1999. *Powers of Freedom: Reframing Political Thought*. Cambridge, MA: Cambridge University Press.

Roth, Philip. 1973a. *Great American Novel*. New York: Holt.

———. 1973b. "My Baseball Years." *New York Times*, April 2. https://www.nytimes. com/1973/04/02/archives/my-baseball-years.html.

Rowe, David. 2003. "Antonio Gramsci: Sport, Hegemony and the National-Popular." In *Sport and Modern Social Theorists*, edited by Richard Giulianotti, 97–110. London: Palgrave Macmillan.

"San Antonio Sports Hall of Fame 2012—Leticia Morales-Bissaro." 2012. https://www. youtube.com/watch?v=JotaMw4Ip9Y.

Sanchez, George J. 1995. Becoming Mexican American: Ethnicity, Culture, and Identity in Chicano Los Angeles, 1900–1945. New York: Oxford University Press.

Santillán, Richard. 2008. "Mexican Baseball Teams in the Midwest, 1916–1965: The Politics of Cultural Survival and Civil Rights." In *Sports and the Racial Divide: African American and Latino Experience in an Era of Change*, edited by Michael Lomax, 146–165. Jackson: University Press of Mississippi.

Santillán, Richard, Gene T. Chávez, Rod Martínez, Raymond Olais, and Ben Chappell. 2018. *Mexican American Baseball in Kansas City*. Mount Pleasant, SC: Arcadia Press.

Santillán, Richard, Jorge Iber, Grace G. Charles, Alberto Rodríguez, and Gregory Garrett. 2015. *Mexican American Baseball in the Alamo Region*. Mount Pleasant, SC: Arcadia Press.

Sauceda, Loney. 2011. "The History of American Legion Post 213, Kansas City, Kan." Oral history given to Linda Blount. http://www.legiontown.org/story/4089/history-american-legion-post-213-kansas-city-kan.

SB Nation Rock Chalk Talk. 2014. "Know Your KU History: Ray Evans." https://www. rockchalktalk.com/2014/11/19/7229471/know-your-ku-history-ray-evans.

Schmucker, Kristine. 2019. "'But It Was Too Late for Me.'" Newton, KS: Harvey County Historical Museum. http://hchm.org/but-it-was-too-late-for-me/.

"Soft Ball Season Starts: Formal Opening Monday Night on Bethel College Field." *1934. Evening Kansas Republican*, April 28.

Solis, Gil Sr. 2018. "More Than Just a Softball Tournament." *Newton Kansan*, July 3. https://www.thekansan.com/news/20180703/more-than-just-softball-tournament.

Soto, Sandra. 2011. "Wearing Out Arizona." Rappaport Human Rights Center working paper series 4. http://hdl.handle.net/2152/27713.

———. 2012–2013. "Neoliberalism and Attrition in Arizona." Scholar and Feminist Online 11 (1–2). https://sfonline.barnard.edu/gender-justice-and-neoliberal-transformations/neoliberalism-and-attrition-in-arizona/.

Spear, Jeremy, dir. 2000. *Fastpitch*. New York: New Video. DVD.

Stewart, Kathleen. 2017. "In the World That Affect Proposed." *Cultural Anthropology* 32 (2): 192–198.

Thangaraj, Stanley. 2015. *Desi Hoop Dreams: Pickup Basketball and the Making of Asian American Masculinity*. New York: New York University Press.

Trueba, Henry T. 2002. "Multiple Ethnic, Racial, and Cultural Identities in Action: From Marginality to a New Cultural Capital in Modern Society." *Journal of Latinos and Education* 1 (1): 7–28.

Turner, Victor. 1986. *The Anthropology of Performance.* New York: PAJ Publications.

Valencia, Richard R. 2005. "The Mexican American Struggle for Equal Educational Opportunity in *Mendez v. Westminster:* Helping to Pave the Way for *Brown v. Board of Education.*" *Teachers College Record* 107 (3): 389-423.

Vega, Sujey. 2012. "The Politics of Everyday Life: Mexican Hoosiers and Ethnic Belonging at the Crossroads of America." *City and Society* 24 (2): 196–217.

Villa, Raúl Homero. 2000. *Barrio Logos: Space and Place in Urban Chicano Literature and Culture.* Austin: University of Texas Press.

Westly, Erica. 2016. *Fastpitch: The Untold History of Softball and the Women Who Made the Game.* New York: Touchstone.

Wilkerson, Isabel. 2020. *Caste: The Origins of Our Discontents.* New York: Random House.

Willis, Paul. 1981. *Learning to Labor.* New York: Columbia University Press.

Willms, Nicole. 2017. *When Women Rule the Court: Gender, Race, and Japanese Basketball.* New Brunswick: Rutgers University Press.

Witcombe, Mike. 2011. "Home Run or Strike Out? Reimagining Baseball in Philip Roth's *Great American Novel* and Michael Chabon's *Summerland.*" *Emergence,* 35–36.

Zipter, Yvonne. 1988. *Diamonds Are a Dyke's Best Friend: Reflections, Reminiscences, and Reports from the Field on the Lesbian National Pastime.* Ithaca, NY: Firebrand books.

INDEX